TWAYNE'S WORLD AUTHORS SERIES

A Survey of the World's Literature

Sylvia E. Bowman, Indiana University

GENERAL EDITOR

SPAIN

Janet W. Díaz, University of North Carolina at Chapel Hill
Gerald Wade, Vanderbilt University

EDITORS

The Moorish Novel

TWAS 375

THE MOORISH NOVEL

"El Abencerraje"
and
Pérez de Hita

By María Soledad Carrasco-Urgoiti

Hunter College

TWAYNE PUBLISHERS

A DIVISION OF G. K. HALL & CO., BOSTON

Library of Congress Cataloging in Publication Data

Carrasco, María Soledad, 1922–
  The Moorish Novel.

  (Twayne's world authors series)
  Bibliography: pp. 177–87
  Includes index.
  1. Pérez de Hita, Ginés, 1544?–1619? Guerras civiles de
Granada. 2. Granada (Kingdom) in literature. 3. El Abencerraje.
PQ6419.P8G833   863'.3   75–25977
ISBN 0–8058–6178–0

MANUFACTURED IN THE UNITED STATES OF AMERICA

To the memory of my cousins
Ricardo and Fernando Urgoiti

Contents

About the Author

María Soledad Carrasco-Urgoiti studied at the University of Madrid and at Columbia University, under the guidance of Federico de Onís and Angel del Río. Her dissertation, *El moro de Granada en la literatura,* treated the themes derived from *El Abencerraje* and Pérez de Hita's *Civil Wars of Granada* as they appear in the literatures of various periods and countries.

Her most recent studies of the sixteenth-century Moorish novel consider the stylized vision of Moorish Granada and of Moorish Christian confrontation as resulting from the interplay of literary trends and other incentives related to the authors' experience of living in a society with a diversified Morisco population. Miss Carrasco has also been concerned with Golden Age plays and with the history of the Moriscos. Her work on other subjects includes a study of *vejámenes de academia* and an annotated edition of Vicente Espinel's *Marcos de Obregón* for Clásicos Castalia.

In 1960 Miss Carrasco joined the faculty of Hunter College. She is Professor of Romance Languages and a member of the Doctoral Faculty of The City University of New York.

Preface

This book attempts to assess the significance of the fictional genre designated in Spanish literature as the Moorish novel, which emerged in the little masterpiece *El Abencerraje* and was expanded in Pérez de Hita's *Historia de los vandos de los Zegríes y Abencerrages*, better known as the first part of *Guerras civiles de Granada* (*Civil Wars of Granada*). I have tried to acquaint the reader with new critical approaches to both works, taking into consideration recent studies, which are more frequently concerned with the anonymous short novel than with Pérez de Hita's work.

Américo Castro has made us aware of many hitherto unnoticed links between literary creativity in sixteenth century Spain and the predicament of the descendants of Jews and Moors. Within this context the present book reflects the opinions I have reached as a result of previous research concerning the connection between certain conditions of the society in which the authors lived and the genesis of *El Abencerraje* and Pérez de Hita's *Civil Wars of Granada*. The stylized portrait which is offered by each of these works of the struggle at the frontier of Granada underscores the affinities, within the spirit of chivalry of Moorish and Christian contenders, who ultimately achieve harmony, be it in a situation of loyal adversaries or by means of the convert's integration into Christian society. I submit that such an approach, which may be said to define the genre, reflects the authors' desire to promote a spirit of reconciliation and harmony between the old Christians and the descendants of converts. To support my point of view I have had recourse to sources of local history, which have helped to explain the anxieties, as well as the aspirations prevalent among the mixed social groups wherefrom I believe the Moorish novel to have arisen. When this book was in galley-print, further arguments which concur with the position taken in my study were presented by Francisco

Márquez Villanueva in an illuminating analysis of the controversy which preceded and followed the Moriscos' expulsion.[1]

Keeping in mind that the Moorish novel of Spain had in the past a nonspecialized international public, I have included, for the benefit of readers who are not Hispanists, a chapter about Moorish Granada, with a general introduction on Moslem Spain, and another about the Moriscos in the sixteenth century, as well as a brief discussion in the third chapter of literary trends in which the idealized portrayal of Moorish types and customs first appeared. The next four chapters focus specially on *El Abencerraje* and Pérez de Hita's *Civil Wars, I.* The interpolated *romances* (ballads) are also considered in some detail as being a primary source, as well as an integral part of the work. Chapter 8 discusses the so-called second part of the *Civil Wars of Granada*, which deals with the 1568 revolt of the Moriscos. Mateo Alemán's "Historia de Ozmín y Daraja," appearing in his picaresque novel *Guzmán de Alfarache*, is not treated in detail, since such an analysis must be made within the context of the complex structure to which it belongs. The novelette is touched upon in the concluding chapter, which surveys the influence of Moorish novels and gives a general impression of literary developments inspired by this genre in later periods and in non-Spanish literatures.

It is a pleasure to acknowledge that Don Luis Vázquez de Parga, of the Biblioteca Nacional, and Doña Consuelo Gutiérrez del Arroyo, of the Archivo Histórico Nacional, have graciously answered my inquiries and given me valuable advice. I have met with the same generous attitude in the Hispanic Society of America, and my thanks go to Dr. Theodore S. Beardsley, Miss Jean R. Longland and Mrs. Martha de Narváez. The present book owes much to the editorial revision of Professor Gerald E. Wade. It should also be appreciatively acknowledged that a fellowship of the American Council of Learned Societies provided the time needed for research in the field.

Among those who have shared in the effort and excitement of writing the book are in the first place my mother and Mrs. Conchita Chaves de Florit. The efficient assistance of Miss Paquita Martínez is also sincerely appreciated.

Chronology

1577   The latest recorded participation of Pérez de Hita in the festivities of Lorca.

1579   Publication of Lucas Rodríguez' *Romancero hystoriado,* which includes poems on the themes of Granada.

1580   Pedro de Padilla publishes his *Thesoro de varias poesías,* which includes Moorish ballads.

1585   Earliest possible date when Pérez de Hita could have visited in La Mancha El Tuzaní (who retired after the death of Don Lope de Figueroa) and other Moriscos, on the occasion of a trip to Madrid for the publication arrangements.

1589   *Flor de varios romances nuevos y canciones* by Pedro de Moncayo. Includes poems used by Pérez de Hita in *Guerras civiles de Granada.*

1591   *Flor de varios romances nuevos y canciones. Primera y Segunda Parte* by Pedro de Moncayo.

1595   Publication in Zaragoza of *Historia de los vandos de los Zegríes y Abencerrages* (*Guerras civiles de Granada, I*). Pérez de Hita resides in Murcia.

1596   Pérez de Hita concludes the manuscript of "Los diez y siete libros de Daris . . ." (*De Bello Troyano*).

1597   Pérez de Hita finishes in November the *Segunda parte de las guerras civiles de Granada.*

1598   Death of Philip II. Beginning of the reign of Philip III. "El licenciado Berrio" issues an *Aprobación* for the publication in Castile·of *Guerras Civiles de Granada, I.*

1599   Mateo Alemán publishes *Vida de Guzmán de Alfarache,* which includes the "Historia de Ozmín y Daraja."

1600   Pérez de Hita contributes to a memorial volume compiled in Murcia on the occasion of the funeral for Philip II.

1601   The first known Castilian edition of *Guerras civiles, I* is published in Alcalá.

1604   The original in three parts of *Guerras civiles de Granada* is returned to the author or his heirs, permission to publish having been denied.

1609--   The Moriscos are expelled from Spain.
1611

1610   An *Aprobación* for the publication in Castile of the three parts of *Guerras civiles de Granada* is issued.

Chronology

1613   A substantially revised edition of *Historia de los vandos* appears in Sevilla.

1619   *Segunda parte de las guerras civiles de Granada* appears in Cuenca and in Barcelona.

The date of Pérez de Hita's death is not known. There is no absolute proof that he was alive after 1600.

CHAPTER 1

The Moorish Kingdom of Granada

I *The Beginning of Moslem Spain and
the Rise of the Christian States*

THE political existence of Al-Andalus, Moslem Spain, spans a period of approximately eight centuries.[1] If any generalization about the people and the culture encompassed by the term Moslem Spain is valid, it must take into consideration the creativity of the period as well as the political factionalism which undermined the splendid performances of the Spanish Moors both in military enterprises and in artistic and intellectual pursuits.

In the year 711 a small Mohammedan army, which had apparently crossed the Straits of Gibraltar in response to an appeal of the political enemies of the Visigothic monarch Rodrigo, destroyed his forces. If plans for an immediate conquest of the Iberian Peninsula were not made even before the battle by the Moslem leaders, such aims were certainly consistent with the pattern of sweeping invasions which had brought under Islamic rule the Middle East and the northern part of Africa. Rodrigo was never seen thereafter, and the conquerors subjugated in a short time almost the entire territory of his kingdom. For posterity the memory of the last of the Goths became a symbol of bereavement not dissimilar to that other historical and legendary figure, Boabdil, the last Moorish king of Granada in 1492. In a popular view of history the parallel destinies of Rodrigo and Boabdil mark, with a poignant note of human suffering, the beginning and the end of Moslem dominion in the Peninsula.

The victorious army that defeated Rodrigo numbered approximately twelve thousand men. The majority of them were

15

Berbers from Mauritania, at that time a province of the Empire
of Damascus, although the Arabs constituted the most influential
portion of the army. A contingent of Syrians, who arrived during
the period of expansion, should also be counted among the
conquerors. Cordova became the residence of the emir governing
the territory, which had been won, at least in theory, for the
caliph of Damascus. Military victory was not the only means
by which most of the Peninsula was swiftly brought under
Moslem domination. A few of the Visigothic lords offered no
resistance but preferred to negotiate a settlement that allowed
them to live in relative autonomy as feudatories of the new rulers.
Even where capitulation followed fighting, Christians were
permitted to practice their religion, under the stipulation that
they pay a special tax, the same principle being applied to
the Jews.

Approximately ten years after the collapse of the Visigothic
monarchy, a contingent of the conquerors' army suffered defeat
in the mountains of Asturias at the hand of a small Christian
host, whose leader, Pelayo, became the founder of the independent kingdom of Asturias. Future generations in Christian
Spain would view as miraculous this victory at Covadonga, and
it is considered to have been the starting point of the Reconquest, a term applied in Spanish history to the gradual recovery
by the various Peninsular Christian states of the territory lost
by the Visigoths to the Moors.

Around the same time the army of Moslem invaders crossed
the Pyrenees and made important inroads upon Frankish
territory, but in 732 they were defeated near Poitiers by Charles
Martel. Soon thereafter, another nucleus of resistance to Moslem
rule appeared in present-day Catalonia. This area strengthened
its ties with the Franks, while, in the western section of the
Pyrenees, Pamplona became the capital of a dynamic and
fiercely independent new state. Thus, in the mountainous
regions of the north the ferment and energy for the long strife
of the Reconquest were nurtured. In the ninth century settlers
from those areas moved into thinly populated regions along
the Ebro and Duero rivers, which had previously served as
protective buffer zones. According to Américo Castro's interpretation of Spanish history, the devotion of the Apostle

Santiago as this developed in northwestern Spain was not only a spiritual rallying force for Christianity, but also a counterpart and a challenge to the bellicose aims of Islam.[2]

During the first quarter of the tenth century, the sovereigns of Asturias established themselves in León, and expanded their territory south of the Duero. The embattled frontier zone of this growing state is said to owe its very name, "Castilla," from the circumstance that it was a garrisoned land with a defense system of castles and fortresses towering over its immense plain. The people in this area soon claimed their independence from León and pursued with renewed vigor the struggle against the Moors. Meanwhile Moslem Spain reached the peak of its power and opulence under the rule of Almanzor, the minister who was to all practical purposes sovereign of the country during the two last decades of the tenth century. This period was characterized by frequent military expeditions against the northern Christian states. Successful as such raids were in inflicting severe hardship and humiliation, they may have had in the long run the effect of strengthening the ravaged land and encouraging its leaders to establish closer ties with France and other European states. And shortly after the death of Almanzor the political structure of the caliphate collapsed, while Christian Spain witnessed the resurgence of a spirit of dynamic expansion which found its greatest leader in the Castilian Rodrigo Díaz de Vivar, better known as El Cid.

II *The Caliphate of Cordova: Its Splendor and Fragmentation*

The first three centuries of Islamic domination in Spain saw the gradual and complete emancipation of the Spanish Moslem state from the distant metropolis of Damascus. The fall of the Omayyad dynasty had important consequences in this regard. A prince of that family, who had had to flee his native land, arrived destitute in Al-Andalus and consequently succeeded in obtaining the allegiance of the faction opposed to the emir, whom he defeated in 756. The young Omayyad, Abderrahman the First, also used the title of *emir* ("governor") but he was really an independent sovereign. After a frustrated attempt to regain control over the Cordova Emirate by the Abbasides, now ruling as caliphs in Bagdad, normal relations were established between the new capital of the Moslem world and its autonomous enclave in the Iberian Peninsula.

Due in great part to the initiative of the Omayyad prince, who could never overcome his nostalgia for the court of his ancestors in Damascus, the city of Cordova became a western outpost of Islamic culture, and soon its influence would radiate to Christian Europe.[3] At the same time, partly through contact with the very different traditions alive on Spanish soil, the art of Al-Andalus developed new and original trends which spread through the Moslem world. Protocol in Abderrahman's court was fashioned after the model of Damascus, and Arabic poetry flourished in the entourage of the emir, who himself wrote with skill in the elaborate styles prevalent at this time. He also conceived grand architectural projects, and began the construction of the great mosque which spans the classical period of Hispano-Moorish art.

Moslem Spain was populated by highly heterogeneous groups. Even after the vast majority of the population had adopted the Islamic religion, both the Christians under Moorish rule, who were known as Mozarabs, and the Jews constituted important segments of the population of Al-Andalus. According to Moslem and Christian sources, the Mozarabs imitated many of the customs of the Moors, whose cultural achievements they admired. On several occasions this minority was divided with respect to the degree of restraint or militancy with which they bore witness to their Christian faith. The policy of religious tolerance was not always to prevail in Al-Andalus; in certain periods not only the Mozarabs, but also the "Muladíes," or Moslems of Christian origin, suffered persecution. There were times when the Mozarabs were close to establishing insurgent states, and in fact toward the end of the emirate their powerful leader, Omar-ben-Hafsun, maintained an independent stronghold for thirty years. In later periods Mozarabic communities, with their mixed cultural patterns, established themselves in large areas that had just passed into Christian hands.

A minority group of considerable importance in Moslem Spain was that of the slaves, who were brought in large numbers by professional traders from eastern Europe and Africa. Although their civil status was that of slavery, many of them held important administrative positions and some became extremely wealthy and influential. Undoubtedly, religious and ethnic differences in the urban and rural population contributed to the tensions that prevailed during the greater part of the history of Al-Andalus, but the main cause of unrest seems to have been the perpetuation of tribal rivalries and the lack among the ruling class of a spirit of national solidarity.

Among the successors of the first Omayyad, Abderrahman the Third (912–961) bore the sign of greatness. Although he was for the most part successful in military encounters, it was in the government of his own country that he met his greatest challenge and success. Under his rule the turbulence of enemy factions was checked, important institutional reforms took place, and commerce with European and African states was considerably increased. Abderrahman also promoted learning and public education, which reached in Cordova a degree of excellence unparalleled at that time anywhere in the Western world. Although his interest in scholarly pursuits was lively, in this respect he was to be overshadowed by his son Alhakem II, whose library included 400,000 titles. Medieval Arabic philosophy was to a large extent Aristotelian, and the scholars of Al-Andalus distinguished themselves as interpreters of ancient thought. It was through translations produced in Castile by teams of Jewish, Christian, and Moslem experts that their major contributions would find their way into the mainstream of European learning.

When his government was consolidated, Abderrahman III assumed the title of caliph. By so doing he severed Al-Andalus's symbolic link of bondage to the Empire of Bagdad and claimed the spiritual leadership of the western part of the Islamic world, which included the north of Africa. His prestige was also great among the Christian monarchs, in whose disputes he was sometimes asked to intervene as mediator. Aware of his position as a world leader, Abderrahman established diplomatic relations with the emperors of Byzantium and of the Holy Roman Empire. His capital, with its heterogeneous population of half a million inhabitants, its schools and libraries, its flourishing commerce, its monumental and beautiful public buildings and parks, might well have been the only city in Europe possessing, at that time, some features of a modern metropolis. The palace and fortress of Medina Azzahra, built for the residence of the caliph in the vicinity of the capital, was considered to be, together with the mosque, one of the architectural wonders of the world, and the fame of Cordova as a brilliant center of art, science, philosophy, and poetry loomed large in the Islamic and the Christian worlds.

The era of outstanding achievements includes that of Almanzor. The military genius and statemanship of this minister, who supplanted the caliph for all but ceremonial purposes, kept the country together and restored temporarily its supremacy in the Peninsula. A few years after his death in 1008 the caliphate was torn by violence and confusion. A proliferation of small states, called *reinos de taifas*, resulted. Some of them may be defined as microstates, whereas others, like Seville and Toledo, attained a high political and cultural level.

Intellectually this agitated era was remarkable. The poet and polygraph Ibn Hazm was one of the great minds of the generation which witnessed the disintegration of the Omayyad Cordovan empire. Taifa kings encouraged henceforth artistic and intellectual pursuits. Some of their little courts became important centers for music, others for science and various kinds of learning. All of the kings shared an interest in poetry. Unfortunately individual ambitions and intrigue prevented most of the Taifa states from living in peace with each other or from achieving internal stability.

A temporary solution to the political chaos of the eleventh century was the subjugation of the Taifa kings by leaders of belligerent sects that had originated in the Berber countries. First the bellicose and unlettered Almoravids gained control of Moslem Spain and launched in the early years of the twelfth century successful campaigns against the Christian states. Heads of small Moorish states found themselves in the painful dilemma of either surrendering to Christian Spain, represented mainly at that time by the vigorous kingdoms of Castile and Aragon, or placing themselves under the protection of fanatical forces, which would inevitably destroy their way of life. Such was the fate of Almotamid, the poet king who died as a prisoner in

Africa after losing his kingdom to his powerful ally, the Almoravid Sultan.

The new empire succumbed very soon to factionalism, and around 1150 the Almoravids were overruled by the Almohads, a Berber people led by more enlightened minds than those of their predecessors. Scientific and speculative studies were encouraged by the Almohad Sultan Yusuf: both Averroes, one of the most significant figures of medieval thought, and the Aristotelian scholar Ibn Tofail worked under his patronage. In the twelfth century the Jewish religious poetry and philosophy of Al-Andalus reached also, with Ibn Gabirol and Maimonides, its finest hour.

In 1212 the Almohads were defeated at Las Navas de Tolosa by a coalition of Christian monarchs, and in the next thirty years sweeping campaigns were conducted by the Aragonese in the Mediterranean area and by the Castilians in the southern and southwestern regions of the Peninsula. The Balearic Islands, Valencia, and several Andalusian capitals, including Cordova and Seville, fell into Christian hands. This was the historical situation which saw the birth of the kingdom of Granada.

III *The Nasrid Kingdom of Granada*

Granada, an important town since Roman times, had become after the fall of the caliphate, the capital of a Taifa kingdom ruled by a Berber family and later by Almohad leaders. A period of turbulence and struggle for power among various factions followed the Almohads' loss of power in the first half of the thirteenth century. A young man of Arab descent, the nephew of the king of a small Taifa, emerged as the victor and became Mohammad-al-Nasr I of Granada, better known in Western literature as Alhamar.[4]

Although the founder of the new Moorish state had mastered the arts of war and intrigue, he was above all a man of peace, with a genius for effective government and a pragmatic and hedonistic attitude. He transformed the divided land, newly brought under his rule, into one of those small states that represent at their best the achievements of a mature civilization. The country covered the territory of the present provinces of

Granada, Málaga, and Almería. It comprised, therefore, a sea-
board zone and high mountain ranges, including the Sierra
Nevada, at whose feet the ample *Vega* ("valley") of Granada
spreads, crossed by the rivers Darro and Genil. The town lies
between two hills separated by the Darro, on which the
Alhambra and the Albaicín stand today. Even if no civilization
had left its trace in this region, it could still be considered
outstanding for its natural beauty.

Moreover in the southern Mediterranean area the proximity
of the mountains and the coast results in a temperate, moder-
ately dry climate. The abundance of water is a blessing that
few of the neighboring regions share, and it has become a
poetic motif related to Granada. Likewise, the contiguity of
heights and plains and the luminous atmosphere characteristic
of the region may have contributed to some of the themes of
Granada. Indeed, the legend of the Moor's sigh[5] or poetic
reports of combats in the Vega,[6] take into account, not just
the visual impression of landscape, but also the experience of
contemplating it in a special mood or situation.

The Nasrid kingdom was founded at a time when the tide of
history had taken an adverse turn for Moslem Spain. After
Cordova and Valencia fell into Christian hands, and a victorious
campaign launched by Ferdinand III of Castile swept over
Alhamar's native Arjona, the strong citadel of Jaén became in
1245 the next target. In a gesture inspired by political realism,
as much as by a chivalric feeling of trust toward a noble
adversary, King Alhamar presented himself unescorted at the
Castilian camp and offered his friendship and his allegiance
to the Castilian sovereign. The treaty that was negotiated made
of Granada a feudatory state pledged to pay a tribute and
lend military assistance to Castile, and entitled to participate
in its *Cortes* ("parliament"). In 1247, a Granadine contingent
led by Alhamar fought valiantly on the side of the Christians
against the Moors of Seville, many of whom would become
refugees in Granada soon thereafter, when their country was
lost. Throughout the long struggle of the Reconquest the pattern
of alliance and enmities was so complex that the presence of a
Moorish warrior in a Christian camp or vice versa was by no
means exceptional and carried no connotation of treason. And

yet, the participation of the first king of Granada in the undoing of the last and the most brilliant Taifa state does ring a poignant note and underscores the inherent weakness of the country that was to be the epigone of Moslem Spain.

Granada, a zealous Islamic state with no Mozarabic minority, had to absorb a great number of refugees from the fallen Taifas, although the vast majority of the latter's population remained in their native land as *mudéjares,* that is to say, Moors living under Christian rule. Faced with the problems of overpopulation, Alhamar understood the importance of developing all the resources of the country. He encouraged farming, mining, and commerce. With the planned increase in the cultivation of white mulberries and in silkworm breeding, the Granadine textile industry flourished. In this and other crafts, the artisans of Granada, who had inherited the techniques developed during the caliphate, were considered to be among the most skilled of their time. Brocades and taffeta, woolen and linen cloth in exquisite colors, leather repoussé, ceramics, inlaid wooden objects, finely carved arms, jewelry, and ornaments were among the products exported to European and African countries. Alhamar is known to have taken great pride in the delicate shaping of Granadine silver and gold coins, which were first stamped during his reign. Throughout the existence of the kingdom of Granada commerce with neighboring Castile was normally quite active.

In the tradition of the caliphate, irrigation systems and agricultural policies were constantly being revised and improved in Granada. Successful efforts were made to acclimatize a great variety of trees and plants, and soon the fame of the orchards and flower gardens of the Vega spread through the Islamic and the Christian world. Vineyards and olive groves yielded splendid harvests. In spite of the Koran's prohibition, drinking songs were common in the poetry of Al-Andalus. Wine was produced, exported, and also consumed. Cattle breeding, although far less important than in other Peninsular states, was promoted by the Nasrid monarchs, and the spirited horses ridden by the knights of Granada were coveted by horsemen everywhere.

Successful as Alhamar was in consolidating the economy of his country, the image he projected was that of an artist king and a contemplative man. From his time on, the fine cultural traditions of caliphal Cordova and of the most refined Taifas were continued in Granada. Like many Oriental rulers, the Nasrid monarchs took great pride in the beauty and splendor of those mansions that they intended to be both their dwelling place and their lasting memorial. The high gardens of the Alhambra were planned with meticulous foresight by Alhamar, who constructed the canals that made possible the shady groves. (The fountains and ponds were added in a later period.) Legend tells us that before his death the first Nasrid king had a vision of the Alhambra, complete and perfect in its delicate beauty.

It may be said that the art styles exemplified in the Alhambra and the Generalife reflect well the refinement and the frailty of the Nasrid state. Depending on perishable materials, mostly wood and polychromed plaster, this art lacks the majesty of the architecture of the Caliphate, but it has an incomparable grace. The Granadine builders knew how to encompass both landscape and architecture in their planning, and the view framed within the arabesques of a window is an essential element of the experience of beauty and pleasure conveyed by Nasrid art.

Granada was not free of the factionalism which had plagued early Moorish states. In less than a hundred fifty years more than twenty princes occupied or claimed the throne, and the number of sovereigns, princes and dignitaries who lost their lives in civil strife or were the victims of assassination is appalling.[7] On the other hand, an intelligently cautious policy prevailed most of the time in Granada's relationships with Castile and the African Moslem states. A complex tax structure was developed to meet the feudatory tribute which was paid, though intermittently, to Castile. In fact, although the Nasrid kingdom had a well-trained militia, the chances it had of survival depended mainly on the wisdom of its diplomacy. In the second half of the thirteenth century the new Berber empire of the Benimerines, after breaking the power of the Almohads, sent well-disciplined troops across the Strait of Gibraltar, in an effort to recover for the Moslems the initiative in the struggle for domination of the Peninsula. The Granadine

Moors used those powerful allies to check the progress of the Reconquest, but they never allowed the balance of power to pass into their hands, and at times they sided with Castile against the Benimerines. With the decline of the latter's power, the danger of the fall of Granada increased. However, more than a hundred years elapsed before a persistent and successful effort to achieve this end was made.

IV *The Frontier*

Although full-scale warfare was only occasionally waged between Castile and Granada, the knights of the Moorish kingdom excelled in the skills and virtues of the warrior. Along the frequently shifting borders, adversaries coexisted through periods of truce and military campaigns. Such a setting offered men stationed at frontier towns excellent opportunities to display feats of individual prowess. Courage, constant vigilance and initiative, as well as an understanding of the enemy's language and customs were required of such leaders and knights, both among the Castilians and the Moors. Warfare techniques like the ambush and the skirmish, and sports like the bullfight and the *juego de cañas*—a kind of tournament in which two opposing teams of horsemen used reeds instead of spears and protected themselves with leather shields—became the common skills of the Christians and Moors of the frontier. And as many readers of medieval chronicles and poems have observed, their encounters took place in a spirit of sportsmanship.[8]

Capture by the enemy was always a possibility for a *fronterizo*, although he could normally expect to be ransomed or exchanged for another prisoner. In exceptional cases the time spent in captivity gave rise to a real friendship among adversaries. To facilitate ransom negotiations and similar contacts the office of a special judge was established.[9]

Coexistence at the frontier encouraged mutual influence between Granadines and Castilians. Ibn Jaldún, one of the Arab historians who lamented this fact. observed that, although the Moors of Granada still considered genealogy important, they no longer had a strong sense of political solidarity among kinsmen.[10] Their habits were deeply influenced by European customs,

as is proved by the fact that paintings of nobles and warriors—
contrary to Islamic prescription against representation of the
human figure—decorated the walls of the Alhambra. On the
other hand, Castilian nobles owned and occasionally used lux-
urious Moorish garments; they also rode horses, fought bulls,
and played cañas in the style of Granada.[11] One continuous
source of admiration and curiosity for the Christians of the
frontier was the beauty of the Moorish capital, crowned by the
Alhambra and other castles. In contrast to the Gothic structures
of the same period, the Moorish palaces expanded into loose
complexes of patios, towers, and gardens, designed for pleasure
and reverie. Such features appealed to the Castilians of the
fifteenth century, who were trained in the subtleties of trouba-
dour poetry and had established contact with the Italian Renaissance. And yet the hedonistic spirit of the builders of the
Alhambra must have remained alien to them.

The fact that the Moors and Christians of the frontier shared
the same activities and problems, and that they had similar
ideas on knighthood and courtesy, should not lead one to
minimize the profound differences in their historical circumstances and consequently in their attitude toward life. Those
Castilians who best represented the spirit of their age and of
their land conceived life as a projection toward the future.
They strove for conquests yet to be achieved, for service
to an expansive faith, for fame that would perpetuate the
memory of their exploits, and for reward in eternity. The
Moors of Granada had perfected a culture for here and now.
Coming into existence at a turning point in the historical cycle
of Al-Andalus, when gradual decline could at most be checked,
the Nasrid kingdom became an example of wordly wisdom.
Their quest in life was to impart beauty to every object, and
joy to every hour. Such an attitude was not incompatible with
a supreme elegance of conduct and an exalted sense of honor.[12]

V   *The Conquest of Granada*

In the last decades of the fifteenth century, Castile and
Aragon were already united under the Catholic Sovereigns
Ferdinand and Isabella, who proved to be capable of holding
together and of orienting toward momentous enterprises the

dynamic and ambitious people they ruled. The conquest of the Moorish kingdom of Granada was an essential part of their program of national unity and expansion. A refusal to send the tribute that Granada paid to Castile gave rise to a ten years' war, which ended with the surrender of the Moorish capital.[13]

Historians give credit to Queen Isabella for her success in keeping under perfect control the unruly Castilian nobility during the period of hardships of the long strife. Unity was achieved in some measure by imposing stern discipline, but a more important factor was the enthusiasm that swept away former differences. Striking examples of mutual assistance in perilous situations were given by powerful Andalusian nobles, who had earlier plunged the region into a situation close to civil war. Formerly disobedient subjects were eager to perform heroic deeds in the service of a queen who tried to be always near the battlefront. And although austerity was the dominant note in her valiant, itinerant court, music, poetry and courtly love were also present.

In contrast to the concerted effort on the Castilian side, the royal family and the nobility of Granada present a picture of discord and cruelty. King Muley-Hacén, a brave and fierce fighter, provoked the principal rift within the royal family when he deserted his wife Aixa for a Castilian captive. The abandoned queen, a woman of great energy and highly adept in courtly intrigues, succeeded in turning against Muley-Hacen their son Abdallah, more often referred to as Boabdil or the *Rey Chico*. She also won for him the support of a powerful faction headed by the Abencerrajes. The old king was deposed after the first setbacks in the war with Castile, but Boabdil could not unite the kingdom under his rule.[14] His authority was challenged by his father's supporters, and his military efforts were doomed to failure. He became a prisoner of the Christians, who understood it was to their advantage to allow him to return to Granada. At the time when Boabdil was taken captive, his uncle El Zagal also proclaimed himself sovereign. This action worsened the internal difficulties of the Moorish state, but it must be recognized that the last of the Granadine rebels was an able and courageous leader, as his stubborn defense of Málaga proves.

The strife within the Moorish royal family was paralleled by feuds among the most powerful clans, such as that of the Abencerrajes, whose prestige seems to have been immense. The faction they led supported Boabdil against his father, a policy which, according to Luis Seco de Lucena,[15] was consistent with the tendency to promote insurrection that members of this clan had exhibited earlier. Pérez de Hita, and after him most authors who wrote about Granada, pictured the Abencerrajes as the victims of Boabdil's ·cruelty and subsequently as refugees in the Castilian camp. This was not true of that particular clan. However, although Granadine warriors defended with courage the citadels and towns of the kingdom, it appears that in the last years of the war a considerable number of them defected and joined the Castilian army.

In the last stage of the campaign the Moorish capital was besieged by the Christians; it was at the Castilian camp, built like a city and called Santa Fe, that Columbus presented himself to the queen. The Vega of Granada became for some time the scene for what was probably the last military conflict resembling a giant tournament, with individual warriors of both sides challenging one another to group or single combats. If the camp in Santa Fe could be viewed as a portrayal of chivalric lore,[16] ballads depicting this phase of the war show the noble women of Granada watching the fighting from the towers of the Alhambra. The war itself was no mere joust cr game, however, and the Castilian side gave no indication that it would loosen its grip.

Boabdil had no alternative but to surrender the keys of the Moorish kingdom, after negotiating an honorable capitulation that guaranteed the lives and property of the people of Granada and granted them the right to remain Muslims, if they so wished, and to keep their usages and language. With the solemn entry of Ferdinand and Isabella in Granada on January 2, 1492, and Boabdil's melancholy departure, which would become a topic of literature and legend, the doom of Islamic Spain as a political entity was sealed.[17]

CHAPTER 2

The Moriscos of Granada

I The Population of the Kingdom of Granada After 1492

SINCE Julio Caro Baroja's penetrating analysis of the changing sociological background that underlies the vicissitudes of the people of Granada during the sixteenth century,[1] considerable research has been done on this historical process,[2] whose general lines should be kept in mind in order to assess the paradoxical appearance of the literary type of the sentimental and chivalric Moor.

During the first ten years after the surrender of Granada the Moorish population was faced with the three following alternatives: migration to a Moslem country in Africa or the Middle East, conversion to the Catholic religion, or acceptance of the status of mudéjares. To the latter group their freedom to practice the Moslem religion was promised in the Capitulations of 1492, although their rights were in many ways restricted. Families belonging to the ruling classes, which in fact included many merchants and landowners (although literary works of the period speak only of gallant knights), chose the first or the second alternative. The vast majority of peasants and craftsmen, as well as the small storekeepers and migrant vendors so typical of Moslem society, stayed in their native land but held fast to the religion and the way of life in which they were born.

The powerful sector of the Granadine society which migrated to Africa included El Zagal, the courageous defender of Málaga, and most members of the Abencerraje family. Eventually, Boabdil, following the first revolt of his former subjects, was compelled to exchange the territory allocated to him at the time of the conquest for a less desirable state. He also became an exile and died a soldier's death fighting for the king of

Fez. A large number of Moors from Granada settled in Fez, Tetuán, and other cities, and they contributed considerably to the prosperity and military might of the Moslem African states. Some of them conceived the dream of returning as conquerors to their native land, a project which, taking into account earlier invasions of southern Spain, was not to be considered an absolute impossibility. Granadine warriors and their sons swelled the ranks of those pirates who frequently attacked the small ports of southern and eastern Spain, ravaging the coastland and taking captives. As the Spanish authorities well knew, such raids were secretly supported by the Moriscos in the Peninsula. Consequently, in every debate concerning this unhappy minority, the advocates of stricter controls of the suspected group were certain to refer to such contacts with outside enemies and to underscore the threat they represented to the country. With regard to Moorish families whose conversion was voluntary, it may be presumed that the higher their social standing, the more advanced was their assimilation to the corresponding, or immediately inferior, class in Castilian society. Thus we see that the noble house of the Granada Venegas, founded by a Granadine prince, intermarried with the Mendozas who, for several generations, held the governorship of Granada.[3]

Less illustrious families participated in local government or became attached to the household of the powerful Andalusian nobility, to whom after the conquest vast domains had been assigned in the territory of the former kingdom of Granada. It appears that still others among the vanquished found some consolation in wealth and in luxury. Following the fashion of Moorish times, the leisure class of Granada divided its time pleasantly between comfortable city homes, which they continued to build and decorate in Moorish style during the sixteenth century, and estates in the country.[4]

The erosion of Moslem belief and practice among the members of this class dated from the period of Moorish independence, and, whether they were sincere or not in their conversion to Christianity, a few of them would risk persecution by adhering secretly to the rites of Islam. Regarding dress, home furnishings, and social customs the pattern must have been mixed. The clothes of peasant women remained unchanged after the conquest and the nominal conversion of 1526. In contrast, men of Moorish descent dressed usually like the old Christians. At the same time, Moorish attire and Moorish sports became fashionable in Spain, and Morisco entertainers, who played their typical instruments and danced the *zambra*, were greatly appreciated. After the conquest, some of the prominent families of Granada adopted names that gave an indication of their Moorish origin, such as Núñez Muley or Alvaro de Fez, but the majority of converts took on Spanish names. Ethnic differences were not strong enough to clearly differentiate the Morisco community from the Old Christians, although, contrary to what Moorish ballads composed in the sixteenth century seem to indicate, certain physical traits were considered to be characteristic of this group.[5]

The conditions stipulated at the time of the surrender of Granada seem to have been inspired, as Caro Baroja has remarked, by the medieval attitude that recognized the right of religious minorities to coexist, though not on an equal basis, with the dominant people and its creed.[6] Some of the factors which quickly undermined this liberal opinion were of a political nature. It was felt that the balance of power in the Mediterranean could be adversely affected by the presence in the south of Spain of a Moslem population which, unlike the mudéjares of Aragon and Valencia, was used to being independent and to seeing in the Christian a foe rather than a master. And so it was that both political expediency and missionary zeal prompted some of the chief advisers of the Catholic Sovereigns to advocate strong measures conducive to the conversion of the recently subjugated Moors.

The first appointments made by Ferdinand and Isabella after the conquest of Granada show the willingness of the monarchs to deal fairly with the Moorish population. As governor they selected the count of Tendilla, Don Iñigo López de Mendoza, who came from a family with a reputation for literary accomplishments as well as for military feats. Those traditions were never belied by Don Iñigo, whose government was marked by a liberal spirit. At the same time he conducted himself with great personal courage at moments when violence

seemed about to erupt. These traits made him extremely popular.
Even more beloved was the first archbishop of Granada, Fray
Hernando de Talavera, a great spiritual leader and a man of
uncompromising virtue, who had been confessor to Queen
Isabella.[7] He envisioned the conversion of the Moors of
Granada as a goal deserving of all his energy and efforts, but
he never resorted to other means than preaching, instruction,
and the example of Christian virtues. Fray Hernando held that
the Moors should be allowed to embrace Christianity without
giving up their own traditional customs. His approach is
well illustrated by the fact that he encouraged young priests
to study Arabic and to become acquainted with Moslem
science and ideology.[8] It would not be accurate to say that
his missionary program failed, because the number of converts
who responded to his teaching was high, and he exerted deep
influence among the educated classes, including Old and New
Christians. However, for those who were mainly concerned
with the country's security and who wished to shape a uniform
Christian society, the progress made seemed far from adequate.

The towering figure of Fray Francisco Jiménez de Cisneros,
future cardinal and regent of Castile, was prominent among
those who favored the use of pressure, if not of force, to
induce the people of Granada to accept baptism. When his
point of view prevailed in 1499, one of Cisneros' first measures
was to burn publicly copies of the Koran and other Moslem
religious texts, although at the same time he was careful to
save scientific works for the recently founded University of
Alcalá de Henares. He resorted to gifts in order to induce
prominent members of the Moorish community to embrace the
Christian faith, and he finally instituted a system of baptisms
en masse. Soon after these measures were taken a revolt broke
out in the capital and spread to the Sierra of the Alpujarra.
King Ferdinand in person led the fight against the rebels, who
were defeated at the cost of many lives. Among those killed
was Don Alonso de Aguilar, the head of the House of Córdoba
and one of the bravest Castilian generals. After such events
the hard line was considered to be justified. Compulsory
conversion or exile was imposed by decree in 1502 on all the
mudéjares living in the territories under the crown of Castile.

With this measure the entire population of Granada fell into the category of *nuevos convertidos de moros,* more commonly referred to as Moriscos.

II *The Plight of the Moriscos*

Throughout the sixteenth century, Spanish theologians argued whether the compulsory baptism received by the majority of the Moriscos was valid. The dispute had important practical implications, since apostasy and heresy were severely punished, and if those involuntary converts were considered to be responsible Christians, their relapse into Mohammedanism would be viewed as a grave crime. The Tribunal of the Inquisition or Holy Office, whose mission it was to watch over religious orthodoxy, had jurisdiction over such matters. The decision taken in 1526 to establish in Granada a branch of this tribunal was a hard blow for the numerous Moriscos who had succeeded so far, in spite of every prohibition, in keeping unaltered their religious belief and their way of life.[9]

In Aragon and Valencia the Islamic religion was officially abolished in the same year of 1526, and all mudéjares were ordered to leave the country or accept baptism. The effectiveness of the Inquisition in those two states, was, however, somewhat restricted by the *fueros* ("regional legislation").[10] Moreover the landowning nobility, in whose domains the vast majority of the Moorish population lived and worked, obtained a postponement for forty years of the enforcement of laws punishing the religious transgressions of the Moriscos. This period was to be used to properly indoctrinate the New Christians. Such a program was not easy to achieve, since the mudéjares of Aragon and Valencia were fervent Moslems, in spite of the fact that in Aragon most of them were not able to speak Arabic. Their communities included *alfaquís,* Moslem priests who performed the rites of the Islamic religion, usually with the tacit consent of the rural lords. In their religious and literary works, which constitute the so-called *aljamiado* literature, Moslem spiritual leaders and other learned Moriscos generally used the Spanish language, but they wrote in Arabic script, partly as a protective measure.[11] Some of the skilled

Aragonese craftsmen who in the sixteenth century decorated churches, halls, and palaces in the elaborate mudéjar style left in the vaults of such buildings secret emblems of the faith of their fathers.[12] Resistance to the decree of 1526 took the form of an open revolt in the Sierra of Espadán in Valencia, and subsequent efforts to win over the Moriscos made during the reigns of Charles V and Philip II by some churchmen, notably the archbishop of Valencia, Juan de Ribera, failed. In rural Aragon officers of the Inquisition were frequently threatened or attacked, and in the last decades of the sixteenth century bands of Morisco outlaws, at war with similar bands of mountaineers, ravaged the land and plunged it into a state of terror.

In the kingdom of Granada a smaller proportion of Moriscos were vassals of the nobles; moreover Castilian law did not give those lords the quasi-feudal autonomy enjoyed by their counterparts in Aragon or Valencia. Another differentiating trait may be seen in the fact that several prominent Granadine families were, at least in part, of Moorish descent. In the eventful year of 1526 the emperor Charles spent some time in Granada and three representatives of the Morisco community presented to him a list of grievances. A commission which included the renowned preacher and writer Fray Antonio de Guevara,[13] was appointed to study the matter. They reached the conclusion that the descendants of the Moors had just causes for complaint but also asserted that they continued to be Moslems, notwithstanding their official conversion. The result of the investigation proved to be, in the long run, detrimental to the interests of the Moriscos. The effort to eradicate the Moslem faith took the form of renewed prohibitions affecting, among other things, the manner in which they dressed, celebrated marriage, and buried their dead. Books in Arabic were forbidden, and in fact every differentiating minority trait came under attack.[14] The Moriscos' history presents a recurrent pattern of prohibitions that did not achieve their goal, but only encouraged unrest and revolts that finally resulted in stiffer repression. In Granada a considerable degree of harmony was achieved between Old and New Christians in the very active artisans' guilds as well as in some spheres of public administration. It is also possible that the assimilation of the Granadine leisure class by that of the hidalgos would have been achieved, if its members had not been drawn into one or another kind of involvement with the problems of an increasingly harassed and belligerent rural population of Moriscos. When violence flared up, the king's officers counted on the principal families of Granada to exert a pacifying influence. On the other hand, discontented Moriscos expected to find among the descendants of the oligarchy of the Moorish kingdom leaders and intermediaries who would take their grievances to the governor or the king.

Ethnic prejudice seems to have been absent among the conquerors of Granada, but toward the middle of the sixteenth century a considerable number of *estatutos de limpieza de sangre* barring the descendants of Moors and Jews from entering religious orders, schools, or branches of government were promulgated.[15]

Among the common people, Moriscos were easily identified by, and ridiculed for, their accent and other peculiarities of their Spanish.[16] All of this contributed to their alienation. Other causes of friction became very acute in the third quarter of the century. Terrorism mounted alarmingly. It was caused by bands of Moriscos, called *Monfíes*, who descended upon the cities, robbing and killing, and then returned to almost impregnable hiding places in the mountains. Some of their local lords, it was rumored, failed to punish such conduct, and disagreement among the authorities as to the extent of the problem and the best way to deal with it ran deep. And the mounting economic crisis that presented itself in the first years of the reign of Philip II aggravated the very tense situation.

III · *The Rebellion of the Alpujarras*

One of the immediate causes for the rebellion that for more than two years kept the former kingdom of Granada in a state of civil war,[17] may be found in the promulgation in January of 1567 of a decree, to become effective one year later, reinforcing earlier prohibitions of Moorish customs, attire, and ceremonies. Another provision stipulated that the use of Arabic would be permitted only during the next three years. Morisco

children were to attend schools where they would be instructed
in the Catholic faith and taught the Spanish language. This
they deeply resented, as they did the order that women keep
their faces uncovered. The decree also made it illegal for the
Moriscos to have Negro slaves, a practice that until then had
been authorized.

The preparation of a "Memorial" requesting the repeal of the
regulations was entrusted to Don Francisco Núñez Muley, an
elderly lawyer who had been raised in the household of Fray
Hernando de Talavera and had represented the Morisco community on other occasions. He produced an impressive document,[18] in which he accused the Crown of not having kept
the promises made at the time of the conquest of Granada
and insisted on the compulsion under which the Moriscos had
embraced the Christian religion. Their persistent commitment
to the Moslem faith was, on the other hand, skillfully under-
played. Núñez Muley made the point that the attachment of a
people to a way of life that is its heritage does not necessarily
imply religious allegiance to a particular belief. Distinctive types
of personal attire characterize, for instance, different nations
within the same religious community, Christian Europe being
an excellent example of such diversity. As a sociohistorical
document, the "Memorial" is of the greatest interest, since
it reveals to some extent the double life that was characteristic
of the Morisco community. It is explained, for instance, that
brides were attired in Christian garb for the wedding in the
church but wore Moorish clothes for the celebration at home,
which included prescribed ceremonies, music, and dances.

The Moriscos' petition was supported by the Marqués de
Mondéjar, governor of Granada. The king, however, upheld
the decree, which had been sponsored by the president of the
"Audiencia" don Pedro Deza, and other members of that powerful bureaucracy, whose role during Philip II's reign was to
become more important than that of the aristocracy. To make
matters worse it was considered necessary to impose a new
tax on the dyers' industry, which was mostly in the hands of
wealthy Moriscos. Significantly, some of these were among the
first leaders of the rebellion.[19]

It is Pérez de Hita who has reported in greater detail how

the Moriscos counted the men available to take arms and how they raised money for a major rebellion.[20] The Monfíes, or Morisco outlaws, were among the first to proclaim themselves independent in a stronghold of the Sierra. Soon thereafter the rebels sought aid from the Turkish-Berber empire. They did not receive the full-scale support requested, but a contingent of Turkish soldiers did fight at their side, and pirate raids against the Spanish coast became more frequent and harmful, since the number of captives that were taken and subsequently sold as slaves in Moslem countries increased considerably. In general terms, however, Turkish and African involvement in the revolt remained relatively small.

The Spanish authorities did not seem to become aware of the gravity of the situation until the rebellion had become well established. Their failure to take prompt action was due in part to personal differences between the Marqués de Mondé-jar and the bureaucrat Don Pedro Deza. The point of view of the marqués was characteristic of the nobility favoring the status quo, partly because harassment of their Morisco vassals was detrimental to their own interests and partly because the medieval virtues of coexistence were not entirely forgotten. During this war, Mondéjar's efforts to pacify the Moriscos with the promise of a pardon were consistently undermined by Deza.

This was the time when all prominent Moriscos were forced to take sides. The decision must have cost many of them considerable anguish and hesitation. Don Alonso de Granada Venegas, who remained loyal to the king and acted until the end of the insurrection as a negotiator between the rebels and the authorities, was not ashamed to admit the conflict in his heart when one of the first insurgent factions offered him the throne of Almería.[21] Like him, interpreters serving the Spanish command[22] and a large number of soldiers and several village priests martyred by the rebel Moriscos were of mixed blood. Even Don Fernando de Válor, the young *veinticuatro* ("council-man") of Granada who became the elected king of the insur-gents, apparently felt compelled to engage in open rebellion after an incident which he interpreted as an insult to his personal dignity.[23]

It was his uncle El Zaguer, a man of great wealth and

prestige, who took the initiative for selecting Don Fernando as head of a small kingdom which claimed to be legitimate heir of the medieval Moslem states. He was crowned in a secret ceremony reviving forgotten Islamic rites and took the name of Aben Humeya, as a sign that he was a descendant of the rulers of the caliphate. Other leaders of the rebellion also changed their names to the original Arabic version, claiming noble genealogies, and a revival of Moorish customs and lore took place in towns held by the Moriscos.

The rebels failed in an attempt to carry the uprising to the city of Granada and were pushed back to the abrupt mountainous region of the Alpujarras, where they resorted with considerable success to surprise attacks and raids, which had been the characteristic mode of warfare on the frontier of Granada.

The Marqués de los Vélez, a man in whom the energy of the medieval crusader could still be recognized, joined the king's troops and won certain advantages. The situation remained, however, uncontrollable, and Philip II sent his half brother, Juan de Austria—the future hero of Lepanto—assisted by some of the most experienced Spanish generals, to subdue the revolt. The victory he obtained after more than a year of hard fighting would have been even more costly, had not violence and factionalism divided the Moriscos. Aben Humeya was killed by one of his associates over a conflict of honor and jealousy. His opponent and successor, Aben Abó, as well as El Habaquí, who negotiated the surrender of the last organized stronghold, suffered the same fate.

In villages and towns dominated by the rebels, Christians who refused to abjure their faith were publicly tortured and killed. Retaliation and looting were carried likewise to extremes by the king's army. Deportation from their homeland was the final disastrous consequence of the revolt for the Morisco population.

IV   *The Diaspora*

The diaspora, or dispersion, of the Moors of Granada began, as has been indicated, shortly after the last Nasrid king surrendered. The vast majority of the population remained, however, in their native region until the outbreak of the Alpujarras revolt. At that point many Moriscos residing in the city of Granada were forcibly transported to other parts of Spain. After the end of the war all descendants of the Moors were officially banished from the territory of the Nasrid kingdom[24] and immigrants from other areas were brought in. The eradication, however, was far from complete. Certain Morisco families were exempted from the order of expulsion, because they could prove that their parents or grandparents had become converts at an early date, while others soon found it possible to return.

The last two decades of the sixteenth century must have been a time of great anxiety for middle-class residents of Granada who were of Moorish origin, but did not differ in their habits, ideas, or religious practice from the rest of the hidalgo class.[25] The awareness of impending disaster in which these people lived and their desperate will to turn back the tide had curious literary repercussions. Learned men and artisans of the Morisco community collaborated in the fantastic forgeries of leaden books found at the Sacromonte and of other documents that established an Arabic origin for Granada, introducing at the same time material very appealing to devout Catholics and most flattering to all Granadines.[26] The *Diálogos de las cosas notables de Granada* (1603) by Luis de la Cueva also seem to be inspired by a desire to spread ideas that indirectly reflected prestige on the descendants of the Moors. More significant is Miguel de Luna's *Historia verdadera del rey don Rodrigo* (1592–1600), which portrays the Moorish conquerors of the Peninsula as models of virtue and tolerance. The author, who was interpreter to the king, presented his predominantly fictional book as a translation of an Arabic historical work. Luna's intention was actually polemical, as James Monroe underscores,[27] for the picture he drew of a humane Moslem domination carried an implicit censure of the severe conditions imposed at this time on the descendants of the Moors.

Meanwhile the Granadine Moriscos who were resettled in other regions had brought with them an element of unrest. Many of them resorted to itinerant trades, and every reader of Spanish classic literature knows that the *arrieros* ("muleteers") who filled with their noisy laughter and quarrels the country inns across the country, were for the most part Moriscos. Those men acted sometimes as liaison agents between different groups of their own people, including those living in strategic points of the Mediterranean coast who had organized the smuggling of arms and other products from Aragon to Valencian ports where the contraband was collected by Turkish or Berber corsairs. But for all their efforts, during the last quarter of the century every attempt to organize a widespread revolt resulted in total failure.

Hatred between Old Christians and converts deepened, and in Aragon, the 1580s saw what almost amounted to a civil war between Moriscos and mountaineers. Supporters of the plan to expel from the country a minority that was considered to be stubbornly hostile and subversive gained in strength, although some still defended the moral rights of the Moriscos.[28] In spite of the hard line he followed, Philip II refrained from taking so grave a measure as expulsion, whose harmful consequences he could foresee, and which the nobility of Valencia and Aragon strongly opposed. It was his son Philip III who issued between 1609 and 1611 a series of decrees ordering the expulsion of the Moriscos from the different regions of Spain, including Granada. His commands were carried out within the next few years and by 1615 the Moorish nation had been officially eradicated from Spanish soil.

CHAPTER 3

The Noble Moor in the Old and the New Romancero

I The Emergence of a Literary Type

THE war against Moslem Spain provided the background and much of the subject matter of Castilian epic poetry. In the only example of this poetry which has been preserved in its original text, the *Cantar de Mío Cid,* the Moors indeed appear as foes and warriors, but are also treated as simple peasants or burghers, viewed with a considerable amount of sympathy.[1] An attractive character in the poem is El Cid's loyal friend, the good Moor Abengalbón. These people are considered to be part of a familiar environment and no effort is made to describe their appearance or their customs. In other medieval epics reconstructed by Ramón Menéndez Pidal, the destinies of Christians and Moors appear closely knit, and no tendency to disparage the latter is evident. The motif of love between a Christian and a Moslem, which would not recur very frequently in Golden Age literature, appeared in a poem about Alfonso VI of Castile and the Princess Zaida of Seville, who became his bride.[2] Such poems reflect to a certain degree the cultural symbiosis that existed between Christian and Moorish Spain, but they fail to stress cultural differences in any way resembling later trends toward the picturesque.

According to María Rosa Lida de Malkiel,[3] the image of the Moor as a chivalric type and the portrayal of Moorish courtly life in terms of its refinement, luxury, and voluptuousness first appeared in the works of Don Juan Manuel. A nephew of Alfonso el Sabio and one of the most influential men of that period, he had had the experience of frontier life at a time when civil strife within the Christian nations had weakened

41

the impetus of the Reconquest and contacts between Castilian
lords and the Moorish court became more frequent. Don Juan
Manuel appreciated the culture of the Moors and gave a
Hispano-Moorish or a Saracen setting to several stories of the
collection of tales he called *El Conde Lucanor*. The wisdom or
ingenuity of a Moslem sovereign, the gallantry of the last
Moorish king of Seville, who fulfilled the delightfully extrava-
gant wishes of the slave girl he had married because she was
able to improvise poetry, the mutual esteem and trust between
Sultan Saladim and a captive Christian knight are motifs that
foreshadow the idealization of the Moor and of his relations
with the Christians.

A great contemporary of Don Juan Manuel, the author of
El libro de buen amor, who identified himself as Juan Ruiz,
archpriest of Hita, lived also in a society permeated by Arabic
influences, but of a different kind. This poet had contacts with
mudéjar and Mozarabic, as well as with Jewish, communities
in Toledo and other cities, and particularly with those of its
members who were minstrels and entertainers. The influence
of their style and the imprint of their outlook on life runs deep
in his work, and, although Moorish society is only represented
by one literary character in the book—a Moorish woman who
refuses to hear the love message of the narrator-protagonist—
the episode may be interpreted as a sign that the author tends
to idealize the Moslem world.[4]

Stylized visions of a given culture may follow different
orientations, and those we have briefly reviewed do not point
in exactly the same direction as the so-called Moorish ballads
and novels of a later period. A precedent for this trend is found
in the anonymous *Gran crónica de Alfonso XI*, as Diego Catalán
has proved.[5] Even if chivalric customs and ideas attributed in
this work to the Moslem society do correspond to a historical
reality, the very wish of writers to describe them extensively
is in itself significant with respect to later literary developments.
Moreover, although the chronicle relates the deeds of the last
Castilian king of heroic stature, the tragic consequences of his
triumphs for the Moors are also considered. The Benimerín
ruler Alboacén is presented as a figure of great dignity. He
also becomes an object of sympathy when his son is killed on

the battlefield. The character of the prince is that of a gallant young knight; it anticipates the prototype developed in the ballads and the novels of the sixteenth century.

The image of the Moor as an adversary who is an infidel but shares with the Christian the concept of honor reappears in several narratives of the fifteenth century.[6] Such texts prove that contacts across the frontier were not always hostile.[7] There are instances where knights of Granada are praised, not only for their courage, but also for their courtesy and magnanimity; and such feelings increase during the last campaign when the court of Ferdinand and Isabella assumes the aspect of a chivalric court.[8] The architecture and other aspects of the culture of the Moorish kingdom are appreciated also by Castilian chroniclers. Some concern themselves specifically with the internal situation of Granada,[9] attesting to an interest that found in the art of the old ballad its finest poetic expression.

Aside from the ballads of the frontier of Granada, Castilian poetry of the fifteenth century took only occasional notice of the neighboring Nasrid state and the wars against it.[10] A few stanzas, for instance, of Juan de Mena's *Laberinto* recount deeds that were the subject of ballads. The genre of the *serranilla* ("a medieval pastoral poem") as developed by the Marqués de Santillana, reflected certain aspects of frontier life. Later on Juan del Encina, an important figure of the early Renaissance, celebrated the conquest of Granada, both in the folkish style of a shepherd's *villancico* ("a type of poem with refrain, common in Castilian folk-song") and in an allegorical poem. More significant is a ballad inviting the deposed Moorish sovereign to become a Christian; the author anticipated the poetic image that would be associated with the figure of Boabdil by stressing the topic of *ubi sunt* in reference to his loss. Interestingly, among the people of Granada an elegiac poem in Arabic language perpetuated in a somewhat similar image the memory of the last Moorish king.[11]

II *The Ballads of the Frontier of Granada*

From the fourteenth century on Castilian epic poetry flourished in the poetic form of the *romance*, a term usually translated

as "ballad." This type of brief poem, built around a single
theme, contains in fragmented form the historical or legendary
subject matter of the old, much longer epic poems, and likewise adapts most of the latter's formal elements to a more
flexible style that captures a large variety of moods and emotions. In contrast with the so-called new or artistic romances
that were composed in the sixteenth and seventeenth centuries
the old ballads, or *romances viejos*, were shaped in oral trans-
mission through an extended period of time. Narration and
dialogue, unexpected transitions, elements of mystery, lyrical
lines along with traditional epic patterns and abrupt endings
are the chief characteristics of the genre.[12]

Following the emergence of cycles of ballads derived from
longer medieval epic poems, the ballad was used to report on,
and interpret, contemporary public life. Not exclusively but most
significantly this practice was followed during the fifteenth
century on the frontier of Granada, where skirmishing and the
risk of captivity lent an adventurous quality to the existence
of soldiers and leaders, among whom the taste for music, literature, and history was not lacking. Poetic chronicles were written
in a style inspired by the ballads that had evolved in oral trans-
mission; more importantly they underwent a similar process of
enlargement, abridgment, or contamination by motifs alien to
the original nucleus of the poem, thus acquiring further structural and stylistic traits of the old ballad style.[13] Moreover a
sense of the dramatic was growing as a result of a more widespread interest in the destiny of individuals, subject to sudden
changes of fortune.[14]

Rather than the importance of the episode related, it was
the pathos of a situation or its power to stimulate the imagination that seems to have guided the selection of subject matter.
At least the frontier ballads that we now possess do not deal
with the great leaders or the most important events of the wars
against the kingdom of Granada. Rather we find incidents carrying an emotional impact which are seen from the point of view
of the person or the community adversely affected. Thus we
are told of Castilian leaders killed—"Buen alcaide de Cañete"—
or captured—'Día era de San Antón." The description of a re-
treating Moorish population builds toward the death of the

conqueror of the citadel in "Alora la bien cercada," and in the case of the ballads on the conquest of Antequera or Alhama[15] the theme is, rather than the victory obtained by the Christians, the loss suffered by the Moors and its repercussion in the Nasrid capital. Gradually a taste developed for picturing certain fascinating aspects of the exotic culture represented by the people of Granada. Attention is paid in fifteenth-century ballads to their expressions of anger or grief, to the beauty of their cities, to their music, and to the colorful luxury displayed by a small group on a raid, or by knights engaging in a juego de cañas.[16]

The place of the action, if not on the frontier, is in Nasrid territory, and, because of their touches of exoticism and the point of view from which the action is presented, such poems as "Abenámar" or the ballads on the loss of Antequera or Alhama anticipate to some extent the more sophisticated genre developed one hundred years later in the new romancero. Accordingly, they have been categorized as early Moorish ballads by Menéndez Pidal.[17] Fictional situations experienced in part by Moorish characters appear in other ballad cycles, particularly those originating in Carolingian epic. Among them are found sexual motifs that do not conform to concepts of love prevalent in the frontier ballad or in the later Moorish ballad, the object of a Moslem's desire being frequently a Christian woman, although the reverse situation is depicted with marked sympathy for the Moorish maid in "Yo me era mora Morayma."

A topic of Arabic poetry, the wooing of a city by a warrior, appears in the "Romance de Abenámar,"[18] possibly the masterpiece of the genre. Seldom was the historical incident at the basis of a ballad more thoroughly transcended. The attraction experienced by the Castilian king for the visible but distant Granada is the theme of the poem, which offers an interesting example of the courteous antagonism in Moorish-Christian contacts, which will be diversely reflected in the literature of the next century. But the image of the Moor in frontier ballads includes also somber traits: rapid references are made to deeds of cruelty and treason, and it is possible that in one such line the literary myth of the Abencerrajes as a symbol of excellence persecuted took root.[19]

Ballads originating in the successful campaign to conquer

Granada conducted by Ferdinand and Isabella sometimes report
on events of the war, such as the capture of Boabdil in Lucena.[20]
The spirit of chivalry is then stressed by allusions to heraldry
and to topical situations, mentioning for instance the ladies of
Granada who view a skirmish or cavalcade from the ramparts.[21]
Most of these ballads have reached us in enlarged sixteenth-
century versions, intricately combining fragments of medieval
and of Renaissance poems. Challenges and duels being a recurrent theme, small cycles arise, either around a famous champion,
such as the Maestre of Calatrava or Don Manuel Ponce de
León,[22] or a legendary deed, like the victory at Santa Fe of the
youthful Garcilaso over ·the strong Tarfe, who had insulted
the Christians in their faith,[23] an attitude contradicting the image
of the Moor of Granada prevailing in the late sixteenth century.
The name of Muza is given to the antagonist in a few ballads
giving rise to later glosses that must have inspired the fictional
role of the brother of the Moorish king in Pérez de Hita's
Guerras civiles de Granada. But it is in a period removed almost
one century from the time of the conquest that the Moorish
protagonist of Spanish ballads becomes a definite literary type.

III   *The Moorish Ballad of the Golden Age*

The first half of the sixteenth century makes little contribution
to the evolution of the ballad, but the genre remains alive, mainly
as poetry for singing. Some romances are printed in pamphlets,
a practice that had become popular in midcentury when two
important anthologies, the *Cancionero de romances* and the
Silva de Romances, appeared. Individual authors also published
collections of rather dull narrative ballads intended for reading,
among which the historical and legendary subject matter of
Granada is well represented.[24]

The bookdealer Juan de Timoneda, who published four ballad
collections in 1573,[25] plays an important role in a transitional
period when such poems were being compiled, enlarged, and
combined, first in somewhat polished but uninteresting style
and eventually with greater descriptive or dramatic interest.
The appearance and success about 1560 of the short novel
El Abencerraje, with its evocation of frontier life and sympa-

thetic portrayal of a Moorish couple, was a factor contributing to the proliferation of similar subject matter in the genre of the ballad.[26] Indeed, the characterization of Abindarráez and the elaborate image drawn at his first appearance anticipate the psychological traits as well as the descriptive technique that will shape in the new ballad the type of the enamored Moor. Other influences, notably that of Ariosto, make themselves felt, but only insofar as they are consonant with the concept of verisimilitude and with the tendency to idealize the relationship of Moorish and Christian knights that characterizes the Golden Age novels and ballads which have been labeled "Moorish." The latter's descriptive style is recognizable, as Maxime Chevalier has noticed,[27] in certain Spanish ballads on Ariostean themes, and conversely the example of Italian narrative poetry may have encouraged authors of Moorish ballads to build interest around an emotional posture, which is frequently one of jealousy or spite, though never Orlando's blind fury. Single combats recur in both types of poetry. One motif that may be traced back to Boiardo's *Orlando innamorato* is the baptism of a mortally wounded Moor administered by his Christian opponent.[28] It was borrowed from certain ballads about the episode of Agricán's death and adapted to the Granadine cycle, either by Pérez de Hita or by the anonymous author of the ballad on Albayaldos' conversion and death incorporated in *Civil Wars, I*.

Three representative poets of the period immediately preceding the Moorish ballad of nonepic motivation are Lucas Rodríguez,[29] Pedro de Padilla,[30] and Gabriel Lobo Lasso de la Vega.[31] They still write about cavalcades, skirmishes, and duels in the Vega, and the first two also found inspiration in the Abencerraje story.[32] Though a mediocre poet, Padilla, who had been trained at the University of Granada, made a significant contribution to the rise of the Moorish ballad and it is possible that he also influenced Pérez de Hita directly. His series of narrative ballads combines traditional subject matter embellished with descriptions of the colorful outfits of Moorish cavaliers and ladies.[33] Spanish aristocratic customs, slightly modified by an occasional exotic note, are attributed to the court of Granada, and one equestrian feast described in the ballad "El gallardo Abindarráez" resembles in specific details the elaborate *juego de sortija* ("tilting at the ring") in the *Guerras civiles*. Fragments of conversation or emotional reaction by the ladies in the audience to what goes on in the arena become as important as the game or the encounter proper, a trait that is found also in some of the poems by Lucas Rodríguez.

Ballads on nonhistorical Moorish themes in the new artistic rather than in the old traditional style, flourished in the last twenty or twenty-five years of the sixteenth century, and then the vogue declined.[34] These poems were composed by individual authors, but they appeared anonymously in poetic collections, thus indicating a resurgence of the concept of the romancero as a musical-poetic repertoire that absorbed and amalgamated individual contributions. The genre accounted for 40 percent of the poems in the *Flor de varios romances* (Huesca, 1589), collected by Pedro de Moncayo. These were borrowed largely from Lucas Rodríguez' collection but included also ballads of the new nonhistorical type.[35] More anthologies by Moncayo and other editors followed, leading to the appearance of the *Romancero General* of 1600, where no fewer than two hundred Moorish ballads were gathered despite the beginning decline of the popularity of the genre. Although the *Guerras civiles de Granada* appeared in 1595, it is not certain that every ballad published after this date whose thematic content is related to the book was inspired by it. Some of these poems might rather have served as a source for certain episodes before finding their way into a printed collection. In general terms one may, however, ascertain that Pérez de Hita helped to consolidate the literary type of the sentimental Moor of Granada.

Traits of the old ballad style recognizable in the new romancero are the occasional swift transitions and a lively tempo adequate to the zest and youthfulness with which the genre endows its protagonists. A few of the latter—Muza, Albayaldos, Aliatar, the Rey Chico—have some characteristics traceable to fifteenth or early sixteenth-century ballads, although most of the new romances were intended to express emotion. In some instances they were also composed as chronicles *à clef* of an event in the life of the author or his patron. Considering this circumstance, it may be argued that modern editors who grouped in cycles ballads which had appeared dispersed but which coincided in the name of the protagonist and the implicit fictional situation were often correct in restoring a link of origin, although it was a mistake to believe, as did Pérez de Hita, that the poems actually stemmed from happenings in Moslem Spain. The fact is that the majority of Moorish ballads with a well-rounded narrative content deal with juegos de cañas, bullfights, or other types of equestrian exercises, and in this connection an effective style for reporting the incidents of the game or fight was developed.[36] The actual occasion was of course strictly contemporaneous.

The poetic convention of portraying Spanish nobles as Moors did in fact conform with the origin of the sport as well as with the attire and weapons pertaining to it. The use of mythological motifs in the emblems, mottoes, and pageantry displayed by knights in Moorish array reflects also a practice of the sixteenth century, which parallels the not infrequent allusions to pagan myths by Moors in the literary works of the period. At the same time, a specialized vocabulary of Arabic origin lends a vaguely exotic touch to the lengthy passages enumerating the arms, clothing, and ornaments of horse and horseman so characteristic of the Moorish ballad. Paradoxically the effect of such descriptions is to convey a mood. Likewise, action and movement are frequently presented as expressions of emotions, rather than as steps in a logical sequence of events. What happens to the protagonist of the ballad or what he does is sparingly reported, in contrast to the elaborate descriptions and rhetorical monologues or dialogues, displaying joy, or rage, or despair variously caused by love, or jealousy, or clannish hatred. Actually men of letters and part of the ruling class in the era that created the Moorish ballad felt that life itself was largely shaped by the poetic imagination, and—as was stressed by Montesinos[37]—the people shared in this attitude sufficiently to appreciate such a genre, in spite, or even because of, the disparity between the dreamed-of society it depicts and actual conditions of existence.

As a nondirect mode of expression for basically lyrical content, Moorish ballads parallel the pastoral, being at the same time its counterpart. If a peaceful nature and simplicity are stressed in the world of idealized shepherds, the human figure appears in the Moorish ballad within an elaborate frame of

precious objects and contrasting colors. The chivalric environment is used to introduce external tensions or acts of violence
if such is the climate required by the mood expressed. And given
the social conditions of the period, the use of a Moorish protagonist may entail a stronger paradox than the pastoral convention.

Such traits, as well as the tendency to introduce the main
theme in the form of a disproportionately enlarged detail belonging to a vaguely defined episode, permit one to categorize as
manneristic the genre of the Moorish ballad. This style is also
characterized by formal patterns of the Petrarchan tradition[38]
that appear in profusion along with colloquialisms and a certain
directness of expression derived from the old ballads. Moreover,
the world of objects—to use Ulrich Knoke's expression—of the
Moorish ballad is most often presented as a fragmentary view
of reality, perceived in kaleidoscopic sequences. The enumeration
of garments and weapons with specific details of color, material,
and workmanship has an evocative value more often than it
conveys a clear total image.[39]

In frontier ballads references to the landscape and famous
buildings of Granada had become a poetic element. In Moorish
ballads this prestigious background is often built in, using the
evocative power of names. Occasionally the gardens of Generalife may be introduced in the tradition of *locus amoenus*,[40]
or the poet succeeds in enhancing the evocative power of topographical description, within the atmosphere removed from concrete reality created in the poem.[41] The awareness of the Moors'
loss of their native land seems to cast an emotional note in
ballads alluding to famous sites, as it happens in more recent
literary works.

Scholarly research has established that ballads on the loves
and misfortunes of the fictional Moors Zaide and Gazul were—
with few exceptions—composed by Lope de Vega in the 1580s
and that a close relationship exists between early sentimental
episodes of his life and the content of such poems, which are
among the most spirited specimens of the genre.[42] They also
correspond to an early stage of the lyrically motivated Moorish
ballads. Since in most other cases authorship and date of composition are not known, it is not possible to weigh the effect
of Lope's youthful contribution to the changing nature of the

ballads on Moorish or frontier themes. Luis de Góngora also composed early in his career a couple of exquisite Moorish ballads; later on he wrote parodies of the genre, but adopted nevertheless its style when dealing with themes of captivity and adventure in the setting of contemporary wars with Africans and Moors.[43]

In other chapters of this book the point will be made that the unknown author of *El Abencerraje,* as well as Ginés Pérez de Hita, intended their works of fiction to inspire a sympathetic attitude toward the descendants of the Moors. With respect to the Moorish ballad any generalization would be inaccurate. The standard opinion among scholars is that they are unrelated to the existence and problems of the Moriscos, unless one considers parodies that used for comical effect the contrast between the idealized Moors, male and female, about whom everyone sang and the commonplace artisans who bore the same names.[44] Recently Manuel Alvar has pointed out that, since the new Moorish ballad emerged in the years following the revolt of the Alpujarras, it might be related to the reputation of courageous fighters that the Moriscos gained in that fierce strife.[45] Fradejas raises the question and arrives at a negative conclusion. However, he suggests that a Morisco may have been the author of a ballad written to defend against ridicule the type of the gallant Moor, on the ground that Peninsular Moslem warriors were no less Spanish than their Christian counterparts.[46] It may be added that, although most writers of parodies either objected for literary reasons to a style that had become a stereotype, or bore a grudge against a poet known to have composed Moorish ballads, one may also occasionally discern the intention of discrediting a chivalric prototype that was antagonistic to the austere Old Christian tradition, and which moreover might be claimed as their heritage by the Moriscos.

Since debates went on, and since both advocates and critics of the vogue seem to be concerned with the prestige or lack of prestige of the Morisco community, one may wonder if some of the poets who helped to establish the genre were not interested in saving from social degradation the class that may be defined as the Morisco gentry. After all, the differentiating cultural traits stressed in the prototype of the gallant Moor were

only those that could be deemed acceptable in a convert, and
they coincided basically with traditional customs that Moriscos
of Granada openly defended. Moreover the latter in 1570 had
lost by confiscation their prized possessions, including jewels
and garments, identical to those so often mentioned and described in Moorish ballads.[47] Considering that the poet Pedro
de Padilla—born in Linares (province of Jaén) and educated in
Granada—was one of the first to place great emphasis on such
objects, one may wonder whether the sense of loss and the
nostalgia of the surviving bourgeoisie of the Nasrid kingdom
was not a factor, though a modest one, contributing to shaping
the lyrically motivated Moorish ballad.

CHAPTER 4

El Abencerraje

THE idealizing tendency in poetic and historical accounts of Moorish-Christian encounters found its most appealing expression in the *Historia de Abindarráez y Xarifa*, more often referred to as *El Abencerraje*. This first of Moorish novels appeared within the decade following the publication of *La vida de Lazarillo de Tormes* (1554), the little book that gave rise to the romance of roguery. Historically that was a period of transition between the era of expansion and grand illusions coinciding with the reign of Charles V and a different age, presided over by Philip II, which brought consolidation of political and religious unity, at the same time that the country experienced serious economic problems and eventually a decline in international power. In terms of artistic and literary history those years mark the beginning of a highly creative era, following the period of absorption of Renaissance thought and style.

I *The Publication of the Three Texts of* El Abencerraje

El Abencerraje has come to us in three distinctly different versions, a circumstance quite common in the case of the ballads, the short tales, or the accounts of contemporary history, but rather exceptional in the field of the novel. The problem is further complicated by the fact that all three texts are undatable and anonymous or of doubtful authorship. Bibliographical data may be summarized as follows:

A. *Corónica.* Printed in Toledo, 1561, by the press of Miguel Ferrer. The only extant copy was seen by nineteenth-century bibliographers and then lost. It was found in 1958 by A. Rumeau,[1] who published the text. The volume lacks a title page and preliminary material, which may be restored in part with the help of the one other edition of the same version. López Estrada has done a critical edition of the Toledo text.[2]

A text almost identical with that above was printed, with no date or place given, under the title *Parte de la Corónica del ínclito infante Don Fernando que ganó Antequera*.[3] The last part of the text is missing in the only extant copy of this edition, but it includes the complete "Dedicatoria," the first fragment of which does not appear in the Toledo text. The book is dedicated to the Aragonese Jerónimo Jiménez de Embún, Señor de Bárboles y Huitura. Facts known about the latter's life establish that the text was not written before 1550.[4] We shall discuss later the social, political, and literary circles with which Jiménez de Embún was connected.

B. *The 'Diana' version.* Following closely upon the Toledo edition of 1561 another version of the novel appeared as an insertion in the Valladolid edition (1561) of *Los siete libros de la Diana* by Jorge de Montemayor. Actually this edition did not come off the press until January of 1562,[5] and by then Montemayor was already dead.

C. *The 'Inventario' version.* A superior version of the short Moorish novel was published as part of the miscellany *El Inventario*, compiled, and possibly written, by Antonio de Villegas.[6] The book includes several poems and the pastoral novelette "Ausencia y soledad de amor." It was published at Medina del Campo in 1565, and issued again with some additions in 1577. Villegas was first authorized to publish the miscellany in 1551, but it is not known whether his draft included at that date the Moorish novel. There is no certainty either as to whether Villegas was the writer or merely the compiler of the text of *El Abencerraje* that he published. This version includes a minor episode not found in the other two texts of the novel.

II   *The Content of the Novel*

An introductory paragraph sketches the profile of a frontier leader of great prestige, Rodrigo de Narváez, who distinguished himself at the time of the conquest of Antequera and was appointed *alcaide* ("governor") of this important town and, according to the novel, also of the strategic frontier outpost of Álora, where he spent most of his time. Inspired by his example, the group of squires under Narváez's command were always victorious in the frequent skirmishes in which they engaged, thus winning considerable honor and booty.

On one clear night the alcaide invited ten of his men to scour the countryside in search of adventure. They divided into two groups and took different roads. The five squires not led by Narváez saw a young Moorish knight of noble countenance, whose splendid attire is described with some detail. He rode in leisurely fashion, singing a song he had composed in memory of his love. The words told that he had been born in Granada and reared in Cártama, that his beloved was now in Coín, and that he lived close to the border line of Álora. The squires were struck with admiration, but not to the point of allowing the Moor to go his way undisturbed. Under attack the latter proved to be a formidable warrior. The skirmish in which he overcame the five Castilian squires, who opposed him first individually and finally as a group, is described in great detail. Narváez comes to the rescue of his men, one of whom has called for his help by sounding a bugle. Narváez orders the squires to step aside, and he himself engages in single combat with the Moor, who, being weary and wounded, is finally overcome.

On the way to Álora, where he is taken as a captive, the Moor shows signs of grief. Narváez expresses surprise to find this weakness in one who has fought with such stamina. The prisoner then asks to be told his captor's name, rejoices on hearing it, and offers to tell the alcaide in confidence the story of his life.

The Moor's name is Abindarráez, and he belongs to the once powerful clan of the Abencerrajes. He first gives an account of the former glory and prestige of his family and then tells of their disgrace and the execution of many of them following an accusation of treason. He also describes the participation of the people of Granada in the jubilant display of gallantry and in the grievous tragedy that are the two sides of the Abencerrajes' legend. After Narváez has expressed sympathy and disbelief in the accusation that destroyed so noble a lineage, the prisoner tells his own personal story.

In observance of a royal order that the sons of the only two surviving Abencerrajes be reared outside Granada, Abindarráez

was placed as a child under the care of the alcaide of Cártama,
who had a daughter, Jarifa, of the same age. The children grew
up together in fond and happy attachment to one another, be-
lieving that they were brother and sister. The transition to a
tormented phase in the adolescent's awareness of his love for
Jarifa is marked by a calm and delicate scene near the fountain
where Abindarráez sees reflected the beloved's face, as he
expresses for the first time doubt and sorrow at the thought of
their relationship. Having learned some time later that they
are not related by blood, their affection develops into a deep
and vehement love. They live days of tormented bliss. This
time is followed by another of utter dejection, because Jarifa
will have to follow her father to his new post in Coín. Abindarráez's narrative becomes more pathetic and lyrical as he
describes their parting and his time of solitude in surroundings
reminding him of his happiness. His one consolation was
Jarifa's promise that she would call him and marry him secretly
as soon as her father's absence or illness made it possible. It
was after he had received word from her and was riding to join
her, that he had encountered Narváez's men. He winds up his
story with the remark that lack of feeling in such circumstances
would be a greater weakness than giving way to his distress.

Rodrigo de Narváez declares that his virtue will overcome
the young Moor's evil fortune. He obtains from his squires permission to dispose of the prisoner and grants him a three-day
absence under the promise that he will return to captivity.
Grateful and overjoyed, the young man continues his journey
to Coín. He makes his presence known and is taken by a duenna
to the presence of Jarifa. She tells him that she will now fulfill
her promise to him and they exchange their vows. Later that
night, Abindarráez, lying in Jarifa's arms, remembers his promise to return to Álora and the thought causes him to sigh with
anguish. The lady is deeply disturbed and expresses the fear
that she has displeased him or that his thoughts go to another
woman. Abindarráez reveals the situation in which he finds
himself. The first solution that occurs to Jarifa is to send to
Narváez a generous ransom, but the Abencerraje insists that he
is bound in duty to surrender to Narváez. It is now Jarifa's

turn to act with magnanimity. She will leave her father's house, follow her husband, and share his captivity.

In Álora Abindarráez and his beloved are received with utmost courtesy and treated as friends of the alcaide. When the young Moor has recovered from his wounds, he begs Narváez to use his influence with the king of Granada to obtain for the lovers the pardon of Jarifa's father. The Castilian leader agrees to intercede, and, in return for the favor, he offers the Moorish king to give Abindarráez his freedom without requiring a ransom. The proposal is accepted; the alcaide of Coín arrives in Álora and takes his children back home. The novel ends with an exchange of presents and courteous letters between the Moors and Rodrigo de Narváez.

III *Historicity*

Today's readers of *El Abencerraje* might describe it as historical fiction, a novel. In the sixteenth century it was read in all probability as a true story. Rodrigo de Narváez, one of the protagonists, was a well-known figure, whose participation in the conquest of Antequera and subsequent appointment as the town's first Christian alcaide were established facts. Moreover, he was the hero of at least one historical ballad.[7] Other fifteenth-century texts extoll his courage and virtue, all of which bear witness to the attributes given to him in the novel. The Moorish protagonist, on the other hand, could claim some historicity as a member of the Abencerraje clan. At the time of the composition of the novel, this name was mentioned with emotional overtones in a few ballads and chronicles. Abindarráez's account, which does not specify the nature of the slanderous accusation against his family, partakes of the aura of a legend at that time not fully developed, rather than directly reflecting any of the historical incidents in which the Abencerrajes were chastised.[8]

It is important to consider the geographical setting of the novel in relation to its historical background. The action involves Castilians stationed in Álora and Moors living in Cártama and Coín. These are towns in the precipitous Sierra of Ronda. All three towns were strategically situated fortresses along a

war route leading to Málaga, and they remained in Moorish
hands until the last war of Granada, which began in 1482. It
is a gross anachronism in the novel to identify a Castilian alcaide
of Álora with the first alcaide of Antequera, a town which had
been conquered as early as 1410. On the other hand, the local-
ization of the Moorish and Christian towns is consistent with
the situation of the borderline between the conquest of Álora
on June 20, 1484, and the subsequent capture of Cártama and
Coín in 1485. Such partial accuracy may well stem from a
prose text or a poem concerning the short period when the
frontier line corresponded to that delineated in the novel. Indeed,
Abindarráez's topographical song, in each of the variants preserved by the extant texts of *El Abencerraje*, mentions the three
frontier towns, as well as Granada.[9]

IV   *The "Historia del moro y Narváez," a Possible Source.*

A manuscript codex of the sixteenth or early seventeenth
century, containing miscellaneous texts of the Middle Ages and
the Renaissance, includes a story of approximately one thousand
words entitled "Historia del moro y Narváez."[10] It is written
in a rather slovenly and unpolished style, although it includes
certain topical expressions of chivalric literature. No part of the
text reveals in its wording a direct relationship with any of the
extant versions of *El Abencerraje*. However, the parallelism of
plot and structure leaves no doubt that this brief narrative is
related to the novel.

The novel and the short narrative begin with brief indications of historical background, including some specific references to the manner of life at the frontier, although the Narváez
of the story is not identified with Rodrigo de Narváez, the first
alcaide of Antequera, and his headquarters are not in Álora but
in Ronda, a town of the same region, which is not mentioned
in *El Abencerraje*. In both works brief and colorful, though not
identical, descriptions of the Moor's attire are given, and Narváez allows the captive to join his ladylove, after listening to
the young Moor's story. The Moorish couple behaves subsequently just as nobly. An important similarity of composition concerns the function of the dialogues—two in each work—in which

the lover is asked to justify his grief. The Castilian knight's inquiry serves to present flashback material, and it also provides, as does to some extent the lady's question, a turning point in the course of events.

There are two striking divergences between the short story and *El Abencerraje*. In contrast to Abindarráez, who downs five assailants before engaging in single combat with Rodrigo de Narváez, the Moorish protagonist of the short story makes no attempt to defend himself. The other difference concerns his identity: no name is given to the lover, who only declares that he is the son of a brave alcaide. In my opinion, it would be difficult to account for these differences if the "Historia del moro" is considered to be an abridged version of the novel. The suppression in the first case of meaningful action of an epic nature and its replacement by a prosaic sequence of events would be most unlikely. Similarly, the legend of the Abencerrajes, which had in its own right a strong appeal, could hardly be forgotten once it became part of the plot. It is more believable that the short story represents an early casting in literary form of an anecdote that may have occurred in real life, since noble acts of Moors or of Christians found their way easily into one form or another of historical writing. The harmonious balance established in the "Historia del moro," where one noble action leads to a reciprocal proof of trust, is, of course, exceptional; here we are dealing not with the fragment of a chronicle but with a tiny literary work whose clear pattern of composition anticipates the structure of *El Abencerraje*. As for the concept of love, it is restricted in the short story to the approach found in books of chivalry, whereas in the novel it reflects the broad influence of the pastoral genre.

If the briefer text is considered to be the earliest, the addition of the skirmish can be easily explained, since accounts of similar combats are quite common in the literature of the period. The incident serves to establish, moreover, the prestige of Abindarráez as a warrior, making the Moor and the Christian chivalric heroes of the same stature. Likewise, for the purpose of transforming the attractive characters of the "Historia del moro" into exemplary figures, it was logical to provide them with a prestigious legendary background. As to the historical setting of a narrative theme taking shape—not unlike the traditional ballads—through successive recastings,[11] the artistically meaningful but inaccurate data of the novel should correspond logically to a more advanced stage than the simple references of the short story.[12]

V *The Background of the Aragonese Version*

In contrast with the other two versions of *El Abencerraje*, the text issued under the sponsorship of the Aragonese baron Jiménez de Embún was printed independently as a small book, both in the undated and in the Toledo, 1561, editions. A comparative study of the variants of the two editions prompted Keith Whinnom to judge that this was the original version of the novel.[13] The title *Parte de la Corónica del ínclito Infante don Fernando, que ganó a Antequera*, under which it appeared, as well as the opening phrase, relate the subject to the history of a Castilian prince who had conquered Antequera while he was regent of Castile and became shortly thereafter Ferdinand I of Aragon. It is difficult to ascertain how credible the dedication's statement is that an unknown and unpolished work or chronicle fragment had come to the attention of the writer some time before, and that he was encouraged by friends to edit, revise and publish the text.[14]

In his dedication the Aragonese author or adapter describes himself as a man deeply indebted to the señor or baron of Bárboles and Huitura, Jerónimo Jiménez de Embún, of whose household he might possibly have been a member. Situated in a fertile region near Zaragoza and in the vicinity of the important trade center of Épila, the village of Bárboles, with approximately forty Morisco families, lay at the foot of an abrupt cliff, crowned by the castle of the De Embúns. This family was one of the most prominent and wealthy among the "caballeros e hidalgos," the father of Mosén Jerónimo as well as members of his wife's family having held the office of bailiff of Aragon. Since both this lineage—the Sessés—and that of the baron's mother were of Jewish ancestry, it has been suggested by López Estrada[15] that a story emphasizing mutual esteem between persons of different faiths would be particularly appealing in the De

Embúns' household. The point has been further developed by Claudio Guillén in his structural and thematic analysis of the novel.[16] According to this critic, a relationship exists between the situation of members of the converso class, which included prominent families of Jewish origin, and the numerous symbols of cleavage found—though counterbalanced by a movement toward unity—in the story of Abindarráez.

Germane to the implicit meaning of the novel as an example of mutual loyalty between Christians and Moors is the role played by the baron of Bárboles in a confrontation concerning the Moriscos which took place in 1558 and 1559.[17] The Inquisition, used then by the king as an instrument of centralization, clashed with the landowning classes that were in control of the state's autonomous institutions. The barons, most of whom gave tacit consent to Moslem practices—officially abolished since 1526—tried to create legal barriers in order to keep their domains free from interference by the officers of the Holy Office. When this procedure failed, some rural lords were prone to encourage armed defiance on the part of their Morisco vassals or at least to abstain from punishing such resistance when it occurred. Undoubtedly the nobles and gentry who took this attitude protected their own interests, but they upheld at the same time medieval traditions of coexistence. In the late 1550s Jerónimo de Embún was a strong supporter of these policies favoring the status quo. It is conceivable that when he visited Toledo in March, 1560, on a special mission on behalf of the Moriscos and their lords, a member of his staff made arrangements for the publication in Castile of the *Parte de la Corónica*, which had appeared some time before in Aragon.

The baron of Bárboles was, in the words of the dedication, familiar with the Muses, as were, indeed, many members of the Zaragoza gentry, for the prosperous Aragonese capital had a long tradition of courtly refinement and esteem for art and poetry. The patron of *Parte de la Corónica* and members of his staff must have been participants or at least welcome visitors at the small, culturally oriented courts held by some of their powerful political allies. Among them was the count of Aranda, who at a given moment made De Embún his representative in the legal battle mentioned above, and held firmly to his right of keeping a small, well-armed, private force of Morisco vassals, recruited presumably among the peasants who cultivated the splendid orchards he owned on the banks of the Rivers Ebro and Jalón. Épila, with its high-looming Renaissance palace, was the capital of his domain. The middle class of the town included families of Moorish as well as of Jewish origin. It may have been no coincidence that this was the site for the assassination of the first Inquisitor of Aragón in 1485, and that more than a hundred years later Épila became the last refuge of the insurgents who supported Antonio Pérez. In the late 1550s and the 1560s the count of Aranda patronized a group of historians and poets, some of whom were related to Jorge de Montemayor. Another interesting influence exerted on this circle was that of the count's kinsman Jerónimo Jiménez de Urrea. A captain of Charles V's army, this prolific writer spent many years away from his native land, living mostly in Italy, but he kept in touch with the Épila circle. Urrea's translations helped considerably to disseminate in Spain new trends in literature, and his main work, the *Diálogo de la verdadera honra militar,* critically examines standard concepts of honor.[18] One of the two characters who discuss in this book the just causes for challenges and duels describes himself as an ardent reader of the chronicles of the wars of Granada as well as of ballads and chivalric stories. Urrea is also the author of the novel of chivalry *Don Clarisel de las Flores* and of the pastoral novel, now lost, *La famosa Epilia,* which related in some manner to the literary group that has been mentioned.[19]

An appropriate setting for a reading of the story of Abindarráez would be indeed the little Arcadia housed among Morisco-cultivated orchards, presided over by a man of Urrea's interests, and including among its members local writers of New Christian origin as well as barons and nobles engaged in a struggle to keep undisturbed the formerly mudéjar communities over which they ruled. In this connection a trend worth noticing in Aragonese culture of the period was the interest in historical studies. At a time when medieval chronicles and documentary sources were sought after with great interest, a text such as the "Historia del moro" could easily fall into the hands of a man of letters, who might feel prompted to expand the

frontier anecdote. The norms for the composition of the Abindarráez novel conform to the taste for the chivalric and pastoral
genres, the concern for the ethical implications of the concept
of honor, and a liberal approach to Moorish-Christian relations,
which are so conspicuously present in the Épila circle. Such
interests and attitudes are, of course, part of the Renaissance,
and the manner in which they merge with a subject matter
derived from national history and germane to the spirit of the
frontier ballad is characteristic of Spanish literature in the
Golden Age. Still, the degree to which trends and ideas relevant
to the genesis of *El Abencerraje* strikingly characterize Jerónimo
de Embún's milieu corroborates bibliographical data indicating
that on this soil the frontier anecdote may well have blossomed
into the first Moorish novel.

VI *The Text Inserted in Montemayor's* Diana

Jorge de Montemayor had died only a short time before the
publication of the Valladolid 1561 edition of *La Diana,* which
actually came from the press in 1562. It is not impossible that
the insertion of the Moorish novelette at the end of book IV
was done with his consent.[20] Very appropriately the story of
Abindarráez is narrated in the palace of the Sage Felicia by
Felismena, who is not a shepherdess but a lady from Vandalia,
that is, Andalusia, who performs the only heroic action in *Diana.*

When the narrative reaches the point of the skirmish between
the Moor and Narváez's men, mention is made of two earlier
accounts, which do not seem to correspond exactly to either
the *Corónica* or *Inventario* versions, and the combat is described in a simplified manner. Other details related to military
action were also abridged or omitted, whereas the love story
was slightly amplified, to conform more closely to the new pastoral frame.[21] In *Diana,* Abindarráez's account of his love
for Jarifa is more restrained, his emotions are portrayed
with finer nuances than in the other versions, and exchanges of
courtesy appear more refined. At the same time that directness
of expression was sacrificed in favor of polished artificiality, the
novel's exoticism, or Moorish local color, was stressed by a
more detailed description of Abindarráez's arms and attire as

well as by occasional invocations to Allah and the omission of all but one mythological allusion. From the point of view of style the text was also modified to conform with the refined tone of *La Diana*.

No one has claimed priority for the *Diana* version of *El Abencerraje*, which in general terms is closer to the *Corónica* than to the *Inventario*. Mérimée argued in his cited study that all three versions were based on a lost archetype. López Estrada considers it probable that the *Diana* adapter used early manuscript copies of the *Inventario* and *Corónica* texts, whereas Keith Whinnom thinks that *Diana* followed *Corónica* and that the two combined provided the basis for *Inventario*.[22]

The text of *El Abencerraje* inserted in *La Diana* became the most widely read, and it was occasionally translated or imitated in the literatures of other countries and periods. Thus, after the first French translation of Montemayor's work appeared in 1592, the inserted Moorish novel was highly praised in the circles of the Précieux and an adaptation was produced by Pierre Davity. Two centuries later Florian was influenced by the theme, and in the Romantic period Washington Irving wrote an abridged version of *El Abencerraje*, which he had read in *La Diana*, and made it part of the picturesque Granada he cherished by pretending that the story had been told in the Alhambra by an Andalusian girl.[23]

VII El Abencerraje *in Villegas'* Inventario

Little is known about the life of Antonio de Villegas, except that he was authorized in 1551 to publish the collection entitled *El Inventario*, which was finally printed in 1565 and again with additional material in 1577. López Estrada, who has done extensive research on the subject and has edited Villegas' book, believes that, contrary to Menéndez Pelayo's opinion, the little pastoral tale "Ausencia y soledad de amor" and the text of *El Abencerraje* included in the miscellany were most likely written by the same person. He also supports the hypothesis that Villegas probably was a New Christian of Jewish origin. This possibility was first advanced in 1952 by Marcel Bataillon, who commented upon the interest in the scriptures and the melan-

choly that the author of the short works in *Inventario* shared
with Montemayor.[24] The same critic had advocated in an earlier
study[25] the priority of the text of *El Abencerraje* published in the
Villegas miscellany, primarily on the ground that an artist so
gifted as to produce a masterpiece of composition and style
would be more inclined to do purely creative work than to spend
his time perfecting and rewording somebody else's story. According to this theory, the Aragonese responsible for the *Parte
de la Corónica* recast in a somewhat cumbersome style the
Inventario text, whose simple elegance he was not capable of
appreciating.

Aside from minor variants, the version of *El Abencerraje* in
the Villegas collection includes an episode, borrowed presumably from an Italian *novella*, that does not appear in the other
two. On their way to Álora, Abindarráez and Jarifa meet an old
man who tells them a little story illustrating, in his view, Rodrigo
de Narváez's sense of honor. It was reported that the alcaide
withdrew in a gallant adventure upon learning from the woman
he had been wooing for a long time that she was now willing
to be his mistress because her husband had spoken highly of
him. J. P. Crawford found the probable source of this episode
in the first story of Ser Giovanni Fiorentino's *Il Pecorone*, which
was printed in 1558.[26] In view of this, he concluded that the
text of *El Abencerraje*, at least as it was published in 1565, had
not been written in 1551 when Villegas received the first
authorization to publish *El Inventario*.

None of this argumentation is altogether conclusive, according
to López Estrada,[27] since *Il Pecorone* may have been known
in manuscript before its publication, and moreover the story
was based on a narrative motif that had been rather widespread.
It has been rightly observed that an anecdote stressing self-
discipline fits well into the exemplary meaning of *El Abencerraje*.[28] At the same time, the insertion of an incident stemming
from sources alien to the main theme may be interpreted as
an indication that this little masterpiece was perhaps viewed
in the sixteenth century as a historical tale that belonged to
everybody and could be perfected. The manner in which the
story is told during a journey corresponds to a topical situation
frequently found in later Golden Age fiction.[29]

Very few passages of *Inventario* compare unfavorably with the corresponding *Corónica* and *Diana* texts. One of them is the account of the skirmish, which, as Whinnom[30] has remarked, appears somewhat confused in *Inventario*. A variant worth noticing occurs when Abindarráez refers to the many accomplishments of the Abencerrajes in a passage which derives, as López Estrada has proven, from Diego de San Pedro's sentimental novel *La cárcel de amor*.[31] The *Corónica* version is the only one including musical talent and—quite inaccurately, as the critic notices—the ability to compose ballads as part of their skills. In this, the Aragonese text remains much closer to the content and wording of the fragment's source, a circumstance which, we feel, is in favor of its priority.

The title *El Abencerraje* is used for the first time in *El Inventario*. It appears after a short introduction which brings out explicitly the exemplary value of the conduct of Narváez and Abindarráez, and in a lesser degree of Jarifa, her father, and the king of Granada. Those preliminary words, as well as the anecdote illustrating Narváez's self-control and some minor variants, indicate an awareness that the other versions do not show in the same degree of the value of the novel as an illustration of neo-Senecan ethics.[32] The *Inventario* text must also be considered by virtue of its style as the definitive form of *El Abencerraje*. Castilian narrative prose seldom attained such excellence before Cervantes. The serene quality and carefully balanced sentence structure of Renaissance prose is allied here with a direct, functional style that reminds one of the best historical writings of the period. Unhampered by gratuitous stylistic embellishments, the story moves forward in clear, vibrant language that can convey the finest shades of meaning, with regard to emotions as well as to the epic or the moral content of the work.

In our opinion, the limited evidence available concerning the origin of *El Abencerraje* does not permit the formulation of a definitive solution to the priority problem. However, the precedence of the *Inventario* text appears less likely after the discovery of the *Corónica* edition of Toledo, 1561, and the studies that followed. It seems proper to place the first Moorish novel in the category of literary works which, like the old ballads, the *relaciones* ("prose accounts of events, chiefly contemporaneous") and, to a certain extent, a masterpiece as great as *La Celestina* are not entirely attributable to a single artist.[33] The perfection of the Moorish novel in Villegas' miscellany was attained, we are now led to believe, through progressive steps.

VIII *The Artistic Significance of* El Abençerraje

El Abencerraje impresses the reader as a small work of fiction of remarkable complexity. Like the strictly coetaneous *Lazarillo*, also an anonymous masterpiece, the story of Abindarráez is written with a new sense of fictional coherence and depth that forecasts the renovation of narrative genres that took place a few decades after. Its subject matter is derived from the late Middle Ages, and it draws largely from early Renaissance literary trends, blending with great ease these elements into an original and meaningful sequence.[34]

The portrayal of frontier life, with its concrete references to time, place, and renowned figures or facts, provides a seemingly accurate setting that enhances verisimilitude. The alertness and discipline of Castilian soldiers, their ambition, and their cult of fame are pictured in a manner akin to the chronicles and other writings of the period about the conquest of Granada, as well as to the old ballads or their imitations of historical subject matter that find their way into printed collections around the time of *El Abencerraje*'s composition.[35] The capsule profile of the leader, Rodrigo de Narváez, sketched in the opening sentences and developed through the novel, is consistent with the standards set by fifteenth-century biographies of famous men, while it also reflects the neo-Senecan ethics that were deeply embedded in the Spanish Renaissance.[36] In contrast to him, the squires, who seek riches as well as honor, represent estimable but nonheroic standards of virtue. On the one hand they provide a hold on reality, thus contributing toward shaping a realm of fiction, placed between romance and the empirical approach that would soon assert itself in narrative literature. A balance between the goals of exemplarity and verisimilitude is also apparent in the account of admirable but credible exploits. The skirmish and duel are presented with a minute

technique that helps to visualize the scene; this effective
reportorial style is found also in certain passages of the books
of chivalry as well as in chronicles of actual encounters and
tournaments.

In the characters of Abindarráez and Narváez we see a dual
portrait of knightly virtues which is a subtle study in harmony
and contrasts. Both show allegiance to love and honor, but
each of them has only one of these aspirations ever present
on his mind. Loyalty to his king and the pursuit of fame are
so intense in Narváez that his example kindles the same ambitions in others.[37] The Moor, whose youthful exuberance contrasts
with the mature and self-possessed attitude of the alcaide, is
not characterized as inferior to the latter in courage or ability
to fight, but being exhausted when their confrontation starts
he is overpowered. One significant difference lies in the fact
that Abindarráez, who represents the refined but almost decadent
culture of Granada, has accepted his lot as an outcast and
performs no specific service to his country. Neither does he
show ambitions of power or of fame, engrossed as he is in his
love for Jarifa. Characteristically, the wrong done to the Abencerrajes' good name is denied by Narváez with indignation;
this contrasts with the melancholy with which the last survivor
of the clan accepts his fate. And yet, when put to the test,
the Moor will give priority to his commitment to fulfill a
promise, subordinating his and Jarifa's happiness. Earlier the
Castilian captain had allowed the young captive to continue
his journey, yielding to an impulse of sympathy for the separated
lovers. One may say that in such noble gestures exchanged by
the main characters each one of them exercises a virtue more
characteristic of the other, although the alcaide's wish to free
Abindarráez must assert itself in an action requiring authority,
as well as the sacrifice of selfish interests.

The novel formulates, perhaps for the first time, the legendary
theme of the glory and fall of the Abencerrajes, although references to the persecution that they allegedly suffered as well as
to their proverbial prestige were not rare in Castilian literature.[38]
The ill fortune of this particular Abencerraje will be reversed
by the love and friendship that he inspires and reciprocates,
but the forebodings which the theme suggests somehow linger.

The reader knows, although it is not part of the plot, that Moorish Granada was doomed at the time of the action and the future could hold little promise for Abindarráez's race. Because of this connotation, when the captive Moor speaks of himself as the last of his kin, the legendary theme of the last of the Abencerrajes that was to be so appealing to the Romantic imagination, begins to take shape.

The description of the Moorish horseman's colorful garb and arms reflects a practice· of frontier ballads, as well as of the *relaciones* describing the pageantry of sixteenth-century festivals and tournaments. Similar descriptions may be found in the books of chivalry, a genre in which details of a knight's attire almost have a ritualistic value. The influence of this type of literature is apparent also in the account of the skirmish as well as in details of Abindarráez's arrival in Cártama and the simple ceremony of the secret marriage. The Moorish lover may be compared to Amadís in the perfect love he professes and in his uncompromising commitment to honor. But the parallel has its limits. The Abencerraje is not a knight in search of adventures nor is he dedicated to fight evil in this world. Indeed, the lovers in this first Moorish novel have not been cast in the same mold as the knights and ladies of Granada appearing in the later work by Pérez de Hita, since such characters, which are seen primarily in their actions or the projection in words and gestures of their emotions, still belong to the chivalric world where courtship and the deed performed by a knight in honor of his lady come to the foreground.

Descriptive detail and the fascination of poetry and music are used from the onset to shed the light of romance on the figure of Abindarráez. His appearance is tellingly described and makes a strong appeal to the sympathy of the reader, both by his obliviousness to the danger that surrounds him and by his strong response to the attack. His dejection after he is taken captive proves him to be emotionally vulnerable, an impression immediately qualified by the dignity of his demand that the captor identify himself before listening to the prisoner's story. The character of Narváez, man of honor and seeker of fame, is sufficiently established by his name alone; that of Abindarráez can only be defined in an outpouring of memories and sentiments.

The previously mentioned studies by López Estrada and other critics prove the extensive use of topoi in *El Abencerraje*. This is particularly true of the autobiographical segment. The theme of childhood attachment has a long history, which can be traced back to the Ovidian fable of Pyramus and Thisbe and includes the medieval romance of Floire, a Mohammedan like the protagonist of *El Abencerraje*. Gardens and orchards are the setting—*locus amœnus*—where lovers meet in many literary works of the Middle Ages and pre-Renaissance. Although the simple elements singled out by Abindarráez to depict the place of his meetings with Jarifa may be interpreted as belonging to the Andalusian scene, the pool that reflects in turn the lovers' faces has been related to a passage in Sannazaro's *Arcadia*.[39] The wreath of flowers is a symbol of love in various literary pieces, as well as in folk poetry. Deeply influenced but not confined by Neoplatonic theory, the art of *El Abencerraje* combines in this scene such elements with classical references, and the result is, as Claudio Guillén has shown, an original approach to the expression of love and of the fear of separation, rising when a childhood attachment changes to a new more intense attraction.[40]

The autobiographical story told by Abindarráez integrates credibly within the simple account of a man's experience elements so diverse as the evocation of chivalric lore, the theme of Fortune's whims,[41] and the sentimental nuances of Neoplatonism. It is true that earlier Renaissance poetic eclogues as well as the pastoral of Montemayor, which was composed approximately at the same time as the Moorish novel, depict different emotional predicaments, and allow their characters to explain the circumstances which led to their present sentimental involvement, displaying a correlated state of mind. But even within these genres devoted to sentiment, the beginning and the progress of love is seldom so convincingly portrayed as when Abindarráez reminisces on the fondness he and Jarifa felt for each other as children, then on his conflictive awareness of his passion for her, and the moments of ecstatic bliss that he shared with the beloved or the sufferings caused by her departure. The unifying point of view that controls this part of the narrative requires that these emotional stages be put forward as experience stored by memory and considered to be meaningful in the context of a confidence that resembles a confession, in the Augustinian sense of the word.

After Abindarráez's story, as told to Narváez, the action moves swiftly. Having been united to his beloved, he tells Jarifa, whose question about his sadness parallels Narváez's earlier inquiry about the cause of the prisoner's dejection, of his decision to return to captivity. With this gesture, the Moorish protagonist is now placed on the same moral level as the Christian, and illustrates also the Senecan principle running through the novel of man's victory over himself. Jarifa is also made to share in some measure these exemplary standards. The action that follows conforms to the reader's expectation of a joyous outcome deriving from the triumph of virtue. The final exchange of letters and presents amounts to a ceremonial ratification of the bonds of friendship established among adversaries, who, in this work, keep their different beliefs and allegiances unchanged.

The difference between this kind of ending and the somewhat perfunctory conversion of Moorish characters in the fiction of Pérez de Hita and of Mateo Alemán can be related to Renaissance versus Counter-Reformation ideas and attitudes.[42] At the same time, *El Abencerraje* may well have been to some extent motivated by the desire to counteract the growing animosity between the descendants of the Moors and the majority of the population of Spain, as we have suggested in connection with the *Parte de la Corónica* text. Moreover in the structural and stylistic traits of the novel it is possible to see, as does Claudio Guillén, an interplay of signs of disjunction balanced by others expressing a movement toward unification, that relates to contemporary life. In the words of this critic, history is experienced by the characters as "conflict and division, which will be superseded ultimately by ethical values of universal, unifying import."[43] The more recent study by Joaquín Gimeno Casalduero[44] emphasizes likewise the contribution of every character of *El Abencerraje* to an exaltation of virtue intended to inspire all men. According to this critic's interpretation of the work, the two main themes of love and heroism are articulated around five nuclei of composition. Thus, the flexible symmetry of the novel's structure is accounted for.

El Abencerraje is one of the finest examples of that frequent encounter in Golden Age literature of themes rooted in the traditions of the past with artistic and ethical concepts of the present. A similar approach will characterize throughout different periods and literatures that special category of romance-oriented narrative which future generations of readers in Spain and in France would call *novela morisca* or *roman hispano-mauresque*.[45] The plots of these works invariably include episodes that unite in love or friendship persons separated by their beliefs and nationality, reiterating the lesson embodied in *El Abencerraje* that moral excellence makes men free to reach to one another across all barriers.

CHAPTER 5

Ginés Pérez de Hita

I *Biographical Profile*

NOT much is known about the life of Ginés Pérez de Hita, author of the fictional work *Las guerras civiles de Granada* (*The Civil Wars of Granada*), which delighted many generations of readers from the time of Cervantes until the end of the last century. Except for the information derived from the preliminaries and contents of his books, a source well handled by Paula Blanchard-Demouge,[1] only ten years of his life are suitably documented. They correspond to the period, ending in 1577, of the author's residence in Lorca, which was fruitfully investigated in the local archives by Joaquín Espín Rael in 1922.[2] Both researchers consider unfounded an earlier biographer's contention that Pérez de Hita was born in Mula around 1544.[3] The date of his birth, however, could not have been after 1550, since in 1569 he joined the forces of the Marqués de los Vélez against the insurgent Moriscos. It appears likely that he was by then more than twenty years old, given the fact that he was established in Lorca as a bootmaker and had shared in June, 1568, with the Maestro de Capilla (chapel master) the responsibility for the pageantry and pantomimes of the Corpus Christi procession.[4] We may be certain at least that the author of the *Civil Wars of Granada* belonged to the same generation as Miguel de Cervantes, who was born in 1547. As for Peréz de Hita's birthplace, there is no serious reason to contest the statement on the title page of the manuscript copy of his "Libro de Lorca" that the author was from Murcia, where he also settled later on.[5]

Ginés attended in Granada a solemn funeral mass for Queen Isabella of Valois, the second wife of Philip II, who died on

October 3, 1568. He himself recalled having seen on that occasion Don Fernando Muley, Señor de Válor, who became under the name of Aben Humeya the head of the insurgent Moriscos of the Alpujarras. (*Guerras civiles*, II, 8, chap. 1). Pérez de Hita would soon become involved in the events of this war, but there is no real reason to believe, as it has been assumed, that he was an *escudero* ("squire") of the Marqués de los Vélez. According to the documents found by Espín Rael, Ginés did serve under this strong leader but in a more modest capacity. When Lorca, which lies about thirty-eight miles southwest of Murcia near the border of the former kingdom of Granada, was required to send a reinforcement of one hundred men to the marqués for the defense of Vélez Blanco and Vélez Rubio, two towns belonging to the general's patrimony, Ginés Pérez de Hita enlisted on April 12, 1569, but only in response to a second call and as a substitute for a wealthy landowner.[6] Many years later in his account of the war he criticized the methods used by local officials in recruiting the small force, which he, an artisan with literary leanings, must have joined reluctantly and not without some monetary compensation. In spite of this, he did share wholeheartedly in the emotions and hardships of a soldier's life. The fierce struggle was to be narrated by him with the pride of a participant and with warm admiration for the Marqués de Los Vélez and other leaders. And while he condemned looting, Ginés admitted that occasionally he had behaved as badly as most soldiers taking possession of a conquered town.

When the marqués retired from the campaign in January of 1570, Pérez de Hita presumably also returned to Lorca, where the next year he was put in charge for two weeks of a group of Moriscos. In 1572 he is listed as one of the residents able to use arms. Another document, a *bula*, indicates that at that time his household included two women, Isabel Botía and Isabel Leandro, whose relationship with the head of the family is not specified. That year Pérez de Hita worked again on the *autos* for Corpus Christi, which must have been celebrated with more than the usual solemnity, since the war had come to an end. Subsequently his name appears several times in connection with religious or civic festivities, and he won a contest in 1571 when the birth of a prince was celebrated with pantomimes of chivalric themes, as described in his poem "Libro de Lorca." At about that time Ginés was an officer of his guild—*veedor de zapateros*—and he must have enjoyed at the same time some reputation as a poet, since the municipal council paid him for his work on the long poem just mentioned, which dwelt upon the history of the town and other matters of local interest. After 1577 no document records the presence of Pérez de Hita in Lorca.

In the years that followed the artisan-poet must have settled in Murcia, the capital of the region and probably his birthplace, where he is also reputed to·have practiced his trade.[7] In 1595 he resided in this city, according to the title page of his major work published that year in Zaragoza. The success of the *Historia de los vandos de los Zegríes y Abencerrages* (A History of the factions of the Zegris and the Abencerrages)—the so-called first part of his *Civil Wars of Granada*—must have encouraged him to continue writing. The manuscript of another long poem, *Bello troyano* (The Trojan War) is dated 1596, and his book on the rebellion of the Moriscos was finished the next year, although its publication was much delayed.[8] Pérez de Hita contributed two sonnets to a memorial collection for Philip II published in Murcia, 1600, but he is not represented in the more selective commemorative volume for Margarita of Austria, issued in the same city twelve years later.[9] There is no certainty that he was still living at that time. Espín Rael cites indirectly some documents of 1612 relative to the marriage, in the Murcian village of Molina de Segura, of a Ginés Pérez de Hita, and to the will made in 1616 by the wife, the husband being alive.[10] That this concerns the writer's family is almost certain, since the bride had the same last name as one of the women living in Ginés' home in Lorca, but the groom is only doubtfully our author, who would have then been in his sixties. Paula Blanchard-Demouge considered the approval of the Barcelona, 1619, edition of Part Two of *Guerras civiles* to be an indication that the writer had been alive at that date.[11] It is signed by Fray Onofre de Requesens, who states that Pérez de Hita deserves credit and merits permission to reprint his book several times. It appears doubtful, however, that the censor should have more information about the author than the individual who arranged for the publication of the Cuenca edition of the same year, which is the basis for that of Barcelona, and he merely states that he had come by the book a short time before.[12] One must therefore conclude that the writer's death may have occurred at any time after 1600.

Pérez de Hita of course knew Granada, and he traveled at least once to Madrid at an unknown date, but one not prior to August, 1585. According to his own account, the purpose of this trip was to arrange for the publication of one of his books (II, 339, chap. 24), but he also stopped on his way at Villanueva de Alcardete, where the Moriscos of Vélez Rubio had been deported.[13] There he visited Fernando de Figueroa, formerly El Tuzaní, who gave him an account of the events of the war of the Alpujarras in which he had participated, including his own tragic experience of finding his betrothed dead in a looted town. Ginés was deeply impressed by this Morisco hidalgo and portrayed him in his history of the rebellion as a figure of heroic stature, to whom other writers including Calderón de la Barca would be attracted.[14]

Ginés also interviewed many other Moriscos, who found in him a sympathetic listener. He must himself have been a fine story-teller, for he had immense curiosity and imagination, and he judged human beings in terms of individual merit. Part Two of *Guerras civiles* proves that at a time when hatred ran high this author was capable of compassion, since, at the same time that he condemned the rebellion, he had the courage to express indignation at the sufferings caused the Moriscos. Might we surmise from this that he was one of them? Be that as it may, every judgment in Pérez de Hita's work impresses the reader as profoundly sincere, whether expressed in favor of the Christians or the Moriscos. Thus he wrote pages vibrant with enthusiasm about leaders of the king's army, although they do not become, as do El Tuzaní or El Maleh, heroes of fictional episodes requiring a favorable characterization. Again his chronicle does not silence or make excuses for the atrocities committed by the rebels, and deep reverence is expressed with regard to Christians who were martyred, like Ginés' neighbor the priest Miguel Sánchez, whom he calls a good knight of Christ (II, 17, chap. 2). Although he does it rarely, he is not above using vilifying expressions, such as "los más infames y perros moriscos hereges" (II, 98, chap. 10). This would presumably have been avoided by any Morisco.[15] Such an attitude makes us think of Sancho Panza's friendship with his neighbor the Morisco Ricote, with the important difference that, unlike Don Quijote's companion, Pérez de Hita is consistently critical of punitive measures directed at the entire population of Moorish origin.

To observe that the author of the *Civil Wars of Granada* did not identify politically, and even less in terms of religion, with the Moriscos does not imply that he did not have friends or even relatives among them. For a man of his time, Ginés is unusually silent about his parentage. Unlike Cervantine characters of the peasant class he never boasts of being an Old Christian.[16] Neither did he claim that he was an hidalgo, although scholars have been led to believe that he belonged to this class, because it was so stated without proof by genealogists who lived in the eighteenth century and after.[17] It is true that Ginés showed special fondness for the village of Mula, which was the home of hidalgos named Pérez de Hita, and he introduces in a markedly fictional section of his *Civil Wars of Granada* the character of Esperanza de Hita, a captive Christian woman from that town. It is this loyal attendant to the Moorish queen who advises her, when the latter is falsely accused, to put her defense in the hands of Christian champions and finally persuades her to become a Christian.[18] All of this seems to hint at some sort of connection between Pérez de Hita, the artisan-poet, and the more highly placed family of Mula. Could it have been a blood relationship, or was the link established when a converted Moor took in baptism the name of Pérez de Hita? Either, or even a combination of both, is a possibility, since in real life, as in our author's fictional world, prominent Christians who became godfathers to Granadine Moors gave them their names and often married them to members of their own family or household. Although Moorish parentage was an obstacle for admission to high honors and positions, the fact is that a good number of priests, soldiers, and civil servants, including the ones who negotiated the settlement of the Alpujarras war, came from this segment of the population, or else were the offspring of

mixed marriages or illegitimate unions. Such a background
would not necessarily prevent a man who had participated in
the struggle on the king's side from enjoying the trust of local
authorities, as Ginés obviously did.

Whatever his origin, it is certain that the author of the *Civil
Wars of Granada* belonged to a society comprising a high per-
centage of families of Moorish ancestry. In the area of Murcia
the mudéjar communities of artisans and farmers, living formerly as Moslems under Castilian rule, became officially Christians in the first three decades of the sixteenth century. Both
groups blended more closely than in other regions with the rest
of the population, and they had some influence on the decisions
of local government, although these were frequently reversed
by the crown if such decisions favored the converts.[19] Moreover,
the leather crafts that Ginés practiced had been developed with
distinctive technique and style by Moors and mudéjares, from
whom, directly or through other masters, he must have learned
his trade. When occupational connections do not result in a
dislike of competitors, they promote a feeling of solidarity,
and a man with an outgoing, generous nature like Pérez de
Hita's could not fail to have a fraternal attitude toward his companions of trade. Among them, or at least in the society in which
he lived, were wealthy families of Granada claiming equal
status with the Old Christians. Our author gave such claims
whole-hearted support, representing at a more modest level the
same position as the diplomat and outstanding writer Don Diego
Hurtado de Mendoza, who was also a historian of the war of
the Alpujarras.[20]

Pérez de Hita's trade deserves our attention in another respect.
He was an artisan, not a man of letters or a soldier, by profes-
sion. This circumstance was compatible with a passion for reading, but his knowledge was not that imparted at universities,
nor had he received a gentleman's education. Although he may
have had some schooling, the author of the *Civil Wars of Granada* was a self-taught man who read the best-sellers of his
time, mainly books of chivalry. He was also familiar with some
historical works and with the *Orlando Furioso* of Ludovico
Ariosto which had been translated by José de Acosta and by
Jerónimo de Urrea. The ballads and other forms of traditional

poetry were of course part of popular culture and the new
ballads were enjoyed by all.[21] Like some other members of the
artisan class, Pérez de Hita composed poetry and he wrote the
text of folk plays that were performed in religious and civil
festivities. We can imagine him as a town's poet, like those who
produced in *Don Quijote* the symbolic dance and pantomime
for Camacho's wedding.

This type of semiliterary culture showed at that time great
vitality, paralleling and influencing certain forms of theater
and of decorative art. It is an established fact, for instance,
that Lope de Vega, who was sometimes commissioned to write
plays about a given subject by the organizers of great civic
celebrations, occasionally hired as a collaborator a tailor in
Toledo who was skilled at writing verse.[22] We can assume that
in Lorca Pérez de Hita was responsible, not only for the text,
but also for the triumphal carts, costumes, and machines used
in the play or pantomime. He had therefore a professional, or at
least an amateur's, interest in all aspects of the elaborate pageantry, which he describes minutely in certain chapters of both the
first and the second part of his *Guerras civiles*.[23] There is so
much plasticity in such descriptions and such obvious enjoy-
ment on the part of the author when he praises every small
detail of workmanship that it is not surprising to learn that
he was a man trained to work with his hands in shaping and
decorating useful and beautiful objects. It has been noticed,
for instance, that when Ginés sketched his vivid portrait of the
Marqués de los Vélez, he gave details about the general's equip-
ment that reveal the specialized viewpoint of the author's handi-
craft.[24] His tendency to specify material, color, and shape and
his ability to render visual images, although consistent with
the style of the Moorish ballads, may also be related to the
interests of the artisans' world to which he belonged, and more
specifically to the style of mudéjar art and workmanship.

II *The Interest in Poetry*

Ginés Pérez de Hita was certainly perceptive of poetic values,
but this is better revealed in his selection of ballad material
and in his ability to blend into his fiction elements of compo-

sition, characterization, and style derived from traditional or
Renaissance narrative poetry than in the huge amount of verses
that he produced. Yet the first book he wrote—and it deserves
our attention for reasons other than its literary merit—was a long
historical poem in *ottava rima* about the town of Lorca.[25] Even
after the success of the *Civil Wars of Granada, I* the author
versified, using mainly Italianate metrical forms, an adaptation
of the *Trojan Chronicle* adscribed to Dares Phrygius and Dictys
Cretensis, which was really a product of medieval chivalric literature.[26] This endeavor, undertaken in the very last years of the
sixteenth century, reveals to what extent Pérez de Hita's preferences were attuned to popular taste and traditions. And characteristically, it is as a source of heraldry that he refers to this
Chronicle in his history of the rebellion (*Guerras civiles*, II,
50, chap. 5). Nevertheless he had an interest in new trends and
imitated occasionally the learned mannerisms predominating
during that period in lyric poetry. An example of this is offered
by the two sonnets contributed to Murcia's memorial for Philip
II, published in 1600,[27] in which mythological allusions and other
topics characteristic of this type of composition were amalgamated with a little more refinement than one would expect
from the author's earlier poems.

Before considering other poetic texts included in the *Civil
Wars of Granada,* some attention is due to the *Libro de Lorca.*
It was written on commission, or at least rewarded by the town's
council in 1572,[28] and it falls into the category of predominantly
historical narrative that was not uncommon in the sixteenth
century.[29] The lengthy poem is divided into two parts, each
comprising sixteen cantos. The first canto begins with the
mythical founding of the town by Trojans, companions of
Eneas. Then the poem moves swiftly in time to the Reconquest,
especially when the people of Lorca and the ancestors of the
Fajardo family, headed by the Marqués de los Vélez, participated in the various campaigns against the Nasrid kingdom,
including the conquest of Granada. Pérez de Hita made use
of manuscript material and, although his work contains some
serious inaccuracies, it was considered to be a valid source by
at least one local historian.[30] The episodes of a fictional nature
are inspired by local legends and depict chivalric customs. Part

I ends with a summary of the history of the Moriscos of Granada up to the eve of the revolt, and part II concerns itself with the participation of the people of Lorca in the struggle against the Alpujarras rebels, written out of the understanding gained by the author through his experience as a member of the force sent by the town. The last cantos describe the civic festivities that Ginés had helped to organize, including pageantry and pantomimic plays of the type that the fictional Moors of his main work will be displaying in their tournaments.

P. Blanchard-Demouge saw in the "Libro de Lorca" a kind of sketch of the *Civil Wars of Granada,* in that both pieces have a first part that deals with wars of Moors and Christians up to the fall of the last Moslem state in the Peninsula and in both works this part is followed by an account of the revolt of the Moriscos. Again, each work combines historical facts, chivalric fiction, and descriptions of festivals and tournaments. Although one might argue that the so-called two parts of the *Civil Wars* turned out to be quite dissimilar and really belong in different literary categories,[31] it seems true that the author intended to encompass in a brief series the distant and immediate past of the people of Granada, as he had done in the case of Lorca. Moreover, certain historical events are treated similarly in both works, and, more significantly, the poem includes a few instances of experimentation with topics and subject matter borrowed from frontier ballads. "Abenámar" in particular is paraphrased in one instance and imitated in another. Reversing the situation of a Castilian king wooing a Moorish city, Pérez de Hita makes a Berber leader address Lorca as if the town were a beautiful woman. In that passage, the octave is replaced by a ballad, with consonantal rhyme such as was commonly used in the transitional period between the old and the new types of ballads. The author's imagination was, however, far more restricted by faithfulness to his sources in the poem than it would be in his major prose work and even in the history of the rebellion.

This is not the place to discuss the medieval and modern ballads used in the *Civil Wars of Granada, I,* both as a component of the text and as an inspiration for the fictional plot. One should, however, keep in mind the author's high esteem for the two types of ballads and also the fact that his admira-

tion did not prevent him from tampering with the text of the
poems he inserted, if it suited his approach to a given topic.[32]
The situation was different when he wrote the history of the
rebellion, since only in one or two instances would there be a
ballad already in circulation that the author could use.[33] For
this reason he decided not to disrupt the consistency between the
two parts, as he puts it himself (*Guerras civiles*, II, 10, chap I),
but rather to end each chapter with a ballad of his own sum-
marizing its content or part of it. Among these narrative poems
are "Temeroso de la muerte / estaba Abenabó Audalla" (II,
353-55, chap. 25), which concludes the book, and "Las tremo-
lantes banderas/del grande Fajardo parten" (II, 103-5, chap 11),
which employs the lyrical and musical technique of echoing
the final word of each quatrain. Both of these poems catch a
spark of the traditional style that they imitate. The majority,
however, are factual reports written in grammatically correct
but unimaginative language that recalls the collections of historical ballads issued by Fuentes or Sepúlveda.[34] This is also
the cumbersome style found in series of ballads on the battle
of Lepanto and other episodes of the wars against the Turkish
empire, which addressed themselves to the uneducated public
and are considered to be part of folk literature.[35]

A minor poetic genre in which authorship is relatively unim-
portant is that of the mottos, emblematic phrases, epitaphs,
and the like that are. so richly represented in Pérez de Hita's
work. The examples selected by him avoid extreme obscurity of
meaning and are in general more spirited than subtle. It is interesting that when the subject concerns the festivals of the
Moriscos, as occurs in the history of the rebellion,[36] the poetry
condensed in these tiny capsules loses epic dignity, but becomes
more picturesque, light, and graceful. A dialogue in the *Civil
Wars of Granada, I,* between the Moor Alabez and the Christian
Quiñonero (I, 8-9, chap. 1) reminds us of the verbal confrontations that were and still are part of the "Fiestas de moros
y cristianos."[37] The history of the rebellion includes a handful
of songs in traditional metrical patterns such as a *villancico* (II,
20-21, chap 3), and some *redondillas*, four-line stanzas in octo-
syllables, rhyming *a b b a* (II, 182-84, chap. 14), and *quintillas*,
octosyllabic stanzas of five lines with two rhymes (II, 201-2,

chap. 16). Outstanding in this group are the *endechas,* stanzas of four short lines written for a mournful occasion (II, 185–87, chap. 14), placed on the lips of a Morisco orphan who foretells the doom of her people. The impressively direct poetic language of this poem suggests that at least the first quatrains are in the stream of folk poetry.

Pérez de Hita's understanding of the value of the new style in Moorish ballads was not matched by an appreciation of the parallel trend of pastoral poetry, and this genre is not represented in his work. Two short love poems presented as serenade songs in *Civil Wars, I* that are not in the metrical pattern of the romances conform to widely different styles coexisting in the Golden Age. "Lágrimas que no pudieron / tanta dureza ablandar" (I, 46, chap 5), couched in redondillas creates a dreamy, sentimental mood in the tradition of the fifteenth-century "Lamentaciones de amores" that continued to be very popular.[38] In contrast the style of "Divina Galiana," a poem in *estancias* (an Italianate stanza combining lines of eleven and seven syllables) replete with mythological allusions, is typical of mannerisms that became widespread in lyrical poetry toward the end of the sixteenth century.

Among the possibly original poems in Pérez de Hita's work, Italianate metrical forms are poorly represented, though not neglected. They appear mainly in speeches that use blank hendecasyllables and in two laments, cast in a more complex poetic pattern. To the first group belongs the exposition of Christian faith made by Esperanza de Hita in her successful attempt to achieve the conversion of the Sultana (I, 215–16, chap. 14), as well as an address by an alfaquí entreating the people of Granada to unite and fight the Christians (I, 258–59, chap. 16). In the history of the rebellion, two Moriscos address a Christian leader in similarly solemn speeches (II, 107–9, chap. 11, and 344–46, chap. 25). As is the case in the first part of the *Civil Wars,* the author seemed to conceive those scenes in terms of theatrical situations that occurred in tragedies and heroic plays of the Renaissance.

Worth noticing is the use made by Pérez de Hita in each book of a highly unusual combination of hendecasyllables and pentasyllables apparently introduced in Spanish poetry by Gaspar

Gil Polo in his *Diana enamorada*.[39] The theme of the poem in
Civil Wars, I is the fall of fortune and it is placed on the lips
of the slandered queen (I, 211–13, chap. 14). The lament included in the history of the rebellion appears when Aben Humeya, in a rare moment of introspection, meditates on the para-
doxes of his destiny (II, 30–32, chap. 3). Although this is a
mediocre poem, the author deserves credit for attempting to
express, by means of the topic of *ubi sunt,* a combination of fear,
nostalgia, anxiety, and regrets that relate credibly to the situation of those men of Granada for whom the conflict cut deep
into their own divided personalities.

III   *The Problem of Publishing*

It is a little unusual for an author who spent all of his life
in the area of Murcia and Granada, which belonged to Castile,
to have had his work first published in Zaragoza in Aragon; it
is even more strange that after the successful appearance in
1595 of the *Civil Wars of Granada* a so-called second part,
which the author finished writing in 1597, was not printed until
1619. This delay was due, at least in part, to objections raised
by censorship.

A document of 1604 published by P. Blanchard-Demouge
concerns "three original books on the civil wars of Granada"
by Pérez de Hita, which had remained for an unspecified period
of time in the possession of the Madrid printer Miguel Serrano
de Vargas and were being returned to the author, because permission to print them had been denied.[40] A book dealer in
Madrid and one in Murcia, called Juan Dorado, acted as intermediaries. Six years later a *privilegio* was obtained by the
latter for a book whose description fits *Civil Wars, I;* he claimed
that he had purchased from Pérez de Hita the manuscript, and
that it was lost after being submitted with an *Aprobación* of
the Licenciado Verrio (Berrío). Dorado stated that others had
published the book many times, which is true enough, his
Madrid correspondent Juan Berrillo being among those allowed
to print Pérez de Hita's work, although the text he reproduced
was not the original in three parts that had belonged to the
Murcian dealer. Rather, it was the princeps of Zaragoza, 1595.

Presumably Dorado intended to publish the entire series at that time, since an *aprobación* was issued in Madrid that same year (1610) covering the full text. The censor stated that he recommended publication after having made certain corrections, and he explained that the work comprised three parts. He stated that the first and the third were in manuscript form, whereas the second was a volume published in Alcalá de Henares by Juan Gracián in 1604.

Considering the fact that 1610 was the year of the expulsion of the Moriscos, it appears likely that the publication project had something to do with efforts to counteract the measure. Those trying to obtain exemptions for certain groups may well have wished to disseminate Pérez de Hita's views, and particularly to make known his book on the revolt of the Alpujarras, which was written with compassion for the population of Moorish origin and pointed at the losses that the region of Granada experienced when they were banished. Likewise, opposition to this work could be anticipated, and indeed the publishers must have run into difficulties, for it is almost certain that the history of the rebellion was not printed, or at least not released, in 1610, in spite of the *privilegio* and *aprobación* obtained that year. At least, no copy exists of any edition prior to that of Cuenca (1619), which includes the two documents mentioned.[41]

When Pérez de Hita's second book was finally published, a certain number of copies carried a dedication bearing the name of a former printer of Cuenca,[42] the capital of a region which had been deprived by the expulsion of a useful segment of its population that had come originally from Moorish Granada. The publication was offered to the duke of Infantado, a peer who owned Morisco-populated land and is known to have taken a firm stand in 1612 in favor of the mudéjares of Murcia.[43] The second book by Pérez de Hita appeared, therefore, like the *Corónica* version of *El Abencerraje,* under the auspices of a señor de moriscos who had fought to maintain the status quo.

It is also possible, though less certain, that similar considerations had prompted the Venetian dealer established in Zaragoza, Angelo Tabano, to place Pérez de Hita's book under the patronage of Don Juan de Aragón. P. Blanchard-Demouge has identified this nobleman as the son-in-law of the duke of Villahermosa, Don Martín de Aragón, and now we know that the latter, another señor de moriscos, was involved with Jiménez de Embún in the events of 1559 and remained all his life a bulwark of the fuerista party, which opposed the Inquisition.[44] One more publication detail worth noting concerns the aprobación for Castile of *Civil Wars, I,* signed in 1598. It was issued by the lawyer Gonzalo Mateo de Berrío, who was a graduate of the University of Granada and a member of the literary group that gathered in the home of the Granada-Venegas. These two circumstances indicate that the censor either belonged to, or was closely connected with, the wealthy bourgeoisie of mixed parentage that flourished in the capital of the former Nasrid kingdom, and indeed he must have been in sympathy with the attitude expressed about the past of this land in the book whose publication he recommended, stating simply that it was a book for pleasure-reading translated from the Arabic and contained nothing objectionable, either on religious or moral grounds.[45]

One other question raised by the 1610 aprobación concerns the content of the three parts that were to be published. The second of these is easily identified by the data given by the censor—Alcalá, Juan Gracián, 1604—as a well-known edition of *Guerras civiles, I.* The manuscript continuation must obviously have been the history of the rebellion, still unpublished at the time. It follows that the first book, also in manuscript form as the censor specified, was a different work from the two that we know. It is possible that, after the success of his fictional portrayal of Moorish chivalry at the time of the fall of the Nasrid kingdom, the author concerned himself with an earlier period in history. Though no trace of such a text remains, we must conclude that it existed, for there is no other satisfactory explanation of the statements in the 1610 aprobación.[46] Like his contemporary Miguel de Cervantes, Ginés must have written extensively in his later years. We shall almost certainly never know if his last work conformed to the style of the *Historia de los bandos—Civil Wars, I—*which it was intended to precede in a series on the history of Granada, or whether the author experimented with yet another approach to the blending of history and fiction.

CHAPTER 6

The Civil Wars of Granada, I:
Content and Sources

I *The Plot*

AS authors of historical novels were to do in later times, Pérez de Hita begins his work with a discussion of the geographical and historical background. He offers a brief account of the legendary origin of the city of Granada and refers to the Moslem conquest, adding laudatory comments on this region blessed by nature, where the most noble among the invaders, we are told, made their homes. A perfunctory survey of Nasrid monarchs, from Alhamar to Boabdil, emphasizes a single cultural trait, the beauty and power of their buildings.

The first long digression deals with the unsuccessful offensive launched, around 1450, by the Granadines in the vicinity of Murcia and Lorca, an episode known as the battle of Alporchones. Both the preparations and the actual fighting are reported in considerable detail, quoting in full, along with a poetic insertion of lesser merit, the fine old ballad "Allá en Granada la rica / instrumentos oí tocar." Resuming his historical narrative, Pérez de Hita runs into another contingency immortalized by a ballad: the enthusiasm of Juan II of Castile as he viewed from a distant height the marvels of the Moorish capital. The "Romance de Abenámar" serves at this point to stress the beauty and splendor of Granada, precisely when its two last sovereigns, Muley Hacén and Boabdil, are introduced.

The author announces that he will turn his attention to the noble knights who lived in the Moorish kingdom, and with some erudite pretense, goes on to enumerate thirty-four lineages of Arab or Berber origin, and no less than a hundred towns. A brief discussion of the most important Granadine clans leads

87

again to the years preceding the downfall of the Nasrid state, when the young Boabdil—called in the book Boabdelín, Alman-zor, or El Rey Chico—had supplanted his elderly father.

In the first and central sections of the book, which contain and paraphrase a few old ballads and a sizable group of new ones, this grave phase of history is depicted as a time of un-ending festivals and tournaments. The power of Castile is rep-resented mainly by courteous challengers. First the Maestre of Calatrava offers to contribute to the celebrations held in the Moorish capital by fighting a knight from Granada in the Vega, while the king and queen with their attendants watch from the ramparts. Muza, the Rey Chico's half brother, is selected. As elsewhere in Pérez de Hita's work, a fictional situation—Muza, infatuated with Daraxa, is the object of Fátima's love—lends in-terest to the detailed description of the emblems, arms, garb, and jewels worn by Moorish knights and beauties. The armor and colors of the Christian contender are much more sparingly reported, though enough is said to make his appearance har-monize with the brightness of the total picture. The author describes the exchange of courtesies before the duel, and the different stages of the fighting, noticing the transition in the mood of the combatants from a sportive attitude to one of anger. He also takes heed of the emotions of the spectators. The duel remains actually inconclusive, for the Maestre, aware that his opponent is .losing strength, stops the fight. Such mag-nanimity, which Muza nobly acknowledges, also reflects the farsighted intention to win the friendship of the best among the Moors. The episode is concluded by quoting ten verses from the ballad "¡Ay, Dios, qué buen Cavallero / el Maestre de Cala-trava!" which portrays the protagonist raiding the Vega up to the very doors of Granada.

The Moorish court rejoices over Muza's return after he has recovered from his wounds. Dances, gossip, and teasing end in the first irate exchange between members and friends of the Abencerraje clan and the rival faction, headed by the Zegrís. Soon after, the author develops the little story of the enamored Zaide and Zaida (who drew apart because of pressures from the lady's family and the lover's indiscretion), by quoting the text and enlarging upon the subject matter of three ballads—

actually by Lope de Vega although Pérez de Hita did not know
this. Another of the individual love stories interwoven in the
central part of the book with the description of duels or pageantry is that of Sarracino and Galiana, and here, too, the
narrative conforms to the situation depicted in the interpolated
ballads.

The prestige of the Abencerrajes and the envy of the Zegrís
come closer to the foreground as the author describes the preparation for a bullfight and a juego de cañas. The excitement of
the crowds and the animation of the ring are effectively
rendered. When he discusses the attire of the participants, Pérez
de Hita's style becomes minutely descriptive, and the contest
itself is reported with rapid, precise, and effective strokes. An
element of suspense is introduced as the reader becomes aware
of the bad faith of the Zegrís, who carry concealed arms. When
spears are used in place of reeds the game turns out to be
deadly serious and a Zegrí is killed before the king succeeds in
reestablishing some order, all of which conforms to the interpolated ballad "Afuera, afuera, afuera; / aparta, aparta, aparta."
For the second time a Christian knight, now Don Manuel Ponce
de León, approaches the gate and throws a challenge. It is
answered by Malique Alabez, and the outcome will be again
a bond of friendship between the adversaries, although there
is a moment when the combat spreads, first to the horses of
the cavaliers now fighting on foot, and then to the men escort-
ing them. The episode is closed with the ballad "Ensilléysme
el potro rucio / del Alcayde de los Vélez," although this poem
deals with the Moorish knight's preparation for the encounter
rather than with the fighting itself.

The most elaborate pageantry in the book is presented on the
occasion of a *juego de sortija,* in which galloping horsemen
show their skill by snatching a ring with a spear. Elaborate
details are given about the emblems and attire displayed in
the game as well as about the ornaments and the complicated
mechanical devices of the various cars in which knights con-
vening for a competition appear in the arena, each carrying an
effigy of his ladylove. The author comments on the feelings
of pride or frustration that each phase of the game brings to the
participants and the audience, and he dwells upon the pointed

dialogues of the ladies whose portraits are to become the trophy of the winner as well as on the competition proper. A somber note enters when a Zegrí insinuates that the Abencerrajes are traitors to the king. And the reader foresees the future awaiting this idle and brilliant court when the Maestre of Calatrava unexpectedly appears and performs in a manner that fascinates the great and the small, winning the trophy that he then gallantly offers to the Moorish queen.

Before departing, the Maestre is challenged to a fight in the Vega by Albayaldos, whose cousin he has killed in battle. This becomes a double encounter, for Ponce de León and Malique Alabez agree to finish their duel, which is preceded by an amicable conversation between the Christian and Moorish champions. The latter are overcome, but Ponce de León spares his opponent at the request of Muza, who on this occasion only watches the fight. The dying Albayaldos, formerly adamant in his hatred for the Christians, asks to be baptized. As the Maestre performs this pious rite, Malique makes a secret resolution to become also a Christian. After Muza has paid the last tribute to Albayaldos, he must again witness a fight that he cannot stop; this time a duel caused by jealousy between the knights of Granada Gazul and Reduán, who are in love with the Abencerraje beauty Lindaraja.

In another single combat at the Vega the Maestre cuts off the head of the Moor Alatar, who had challenged him. In the meanwhile the Zegrís have accused the Abencerrajes of being charitable toward Christian captives, and tensions run high in Granada. To restore the happy spirit of his Court the king orders another tournament and bullfight. Gazul excels on this occasion. A royal party follows, during which some of the subplots are brought to a conclusion: Abenámar is married to Fátima; the impetuous Reduán forgets Lindaraja after having rescued the fair Haxa from four Christian captors.

The last episode mentioned leads to an epic theme derived from a frontier ballad on the attack against Jaén by Reduán. From then on the multiple plot is replaced by concentration in a single sequence of events. The Zegrís put into effect their plan of accusing the Abencerrajes of treason, and they report falsely to the Rey Chico that during the zambra which preceded the fight between Muza and the Maestre of Calatrava—precisely the time when the fictional action begins—two courtiers walking through the gardens of Generalife caught a glimpse of the queen in the company of Albinhamad, one of the Abencerrajes, who was seen later gathering roses and making a garland which he placed on his own head. At this revelation the Moorish king surrenders completely to the influence of the Zegrís and gives his consent to the premeditated murder of the Abencerrajes, who are then summoned one by one to the Alhambra and slaughtered in the Patio de los Leones. Thirty-six of them die, proclaiming themselves Christians. A page reveals the treachery to some friends of the Abencerrajes, whose faction then storms the Alhambra killing a large number of Zegrís. The young king saves his life by hiding, while his father temporarily takes control and is hailed by the rebels. Muza sides first with the Abencerrajes, but in response to a lady's plea he helps to restore his brother to the throne. After these events, the king banishes all Abencerrajes and orders his wife to be imprisoned, until her guilt or innocence is established by means of a duel.

Muza and other protagonists of the preceding subplots volunteer to fight in favor of the queen, who is referred to in this part of the book only by the title of Sultana. She refuses, however, their proffered aid and on the advice of the captive Esperanza de Hita, writes to the Castilian Don Juan Chacón revealing her decision to be a Christian and entrusting to him her defense. The Rey Chico, who has become a monster of cruelty, kills with his own hands his sister Morayma, the wife of Albinhamad, and their two children. Meanwhile the confusion in Granada is compounded as the brother of Muley Hazén also claims power. The most courageous knights, following the Abencerrajes, defect to the Christians, and the gallant Moors who were the protagonists of the previously developed subplots become officers under such Castilian leaders as Don Manuel Ponce de León and Don Alonso de Aguilar.

After debating the propriety of taking up arms in defense of an infidel, four Castilian knights—all well-known historical figures, the Alcaide de los Donceles, Don Alonso de Aguilar, Ponce de León, and Chacón—agree to be the champions of the queen of Granada and decide to appear disguised as Turks of the Christian religion. The "Judgment of God," which takes place in an atmosphere of gloom and mourning shared by the entire population, is treated with the same attention to detail as the joyous festivities that precede it. After clearing by their victory the good name of the Sultana, the Castilian knights return secretly to their headquarters.

Turning to history again and mentioning some of his sources, Pérez de Hita deals briefly with certain episodes of the last phase of the war of Granada. Among these are the capture of the Rey Chico when he attempted to conquer the town of Lucena; the loss of Alhama; the attempt of the alfaquís to restore the bellicose spirit of the Granadine people; the renewed division among the three rulers, each of whom called himself king of Granada; the first negotiations toward capitulation; and the founding of the fortress town of Santa Fe. The latter event introduces a reprise of chivalric topics, such as the legendary duel between the formidable Tarfe and the young Christian Garcilaso, who fights to rescue a motto with the words *Ave María*. As the fall of Granada becomes imminent, a number of the fictional gallant Moors, including Muza who supposedly had had a Christian mother, cooperate with the main negotiator Aldoradín, a historical character who had not appeared previously. They will also participate in the celebration of Isabella and Ferdinand's entrance to Granada, while the Rey Chico refuses in his grief to be honored as a king by his subjects and hears from his mother the bitter remark reported in the legend of the Moor's sigh. After their conversion, many of the Moors marry well-born Castilians, but the Zegrís are banished from Granada. Other families of their faction leave voluntarily, as does the Rey Chico who would have been allowed to stay in Purchena. We are told that one of the exiles was the Moorish chronicler who reported the story of the Sultana.

Two expanded episodes, both deriving from ballads and representing in one case the fictional and in the other the historical approach, bring the book to a close. The first instance concerns Gazul, a character with whom the reader is familiar. This passionate and jealous Moor was actually another creation by Lope de Vega alluding to his own feelings, but Ginés seems to ignore it, and he attempts to explain why part of the story of

Gazul is placed by the ballads in the western part of Andalusia by making the assumption that the protagonist was a Moor living under Christian rule. As to the true incident recalled in the last chapter, it portrays the heroic death of Don Alonso de Aguilar as he attempted to quench in 1501 a revolt of Moriscos in Sierra Bermeja. The work is thus brought to a close on a note that forecasts the theme and style of the so-called second part.

II *The Historical and Legendary Content*

The title page of the *Historia de los vandos de los Zegries y Abencerrages* states that it derives directly—"agora nuevamente sacado"—from an Arabic book whose author was Aben Hamin, a Moor of Granada. However, the text itself at no time warrants a literal interpretation of this statement. Rather the contemporary author comes forward in the very first paragraph (*Guerras civiles,* I, 1, chap. 1) to authenticate with his own experience a remark on the gold and silver carried by the rivers of Granada. After "el Arávigo" (the Arab) has been cited in connection with Muza, the half brother of Boabdil who was the son of a Christian woman (I, 16, chap. 2), the first specific mention of Aben Hamin appears in chapter 3 (I, 24), when lineages that will play the most important role in the fictional part of the book are listed. Henceforth, mentions of the alleged Arabic source occur more frequently when the author relies on loose legendary material or on his own imagination. In the last chapter, the background of the pseudosource is made more specific, Don Rodrigo Ponce de León, count of Bailén, being named as the previous owner (I, 291, chap. 17). It is not likely that Ginés would have dared talk about such a gift if he had not received from the count some material, possibly genealogical; the Arabic original must be considered, however, a literary device.

Historical subject matter is predominant in the first three, as well as in the last two chapters—the sixteenth and seventeenth—of the *Historia de los vandos.* Therefore, if we consider the work as a whole, the individual lives of fictional characters appear as enlarged details of a vast canvas, framed between two compact informative accounts. Although factual inaccuracies do occur in these segments of the book, the impression given is that of historical narrative, chiefly because of the apparently objective manner of reporting events, and the pretense of erudition, which is carried so far as to give long lists of people and places. In the final chapters the relevance of material summarized also contributes to the desired effect that the book is a legitimate chronicle.[1]

Like many of his contemporaries, Pérez de Hita accepted as historical truths some fabulous notions concerning ancient history, which he combined with factual information and with the eulogy of the natural beauty of the region. *Civil Wars, I* enhances and defines the geographical setting with a precision that is unprecedented in works of the period that combine history and fiction. However, laudatory descriptions may echo the practice of medieval chronicles, and are found also, precisely in connection with Granada, in the first part of Miguel de Luna's *La verdadera historia del rey Don Rodrigo,* published three years before Pérez de Hita's book.[2] Achievements in architecture under the Nasrids become the first cultural trait emphasized by Ginés, and it serves, in conjunction with landscape and climate, to establish a link between the subject matter of the book and the world experienced by author and readers. As to the sources for this survey of early Granadine history, two are mentioned in addition to the apocryphal "Arábigo" (*Guerras civiles, I*, 2, 3, 16, chaps. 1 and 2). One is a "Chrónica del rey don Rodrigo" that may be identified with the fictional *Crónica sarracina* by the fifteenth-century author, Pedro del Corral, since it mentions a king Balagis of Seville appearing in this work.[3] The other reference is to the legitimate historian Esteban de Garibay, who published in 1571 the last volume, dealing with Moorish Granada, of his *Compendio historial de todos los reinos de España.* As P. Blanchard-Demouge showed, Pérez de Hita followed this text in his survey of Nasrid monarchs and used it also as a general reference.[4]

The space given in early chapters to the battle of Alporchones, which had been treated in the author's "Libro de Lorca," and to some other episodes reflects his preference for writing about the past of the area he best knew and its ruling family, the Fajardos. Throughout *Civil Wars, I*, it may also be observed

that the relative importance granted to events depends less on
their actual significance than on the possibility they offer to
generate emotion and suspense. And for the most part, the
choice falls upon subjects that had been treated in ballads, as
is the case with the Alporchones episode, and with the admiration of a Castilian king for Granada recalled in the "Romance
de Abenámar."[5]

Chapters dealing with duels in the Vega carry only the historical basis that was preserved as content of ballads. Even less
related to Nasrid history are descriptions of festivities, since
neither the refinement and luxury nor the causes of discord
that did exist in Nasrid Granada were the same as those presented by Pérez de Hita. In the second half of the book—chapter 13—the transition from fragmentary subplots to the theme
of the calumny and death of the Abencerrajes is marked by a
reprise of the epic and historical elements occurring in the
account of the Moors' attempt to recapture Jaén. Amalgamation
of chronologically incompatible elements in this episode stems
from the ballad—termed old by Perez de Hita—"Reduán, si te
acuerdas / que me diste la palabra," which provided a point of
departure, although topographical references in this chapter
indicate that the author was familiar with other texts on the
frontier life of this region.[6]

Pérez de Hita's approach to the legend of the Abencerrajes
is consistent with its formulation in *El Abencerraje* and the pass-
ing allusions found in frontier texts,[7] but he fictionalized the
theme to a much greater extent by linking it, according to
suggestions in contemporary ballads and one *glosa* ("a composition on the theme of a short poem, the lines of which are
incorporated at the end of each stanza"),[8] to the enmity of
the Zegrís and the topos of the slandered wife. It is in such
poems that the massacre is imputed to the last king of Granada,
a distortion of history that satisfies the principle of poetic
justice. In the last part of his book, Pérez de Hita likewise
changes the characterization of the Rey Chico to make it consonant with this act of tyranny attributed to him. The place
where the Abencerrajes are killed becomes significant in *Civil
Wars*, and it is quite likely that the tragic story reached the
author as a legend already ascribed to the Alhambra's Patio de

los Leones, in the same way that the Generalife had become both the meeting place of the alleged lovers and the pleasant setting where the calumny was spoken.[9] On the other hand, there is no indication that the theme of the vindication of the Moorish queen by means of a duel was part of the legend before it become integrated in Pérez de Hita's work.

At the same time that the legendary theme expands, the capture of the Rey Chico in Lucena (I, 260, chap. 16) and actual divisions among the Moors are reported without amplifications of a fictional nature, although rhetorical speeches and letters are introduced. The emphasis on debate and on lamentations reflects true circumstances that found an echo in chronicles and in ballads such as "¡Ay de mi Alhama!" which is quoted in full. Blanchard-Demouge wondered if Pérez de Hita could have known texts in Arabic. This is doubtful, since reports on the subject written in this language do not seem to have been in circulation at the time; moreover, it is not probable that Ginés could read Arabic script, even if he was acquainted with vernacular Arabic. Nevertheless, he had possibly at his disposal sources of information for which we cannot today account. The name Isabel de Granada was adopted after the conquest, not by the estranged wife of the Rey Chico, as we read in *Guerras civiles* (I, 289, chap. 17), but by Zoraya, the renegade who had been Muley Hacén's favorite. Like Muza in Pérez de Hita's work, her son became the most important of all converts, and he founded the house of the Granada-Venegas.[10]

The Zegrís were an important family of Granada, but it is not known if the hostility toward the Abencerrajes attributed to them in late ballads and by Pérez de Hita was based on fact. As for the Abencerrajes, they are reported to have migrated, contrary to Pérez de Hita's contention that they became converts and fought on the Castilian side. But at least the characterization he gave them as brave but compassionate knights who were inclined to make friends with the Christians remains within the guidelines of the ballads. And there is no question that large segments of the Granada gentry adopted the Christian faith at the time of capitulating or even before.[11]

If Garibay provided information about the past history of Granada, actual events summarized in the last part of the book derive chiefly from Hernando del Pulgar's *Crónica de los Reyes Católicos,* which is both mentioned (I, 274, chap. 16) and followed, almost verbatim, in certain passages.[12] Although Pérez de Hita was interested in all sorts of *relaciones* and some information must have come to him by word of mouth, his direct account of Granada's surrender is basically restricted to well-known facts and circumstances: the chivalric character of the Catholic sovereigns' court at Santa Fe, the negotiations preceding their entrance into the capital, the ceremony of handing over the keys of the city, the joyous celebrations by the conquerors and the expressions of grief by the vanquished. The legendary scene of the Rey Chico's farewell to Granada and his mother's reproach is reported but not expanded by Pérez de Hita, who follows the text of Pulgar's *Crónica.*[13] Two emphasized aspects of the last days of Granada are the fights between partisans of the three members of the royal Nasrid family claiming the throne and the efforts of the alfaquís to stabilize the political situation and rekindle the bellicose spirit of the Granadine militia and its leaders. Without departing from historical subject matter, the author relies heavily on ballads, as he closes the book on the epic theme of Don Alonso de Aguilar's death in a battle against insurgent Moriscos.

III   *The Topics of Chivalric Literature*

A modern trait of the *Civil Wars of Granada* is the sense of immediacy imparted to subject matter derived from the vast repertoire of books of chivalry and Renaissance epic. The author's reading of such works accounts, however, only partly for this major influence, since a large amount of such material, as well as the approach toward it, appears to have reached Pérez de Hita indirectly through the vehicle of new ballads, which he frequently but not always included in the text of his work.

In the first place, the author's pretense that he is only a translator must be considered. Such practice was common among authors of books of chivalry, whose alleged original was often a Greek, or occasionally an Arabic, manuscript,[14] although, as Márquez Villanueva has shown, dependence on a spurious source was less ironic and artistically meaningful in this genre than it had been in the pseudohistorical work of Antonio de Guevara.[15] In Pérez de Hita's time the device was used with a very specific propagandistic purpose, by the Morisco Miguel de Luna, who succeeded in selling as factual history the invented plot of his *Verdadera historia del rey Rodrigo* (1592), calculated to enhance the prestige of Moslem Spain. In a parallel development, antiquarian documentation was at about the same time consistently forged in Granada.[16] Luna and Pérez de Hita coincide in their use of an Arabic pseudosource to authenticate an amalgamation of history and fiction resulting in the embellishment of at least one segment of southern Spain's Moorish past. Their approach, however, was utterly different. The author of the *Historia del rey Rodrigo* allows himself an occasional marginal annotation, but otherwise he consistently hides behind supposedly relevant historical material that he offers as translation.

Even in the rare instances when one of the royal characters in this book is engaged in a personal conflict of love or devotion to faith, his or her feelings are at most expressed in lengthy and solemn speeches. In contrast Pérez de Hita does not carry beyond the title page his role of mere translator, although he does refer repeatedly to the "Arábigo," or the "Coronista moro," as one of his sources and makes the apocryphal author an impersonation of himself when he states that the purpose of the Moorish chronicler was to deal, not with the war of Granada, but with what was happening right there at the time, including the civil war among the Moors (*Guerras civiles, I*, 269, chap. 16). Moreover, there is no passage in Luna equivalent to Pérez de Hita's little story about the manner in which the manuscript changed hands and was finally given to him by the count of Bailén (I, 291, chap. 17). And if the apocryphal Aben Hamin was mainly introduced for the purpose of giving the appearance of history to the content of the book, the author also made a literary instrument of the spurious source.

As many authors of books of chivalry had done before him, Pérez de Hita described an idealized knightly court where the display of individual bravery and sentiment overweighs other interests and claims the reader's identification with exemplary knights and their fair ladies. Consequently, the themes of duels, equestrian exploits, and courtship prevail, and emblematic manifestation of sentiment becomes important. On the other hand, supernatural or magic elements are not allowed to creep into the embellished but far from fantastic world of the *Civil Wars of Granada*, which stands close to the genre of the books of chivalry, but distinctly apart from it. Another important difference concerns structure, since a protagonist whose adventures are reported in linear sequence overshadows all other characters of books of chivalry, whereas Pérez de Hita correlates, in a manner possibly derived from the pastoral novel, a number of alternating subplots, presented simultaneously with the lyrical expression of the sentiments involved in each situation.[17]

A gallery of heroes coming alternatingly to the foreground is also found in Renaissance epic, a poetic genre that frequently uses the siege of a city as the basic situation unifying a number of adventures, among which duels by champions of both sides predominate. Pérez de Hita shares such traits, along with the great emphasis placed on the description of a knight's appearance and the abundance of chivalric motives. Among the general characteristics which cannot be tied to any particular influence, the theme of the calumny and defense of the Moorish queen should be considered.

This last topic appeared in a number of late medieval and Renaissance texts including the *Chrónica Sarracina* of Pedro del Corral as well as Ariosto's *Orlando Furioso*. Pérez de Hita's dependence on the latter was asserted by E. Ruta,[18] and denied in reference to this specific episode by G. Valli, who considered a more probable source in several ballads dealing with episodes patterned on the same theme; these combine a subject matter derived from chivalric or historical Spanish sources, including Corral, with the influence of the Italian poem.[19]

Likewise new ballads must have been the vehicle by which a motif stemming from Matteo Boiardo's *Orlando Innamorato* reached Pérez de Hita. In canto 19 of the first part of this work, the mortally wounded Moslem king Agricán begs to be baptized by his conqueror Orlando. According to Chevalier,[20] the episode inspired the authors of a few ballads who were interested in either the religious or the epic aspect of the

theme. The situation was then used as conclusion to the duel
of Albayaldos, in "De tres mortales heridas / de que mucha
sangre vierte," inserted by Pérez de Hita (*Guerras civiles*, I, 124,
chap. 11), who stressed in the subsequent prose account of the
same scene its religious and emotional overtones. Earlier ballads
on Albayaldos' defeat deal with the challenge and combat but
do not include the conversion of this legendary character.

The influence of Ariosto on *Civil Wars* seems to have been
directly exerted in other cases. After eliminating some of the
alleged borrowings noted by Ruta, Giorgio Valli concentrated
on specific details relating to duels in the Vega: a friendly
chat, near a fountain, of Christian and Moorish knights who
are about to fight; the noble gesture of the contender who
dismounts when his opponent loses his horse; honors rendered
in the field to a dead warrior by another knight, who composes
an epitaph and laudatory verses and places them on a tree as
a memorial next to the arms of the deceased; and the motif,
appearing also in *Amadís*, of horses attacking each other fiercely
while their owners fight on foot. There are a few passages
when the text of the Spanish novel follows closely the Ariostean
lines, borrowing analogies and an occasional turn of phrase.
The most striking parallel occurs in a parenthetical comment
expressing wonder at the cordiality of the meeting near the
fountain, although as Chevalier has noticed,[21] Pérez de Hita
ignored the irony of the passages he was imitating, which is
related to a situation in *Orlando Furioso* not present in *Civil
Wars*. Whether or not intended seriously, such simplification
enhances the exemplary value given in this book to the friendship of Moors and Christians.

According to Valli, Ariostean models helped also to shape
the characterization of Muza and part of the story of Reduán,
who after fighting with Gazul for the affection of Lindaraja
falls in love immediately with another lady whom he rescues
from Christian captors. However, Maxime Chevalier, taking into
consideration the total picture of Ariosto's influence on Spanish
literature, concludes that such themes may just as well derive
from ballads or books of chivalry. The manner of ending chapters
4, 10, and 14 of *Civil Wars I,* by promising the sequence of an
unfinished story, is also more akin, according to this critic, to

the practice of *Amadís* than to that of Ariosto's poem. In short, Pérez de Hita was stimulated by *Orlando Furioso* in his handling of the most favored chivalric themes, but the direct borrowings of the text of the poem are secondary to the influence that was exerted through certain ballads that offered an adaptation of Ariostean themes and style attuned to the sensibility of the same reading public to which the author of *Civil Wars* addressed himself.

IV   *The Traces of* El Abencerraje

A paradox in *Civil Wars of Granada* is the absence of any reference to the first and only preceding Moorish novel. Although a gallant Moor by the name of Abindarráez and his fair lady, called Xarifa, do play a part as a mutually faithful pair, every situation in which they are portrayed stems from new ballads that do not relate, except for the name of the protagonists, to *El Abencerraje*. Mention is also made of "the good alcaide Narváez" (*Guerras civiles*, I, 255, chap. 16), but here again only the surname and title bring to mind the short novel. Taking into consideration Pérez de Hita's disregard or perfunctory explanations of chronological conflict and his tendency to combine action found in different texts with characters of the same name, the silence he keeps on the Narváez-Abindarráez episode is difficult to explain and raises the question of his knowledge of the short novel.

It is most unlikely that a man who was fond of reading should not come across one of the many editions of Montemayor's *Diana* including the story of Abindarráez. Moreover, Harry A. Deferrari pointed out several passages of *Civil Wars* that he considered based upon the text of *El Abencerraje*.[22] One of them occurs in a description of a combat in which a knight who, leaning down from his horse, swiftly snatches an opponent's lance which had been wedged into the ground, is compared to a bird. In this case the similarity might be deemed inconclusive, given the abundance of step-by-step accounts of combat that use comparable images and which are found in books of chivalry as well as in reports of actual jousts. Other closely related passages appear when the virtues and popularity of the

Abencerraje clan are extolled, and when the people of Granada mourn for them. Such parallelism clearly indicates either Pérez de Hita's knowledge of *El Abencerraje* or the existence of a common written source for the legendary story.

As to the general handling of this theme, it is not dissimilar in both works, although new novelistic elements borrowed mianly from the ballads are introduced in *Civil Wars*, linking closely the king's wrath, which is politically motivated in the story of Abindarráez, to the slanderous reports reflecting on his honor that have been fabricated by the envious leaders of the rival Zegrí clan. In either case, the Abencerrajes epitomize the virtues and prestige of the knightly Moorish court, and the tragic element of the legend becomes a pivotal theme in the structure of the work. In the short novel it starts the chain of events that shape Abindarráez's destiny, and in *Civil Wars* it marks the transition from the radiant to the somber image of Granada. The fall from favor of the Abencerrajes is treated by Pérez de Hita less as an example related to the change of fortune theme than as a catastrophe resulting from the evils of envy and tyranny that will become a determining factor of the collapse of the Moorish state. Poetic justice and Pérez de Hita's interest in presenting as voluntary the conversion of the best among the Moors are well served by this approach, which is moreover in line with an early stage of the legend that may be surmised from the final lines of the frontier ballad on the loss of Alhama.

Basic is the role played by *El Abencerraje* in shaping the type of the courageous and enamored Moor vis-à-vis his sympathetic but sentimentally less vulnerable Castilian counterpart as well as in establishing along exemplary lines their loyal enemy relationship, based on trust, admiration, and discreet curiosity. Along with these similarities, different concepts of love are represented in the novels. The implied thesis concerning the situation of the Moriscos is not exactly the same either, since the conversion of the Moors that Pérez de Hita emphasizes had no place in the short novel. Such divergences reflect the attitude of two generations. *El Abencerraje* was inspired by the uninhibited, humanistic ideals of the Renaissance, whereas *Civil Wars* reveals the tolerant but far more pragmatic approach that the author's era and circumstances permitted.

The problem of Pérez de Hita's silence about the story of Abindarráez and Narváez is difficult to solve. Given the strong indications that not all of his work was printed, the possibility exists that the subject of the short novel, which is placed in the early fifteenth century by the opening reference to the conquest of Antequera, was treated in the lost first part of the original, approved for publication in 1610. Although no similarities of plot exist, what both works have in common is so crucial that it can hardly be accounted for as an indirect influence transmitted by other literary genres which treated with parallel techniques the Moorish theme.

V   *Old Ballads and New Ones*

Because the ballads, particularly those composed by contemporary poets, are not only the source of the vast majority of subplots in the *Civil Wars* but are also an integrating element of the book and provided the impetus for the renewal of narrative form undertaken by Pérez de Hita, their influence will also be considered in the next chapter, where we attempt to assess the significance and originality of the work. At this point we give some indications of the scope and content of the interpolated poems and their fictional content.

Studies on the romancero take into consideration Pérez de Hita's role as a collector of fifteenth-century texts. In *Civil Wars, I,* he inserted thirteen frontier ballads, expressing moderate appreciation for their merit and noting their informative value.[23] The majority appear in the predominantly historical first and last parts of the book. A few are not found in other collections of the period and among these "Allá en Granada la rica / instrumentos oí tocar" (*Guerras civiles,* I, 13–15, chap. 2) and "Reduán, si te acuerda, / que me diste la palabra" (I, 165–66, chap. 16) stand out. The first offers an interesting example of the factual reports often written by *juglares* ("minstrels"),[24] whereas the second illustrates the contamination of two historical subjects stemming from different periods.[25] Its more modern section presents in a well-stressed chivalric setting the last king of Granada at the head of a colorful host, as ladies watch from the towers of the Alhambra. The characters of Alabez and Reduán step

out of those epically oriented poems into the novelistic scene
of Pérez de Hita's Granada.

"Mensajeros le han entrado / al Rey Chico de Granada" and
its recasting in a different assonance (I, 277–79, chap. 17), have
preserved an otherwise unknown ballad on the siege of Granada.
It is built on the motif—previously found in connection with
the loss of Antequera or Alhama—of a messenger bringing bad
tidings. An interesting trait of this poem is that some of its
lines give an emblematic expression of the Crusader's spirit.[26]
Pérez de Hita offers likewise one of the two versions printed in
the sixteenth century of "Cercada está Santa Fe / con mucho
lienço encerado" (I, 280–83, chap. 17), which was to enjoy
great diffusion in oral tradition and inspire some Golden Age
plays.[27] A recasting with altered assonance of one of the old
ballads on the loss of Alhama, "Por la ciudad de Granada / el
rey moro se passea" (I, 254–55, chap. 16), appears next to the
more famous version (with the refrain "¡Ay de mi Alhama!")
"Passeávase el Rey Moro / por la ciudad de Granada" (I, 252,
chap. 16). The author of Civil Wars, I remarks on the sorrowful
character of the poem which he considers to be a translation
from an original in the Arabic language.[28] "Moro alcayde, moro
alcayde, / el de la vellida barba," (I, 256–57), of the same
cycle, brings into focus the family losses of the alcaide and his
daughter's conversion.

Some of the frontier ballads inserted by Pérez de Hita had
been printed around midcentury or later in the Cancionero de
romances, the various editions of the Silva de romances or as
single poems. Such is the case with "Abenámar, Abenámar, /
moro de la morería" (I, 17–18, chap. 2), which is preserved in
Civil Wars in its finest form. The same is true of "Estando el
rey don Fernando / en conquista de Granada" (I, 308, chap. 17)
and the two variants of the "Río Verde" ballad (I, 310–12,
chap. 17) on the death of Don Alonso de Aguilar. All of these
are among the last examples of the genre and close the cycle
of the war of Granada, offering at the same time the first literary
echo of Morisco unrest.[29]

The wide diffusion during the sixteenth century of ballads
on raids and single combats in the Vega is represented, in
addition to the already mentioned "Cercada está Santa Fe,"

by three poems on the Maestre de Calatrava. The ten spirited lines of "¡Ay, Dios, qué buen caballero / el Maestre de Calatrava!" (I, 34, chap. 3), in the traditional style, are quoted by themselves in *Civil Wars*, whereas similar versions of the same fragment appear in other versions combined with an account of challenge and duel. Albayaldos, the challenger of the Maestre, becomes a convert before he dies in "De tres mortales heridas / de que mucha sangre vierte" (I, 124, chap. 11), a new ballad found only in *Civil Wars* which adapts, as already indicated, a theme of Boiardo.[30] A more usual approach to the topic of Moorish-Christian single combat is found in "De Granada parte el moro / que Alatar era llamado" (I, 142, chap. 12), which, before it was used by Pérez de Hita, had been printed several times with a different assonance and certain changes that tend to underplay the animosity of the Moor.[31] It is not always clear to what extent the author of *Civil Wars, I* tampered with the texts of the inserted poems, but quite often the use of bookish relative clauses or prepositional phrases, adverbs ending in *-mente*, and Pérez de Hita's characteristic words reveal that the old text has been altered.[32]

To the intermediate stage between ballads of epic theme and the new romancero belong also three poems not known to have been printed before *Civil Wars, I*, which Blanchard-Demouge considered to be probably original. The first of these, "En las torres del Alhambra / sonava gran bozería" (I, 178–79, chap. 13), is a mediocre composition with consonantal rhyme on the theme of the lamentation of the Granadines for the death of the Abencerrajes. To depict the visible sorrow of a whole town, certain clichés are used which had also appeared in *El Abencerraje* and in the ballad on the capture of the king of Granada, "Junto al vado del Genil / por un camino seguido."[33] As to the second presumably original poem, "Cavalleros granadinos, / aunque moros hijos dalgo," (I, 181–82, chap. 13), Pérez de Hita may at most have modified an existing ballad, which had already been the object of a glosa, "Entre los moros guerreros / granadinos naturales," included in Lucas Rodríguez's *Romancero historiado* (1579). Both texts mention a false accusation of adultery involving the queen of Granada and a member of the Abencerraje family. The slander is the result of the conniving by the envious rivals of the Abencerrajes to make them appear as traitors. The third unidentified ballad, "Muy rebuelta está Granada, / en armas y fuego ardiendo" (I, 205, chap. 14), deals with conflicts, labeled civil wars, arising in Nasrid Granada between the factions headed by Mulahacén, his son the Rey Chico, and a governor appointed by the old king. In the absence of lyrical or descriptive elements, the historical theme of the poem is related to the fictional plot by a single reference to the Zegrís' support of, and the Abencerrajes' and Venegas' opposition to, the young king.

Along with a lively picture of young knights displaying their horsemanship, the topic of two ladies who tease one another as they excitedly watch their cavaliers appears in "La mañana de San Juan, / al punto que alboreava," (I, 79–80, chap. 9), a ballad that had been printed by a Granada publisher in a *pliego suelto* of 1573.[34] Related to the plot of *Civil Wars, I* are a few new ballads not quoted in the text, although they were printed before its publication. The dialogue between Fátima and Xarifa, stemming from "La mañana de San Juan," had been amplified by Lucas Rodríguez in "Quando el ruuicundo Phebo / sus rayos communicaua"[35] and by Pedro de Padilla in "Con Fátima está Jarifa / a una ventana parlando," a poem in which the window has become a strictly urban setting for the speech of the jealous *mora*. The series of Abindarráez-Jarifa ballads, composed by Padilla, which are independent of *El Abencerraje*'s theme, also ·include "El gallardo Abindarráez / tan conorido por fama," where we find the protagonist taking solemnly into the plaza a triumphal cart with the effigy of his fair lady, as is done also in the elaborate equestrian festival described in chapters 9 and 10 of *Civil Wars, I.* With their well-defined narrative content, colorful description, and sympathetic characterization of the Moors' character, Padilla's poems, though uninteresting if judged for their poetic value, carry the seeds of the idealized portrayal of the Nasrid court that Pérez de Hita develops.[36]

The new kind of Moorish ballads in which action, if it occurs, has only an expressive value related to the emotional or purely aesthetic motivation of the poem is well represented in *Civil Wars, I.* Blanchard-Demouge established that the majority of new ballads inserted by Pérez de Hita had appeared in Pedro de Moncayo's first anthology, *Flor de varios romances nuevos y canciones* (Huesca, 1589). The substantially altered—and more modern in taste—*Flor de varios romances nuevos: Primera y Segunda parte* (Barcelona, 1591) of the same compiler includes two other poems of *Civil Wars, I* not found in the previous *Flor.*[37] Equestrian festivals, courtship, and lovers' quarrels are the prevalent themes of the new Moorish ballads appearing anonymously in Moncayo's collections.

A sharp focus on details of precious and elaborate material and a subtle use of the emblematic language of love characterize "En el quarto de Comares, / la hermosa Galiana"[38] (I, 85–86, chap. 10). A fragment from another ballad on Galiana, "En las huertas de Almería / estava el moro Abenámar" (I, 36, chap. 5) combines the emphasis placed on arms and colorful garments by manneristic Moorish ballads with the nature setting and meditative mood of the pastoral. In such poems, epic situations are frequently called to mind only to accent an ecstatic mood, as in "Ensylleysme el potro rucio / del Alcayde de los Vélez" (I, 75, chap. 8), which is considered to be by Lope de Vega.[39]

Some of the new ballads on equestrian festivals do present a narrative content. "Ocho a ocho, diez a diez, / Sarrazinos y Aliatares" (I, 107–10, chap. 10) starts with a brilliant description of the entrance for a juego de cañas, followed by a whirlwind of action, set in motion by the rivalry between the king and a knight, who is the hero of the day and the object of Zelindaxa's love. Similarly, "Estando toda la corte / de Abdilí, rey de Granada" (I, 146–47, chap. 12)—composed to praise, under the name of Gazul, the performance at a bullfight of a Sevillan nobleman[40]—stresses visual effects in the first part and gives in the second a precise report of certain moments of the fight. The author of "Con más de treynta en quadrilla / hidalgos Abencerrajes" (I, 149, chap. 12) builds up a climate of tension and then abruptly closes the poem without developing the expected violence. Lope de Vega may have been the author of this ballad as well as of "Afuera, afuera, afuera; / aparta, aparta, aparta" (I, 61–62, chap. 7), which portrays vividly the colorful entrance and the clash of rival clans, blending skillfully a swift tempo inherited from the old ballad style with a subtle use of dualism and occasionally of aliteration.

The Lope de Vega authorship has been solidly established in the case of certain ballads with a protagonist called Gazul or Zaide, which relate to well-known episodes of his youth. In these two little cycles the enamored Moor runs against family pressures or the power of money. Zaide is dismissed on the ground, or the pretext, of his indiscretion. As to Gazul, he interrupts his Zaida's wedding celebration, kills the groom, and from then on finds happiness in a new love. Presumably, the biographical turning point behind the Gazul ballads was the marriage of a girl loved by Lope, Marfisa, and the beginning of his relationship with the actress Elena Osorio, whereas the Zaide poems relate to their separation a few years later.[41] The accent of sincerity so seldom lacking in Lope de Vega's lines animates in his best Moorish ballads the elaborate patterns of late Petrarchan style.[42]

The gem of the Gazul cycle and actually of all Moorish ballads is "Sale la estrella de Venus / al tiempo que el sol se pone" (I, 300–302, chap. 17). The closing lines of the poem tell of the vengeance of the slighted lover, but this act of violence is handled rather as a flourish sealing his malediction of the unfaithful beloved, which expands in a series of symmetrical antitheses, vibrant with anger and repressed tenderness. Another poem of the cycle, "Adornado de preseas / de la bella Lindaraja" (I, 294–96, chap. 17), uses effectively the description of arms and heraldry to convey a mood of youthful exuberance. In this ballad, allusions to the prestige of the Abencerrajes serve to underscore how precious Lindaraxa is to Gazul. His adoption of the emblems of her clan likewise becomes a fitting symbol of his surrender to her love. Still, "Por la plaça de San Lúcar / galán passeando viene" (I, 292–94, chap. 17) presents an animated picture of the lady's anger when the gallant Moor departs for a tournament, and she offers a feminine counterpart to the scornful speech by Gazul in "Sale la estrella de Venus." The two Lindaraja ballads sum up the small cycle, which places emotional conflict in an ornamental chivalric atmosphere transcending immediate and transitory circumstances.

On the other hand Moorish and pastoral styles blend in "De

honra y tropheos lleno, / más que el gran Marte lo ha sido"
(I, 297, chap. 17), a ballad reminiscent of a love scene of
El Abencerraje in its fusion of mythological evocation, the locus
amoenus tradition, and an understated chivalric setting. Much
less skillfully composed is "No de tal braveza lleno / Rodamonte
el Africano" (I, 303–5, chap. 17), a predominantly narrative
poem similar in subject matter to "Sale la estrella de Venus."

Topics of chivalry recede into the background in the four
Zaide ballads included by Pérez de Hita, except for the virtues
listed to the credit of the protagonist in Zaida's mixed recrimi-
nation and praise, "Mira, Zayde, que te aviso / que no passes
por mi calle" (I, 49, chap. 6).. The tension between the anger
expressed and the love implicitly admitted lies under the apparent simplicity of this spirited dismissal, which soon became
popular enough for a humorous ballad to be composed on the
sad fate of the Moor, who is continuously banished from the
presence of the millions singing Zaida's rebuttal. Parallelisms are
skillfully used in the reply "Di, Zayda, de qué me avisas / quieres
que [muera][43] y que calle" (I, 51, chap. 6). A larger anecdotal
content in keeping with the Elena Osorio episode is developed
in "Por la calle de su dama / passeándose anda Zayde" (I, 42,
chap. 6)–a ballad that has survived in oral tradition, along
with "Mira, Zaide, que te aviso,"[44]—and it likewise provides the
background for the markedly lyrical lament "Bella Zayda de
mis ojos / y del alma bella Zayda" (I, 44–45, chap. 6).

It may be risky to assert the Lopean paternity of all these
poems, but one may reasonably assume that, if not by him,
they were written in imitation of his style by poets aware of the
interrelationship between life and literature that shaped the
Zaide-Zaida theme, as well as the Gazul cycle.[45] However, as
these ballads spread to areas socially and geographically distant
from the poetical circles of the court, the credibility of their
narrative content must have increased. The sentimental stories
of the knights and ladies of Nasrid Granada, supposedly preserved in these poems, became an important element of a popular view of Spain's Moorish past, which, due to the success of
Pérez de Hita's work, would still be considered valid in the
Romantic period.[46]

CHAPTER 7

The Originality of Civil Wars, I

I The Form of Pérez de Hita's Fiction

COMMENTING upon the evolution of plot in narrative literature, Scholes and Kellogg have observed that "traditional romantic narratives of the Renaissance, from *Orlando Furioso* at the beginning to the *Grand Cyrus* at the end, tend to combine the heroic and erotic materials in a more equal balance than either Greek romance, which emphasizes the erotic, or ancient literary epic, which emphasizes the heroic."[1] This characterization fits perfectly *Civil Wars of Granada* [Part One], which was indebted to Ariosto and would inspire the author of *Le Grand Cyrus* to write *Almahide, ou l'Esclave reine*.[2] Pérez de Hita may indeed have been the first writer to effect successfully the transfer of this type of narrative mode from verse to prose, or rather to the peculiar texture of prose inlaid with narrative verse, which he considered to be essential to his art.[3]

Archetypal characterization, as well as a fictional plot rooted in chivalric literature, and the pervasive setting of a besieged city-state, link Pérez de Hita's fiction to the form of the romance, rather than to the novel.[4] At the same time, historical and fictional narrative are combined by him in a singular manner. Contrary to other authors of his time who fictionalized historical events, the author of *Civil Wars* concerned himself with a relatively recent historical occurrence—the downfall of the Moorish kingdom of Granada—which had shaped the society of southeastern Spain where he lived. At certain moments the reader of Pérez de Hita's time is made aware of the fact that few generations separate him from the characters and their actions in the book. The manner in which the author discusses his actual or invented sources lends a degree of credibility to the image of a Moorish society entirely inspired by the ideals

110

of European chivalry, which was an artistic conception con-
scientiously elaborated by him, taking as point of departure
the pseudohistorical background of Moorish ballads.

Pérez de Hita shared with many of his contemporaries the
notion that narrative which did not concern itself with events
having actually occurred was of an inferior literary quality.[5]
Therefore, like other writers of his time, he refers to a spurious
source in order to validate the contents of a book encompassing
the full cycle of a nation's birth, plenitude, and downfall. Unlike Luna, who rarely departs from the point of view of summary
narrative[6] and this only when dealing with royal figures, the
author of *Civil Wars, I* concentrates on the lives of private
people. The unifying point of view in his book is that of the
"histor"—to use Scholes and Kellogg terminology—who com-
pares sources and follows the most reliable ones. Parenthetical
remarks by the narrator, of the type found in epic poetry and
books of chivalry, are combined with comments on the vehicle
by which he has gained information on each episode, whether
it is oral tradition, a poetic text, a well-known history book,
or the mysterious manuscript which is the alleged main source.

The narrator in *Civil Wars, I* steps forward occasionally, as
in the opening page when he confirms with his own travel-
memories a detail concerning the gold and silver carried by the
rivers of Granada (*Guerras civiles*, I, 1, chap. 1). A more deliberate intrusion takes place when the author reports, with expressions of gratitude, that he had been given by the count of
Bailén, Don Rodrigo Ponce de Léon, the translation of the
alleged Arabic text (I, 291, chap. 17). Pretending to feel a
bibliophile's concern about the former whereabouts of his
material, Pérez de Hita tells about a Moorish historian who
migrated to Africa and his grandson Argutaafa. The latter is
reputed to have presented the original to a Jewish holy man,
who in turn gave it to the count of Bailén, after producing a
Hebrew translation. Don Rodrigo, whose ancestors had taken
part in the conquest of Granada, asked the rabbi to write also
a Spanish version. It is this text in Spanish that the author of
Civil Wars claims to have received from the count. Since this
nobleman ruled over Moriscos[7] and was a direct descendant of
Don Manuel Ponce de León,[8] a historical figure who plays a

fictional role in the book, the anecdote provides a significant link between the novelistic world created by the author and the societal realities he shares with his readers.

Such blurrings of limits are frequent in manneristic art and tend to create some form of ambiguity. In this case the main effect is to authenticate as history the subject matter of the book, by highlighting the finding of the spurious source. And yet Pérez de Hita, who stands on ground thus far unshattered by Cervantine irony, forecasts in some way the author's search for the continuation of the story in *Don Quijote* and the discovery, though in different circumstances, of an Arabic manuscript containing it.

When he handles historical subject matter, Pérez de Hita may deliberately create confusion by alternating references to the spurious *moro coronista* with similar mentions of a legitimate *cristiano coronista,* who is in other instances clearly identified as Hernando del Pulgar. Moreover, it is not clear whether the author claims to have used one, two, or more Arabic chronicles. To consider every reference to material that has not been identified as a fabrication may be a mistake comparable to a straight acceptance of the book's alleged historicity. One can, however, ascertain that part of Pérez de Hita's scheme was to blend fictional episodes within a historical content, avoiding a clear distinction between both elements. When dealing with history as in the opening and closing sections of the book, an attitude of fastidious erudition may be adopted; lists of lineages and towns are inserted and facts are reported in the detached and unemotional style of summary narrative, even when a situation with potential pathos is portrayed. As the editor of *Civil Wars* remarked, the author failed to take advantage of the legend of the Moor's sigh. Likewise, the most famous duel in the Vega—in which the arrogant Moorish champion Tarfe, who insults the devotion to the cult of Mary, confronts the newly dubbed knight Garcilaso—is not fictionalized but simply accounted for by the insertion of "Cercada está Santa Fe," plus a perfunctory remark (I, 280–83, chap. 17). This conforms to the treatment accorded to most old ballads, whose subject matter becomes integrated in the prose narrative before or after the poetic text is inserted, usually accompanied by a brief comment, noting its antiquity, the effect it made on the public, the merit of the poem itself, or perhaps the tune to which it was sung.

Within the historical frame, fictional action is organized according to two distinct structural principles. The first, operating well beyond the center of the book, offers a pattern of interlaced subplots, unfolding mainly as a sequence of scenes of courtship, raids, duels, skirmishes, and equestrian games. The latter are structurally important, for they bring together the various gallant stories and initiate the theme that prevails in the subsequent section. Conspiracy, calumny, the slaughter of the Abencerrajes, the murder by the king of his sister and nephews—these are the steps of a scale of horrors coordinated around the theme of the accused queen and leading to the judicial tournament that restores, though now with tragic overtones, the chivalric atmosphere of Granada, before the final historical section is reached.

Pérez de Hita is at his best in the imaginative portrayal of life at the Moorish court. It is here that the myth of the gallant Moor takes shape, though much of the impulse was latent in *El Abencerraje* and in diverse ballads, and a fine shading of stylized chivalric virtues had been achieved in those works. The art of the new ballad stimulated the creative talent of the author of *Civil Wars, I* to recast, with the immediacy of a scene unfolding step by step, the themes of the interpolated poems. These he felt free to cut, enlarge, or change[9] for the benefit of a subplot, which he obtained by selecting and combining in a coherent sequence of events situations depicted in the ballads. When the subject is not related to history and several poems are only held together by the name of the protagonist or a loose thematic thread, the attempt to reconcile conflicting bits of narrative and to treat contemporary poems as scattered biographical records of persons having lived a hundred years ago, is also a clever way of authenticating the elements of the narrative. Readers aware that no less than Lope de Vega was behind the impetuous Gazul, both as composer and protagonist, must have relished then, as they do now,[10] the remark that the author of "Sale la estrella de Venus" had misunderstood the story (I, 298, chap. 17). When this unnamed poet is courteously corrected (I, 302, chap. 17) the irony is pointed enough to suggest the possibility that, in typical manneristic fashion, a second meaning might be implied for the benefit of those who knew the truth about the actual motivation of the ballads.

As the subplots originating in the new ballads are developed, Pérez de Hita changes his point of view, and scenes now are shown rather than told. Contrary to what happens in the pastoral, all lyricism dissolves as the themes of the poems are transposed into the fictional mode. However, the moment of the action selected to come to the foreground unfolds with vivid plasticity and movement, creating the illusion of immediacy that marks the art of the novelist. Specifications of time and place and a good balance of narrative, description, and some dialogue are requisites of the emerging genre of the modern novel, with which Pérez de Hita intuitively complies in his most fortunate pages. Occasionally, a conversation is recorded in the text and somehow a rhetorical monologue serves to express the mood of the moment. Emotion is, however, most frequently rendered through gestures and the symbolism of colors worn, which was at the period an accepted medium of self-expression and communication. Likewise, psychological traits are revealed only by action. Characterization is superficial and only slightly diversified, but none the less effective, in the sense that the reader's sympathy is engaged. Archetypal perfection is stressed in the rather solitary figure of the Christian champion, the Maestre de Calatrava, but the gallant and invariably enamored knights of Granada—uncomplicated, direct, well-bred though impulsive—appeal as human beings, rather than as mythical heroes, to the emotions of the reader.

The best-defined character in *Civil Wars, I* is Muza, whose origin is to be found in a fierce legendary challenger of the same name; he is killed by Don Manuel Ponce de León in a late frontier ballad that Pérez de Hita does not quote and becomes a brother of the Rey Chico in a glosa of the ballad published in 1576.[11] This character is developed with distinctly different traits by Pérez de Hita, who occasionally shows him in moments of frustration or defeat, allowing his moral courage to stand out. Muza acts among the Moors as a peacemaker and as the supporter of the persecuted queen, and he shares with the Abencerrajes the credit for initiating the conciliation with the Christians, leading to the conversion of most Moorish knights. This character is endowed by Pérez de Hita with a feeling for comradeship, an easygoing attitude devoid of pride but reflecting the assurance of a man worshipped by the people, and an unsophisticated and direct manner of speech with a touch of humor. All of this lends a certain degree of verisimilitude and warmth to a literary figure who is of lesser ethical stature, but also less remote, than Amadís or even Abindarráez.

The place of the protagonist is not occupied in *Civil Wars, I* by any individual person, but rather, if at all, by the Abencerraje clan, with the Zegrís acting also collectively as antagonists. Their inherited enmity may be interpreted as representing the divisions within the larger community of the people of Granada. Though seen in a highly stylized image, this is the real subject with which the author is concerned. As to the Castilian conquerors, they loom in the background and will pick up the broken pieces of a nation torn apart, but the author does not make of the war a major source of fictional conflict.

Appropriate to the plural protagonist scheme is the frequent use of outdoor settings. Though some festive scenes take place in a hall of the Moorish palace, it is the broad spaces of the Plaza de Vivarrambla or the Vega which become a sizable element of Pérez de Hita's fiction. Never described in detail, the landscape is effectively evoked by geographical references and mention of famous buildings. Old and new ballads had not only used this technique before but also prepared the public to respond to such evocative traits. A sudden change of focus, not infrequent in the ballads, may introduce unexpectedly before the reader's consciousness one or more distant spectators of a fight or a competition; transitions of this kind are also put to good use in *Civil Wars, I* and impart to certain scenes a more interesting perspective. In other instances the reader's interest is enhanced by introducing a group of witnesses projecting, from within the fictional space itself, some emotional response to the action.

Deeds of arms and displays of prowess in the Vega predominate over accounts of more serious battles, but they are less important than the spirited equestrian games that Pérez de Hita portrayed with real skill and gusto, combining verisimilitude in detail with imaginatively planned total effects. He is indebted to the *relaciones de fiestas* of his time for a technique of description that emphasizes color and detail as articles worn or carried by the cavaliers are enumerated.[12] From contemporary ballads he learned to make meaningful such description of outward appearance as an expression of sentiment or of mood. Both *fiesta* related genres lent him a well-developed reporting technique that captures auditory effects, as well as visual images, and can render the mass movements of the quadrille in the juego de cañas[13] or the precise motions of man and beast in the most tense moments of the bullfight. And his own instinct for generating suspense led him to relate the occurrences of the fight to the fictional plot. The reader who knows that the Zegrís carry concealed arms, follows with vivid interest and with some apprehension the equestrian exercises in which they compete with the Abencerrajes, who somehow win the heart of all those who watch. Descriptive details of the horsemen's arms and attire, which could be tedious, are then absorbed without effort as are stage directions for an unfolding drama.

An elaborate juego de sortija is closely tied to the courtship subplots and the petty rivalries between the proud ladies of Granada, since each of the young knights carries a life-size effigy of his beloved, which will pass, if he loses, into the hands of the victor and be placed below the portrait of the latter's ladylove. In another episode built around a topos common to books of chivalry, the outcome of the judicial duel *à outrance* will decide the fate of the Moorish queen, and the reader, who is aware of the identity of her champions, will sense in their victory the imminence of the end of Moorish Granada.

The type of equestrian festival portrayed by Pérez de Hita as an expression of the Nasrid state's terminal splendor was a product of his artistic imagination, obtained by heightening the luxury of the Spanish fiestas of his time and stressing the exotic touch imparted to them by the use of the Moorish array, which was considered the most proper for the Moorish-originated juego de cañas, or the bullfight. At the same time, members of each quadrille wore identical *libreas* ("liveries"), as was the custom in other European countries, and consequently this was also the outfit displayed by the gallant Moors of *Civil Wars, I*. The participants are reported, likewise, to use versified mottoes and allegorical emblems, frequently with references to pagan deities, as had become customary in the great festivals of the Renaissance. Moreover, the fictional Granadine cavaliers use for the *entrée* to the juego de sortija either triumphal cars, adorned with mythological motifs, or larger floats representing the castle, the vessel, or the garden, which were important elements of late medieval and Renaissance pageantry. The number of cars and their mechanical devices, like the cloud which opens and closes carrying one or more persons, correspond approximately to the features of a solemn procession in a medium-sized town.[14]

The ladies' life-size portraits paraded in the triumphal cars are praised for their accurate details, and evidently they have been imagined by the author with wooden polychrome sculpture in mind, of the type that flourished in southern Spain during his lifetime. Both the effigies of Moorish beauties and their fair originals are clad in magnificent *marlotas*,[15] a type of embroidered gown originated in Al-Andalus that had become fashionable in the Peninsula. As is the case with all other garments, except libreas, mentioned in *Civil Wars, I*, similar or even more profusely ornamented specimens are often mentioned in inventories of the possessions of wealthy Moriscos, taken after the 1568 rebellion; and indeed the two-color scheme of this style characterizes the actual articles of Moorish festive attire, as much as its literary reflection.[16]

One trait of the fiestas spectacle as described by Pérez de Hita that does not conform to the practice in Spain at his time, is the ladies' Moorish attire, which exceeds in luxury that of the cavaliers. However, because the emphasis of his description is placed upon details, such as jewelry, elaborate headwear and, above all, the rich texture and coloring of material and the patterned contrasts obtained by slashing a lined garment, the reader visualizes an image of radiant but strictly controlled elegance. This has a marked affinity with the concepts of style manifest, for instance, in the portraits of Spanish princesses by Antonio Moro or Antonio Sánchez Coello. Like those sixteenth-century painters, Ginés is moved by the beauty of objects.

In his descriptive passages he uses only simple phrasing and avoids expressions that do not convey a meaningful trait. Usually the author begins by giving a simple image in two colors, and then he goes on to enumerate with direct, almost inventory-like language, garments and jewels, noting the material used and pointing out with warm approval certain details of workmanship. When Pérez de Hita depicts in this manner pageantry or array, it is possible to measure this artist-craftsman's feelings for the most precious product of the artisanry of his native region and to understand that the effect he sought in his descriptive passages was akin to the principles of mudéjar style.

Moreno Báez has shown that the mannerism of the period pervades Pérez de Hita's work.[17] Some characteristic traits are the detailed descriptive technique, the use of alien texts as interpolations, the author's intrusion into his fiction, and the tendency to mystify the reader by presenting an original text as a translation. In the second half of the book, a tendency toward thematic unification reverses the principle of episodic composition, as a new source of suspense is built around the character of Boabdil's wife. The author plays with reflected images when a reported love encounter that never took place claims some hold on reality from its location in the Generalife. The sketched scene of the lover wandering slowly through the famous garden and gathering roses rings a note of subdued eroticism and serves as a lyric counterpoint to the agitation motivated by the calumny, of which the scene is part. When the lighthearted Moorish king has acquired the sinister characterization suited to the role he is to play, he becomes the protagonist of a gruesome incident in the macabre taste of late Renaissance plays influenced by Senecan tragedy.[18] The contrast in mood with respect to the episodes inspired by ballads has gone full circle.

The diversity of themes and principles of composition in *Civil Wars, I* is paralleled by considerable variations in style. Predominant is a lively and apparently careless speech, with colloquially conversational overtones, which is not above word repetition and occasionally faulty syntax. In this manner, the narrator's presence makes itself felt, and his judgments and feelings concerning each situation sift through, without interfering with the stream of fictional action. Not infrequently, this style gives way to the emphatic oratorial prose of political speeches, to the sentimentality of lachrymose monologues, or to the rhetoric of epistolary literature. Certain passages adopt a colorless informative style, whereas in others contrived imagery and involved sentence structure suggest that they were written in imitation of the learned prose of the period. Such departures from the author's customary diction detract from, rather than add to, the reader's pleasure. Nevertheless, when Pérez de Hita sacrifices consistency of style to adopt the tone he considers more adequate to a given situation, he is pointing toward the independent evolution of the novel as a genre.

II   *The Underlying Concern*

Pérez de Hita's book has been incorrectly read as a novel of historical interest offering a relatively accurate portrayal of life in the Nasrid state. Nowadays it is considered a purely literary endeavor. This position probably needs also to be qualified by some consideration of the possibility that *Civil Wars, I* reflects the author's views on the predicament of a large segment of the mixed society in which he lived.[19]

We know that Ginés grew up and practiced his trade in a region with a long tradition of coexistence between the mudéjar community and the Old Christians, including those belonging to the peasant and artisan class. He also must have come early in contact with people of different social standings who were children or grandchildren of Moors of Granada. Some among them adhered secretly to the Islamic religion and nourished unrealistic hopes of reestablishing a Moslem state in southern Spain; others would have erased, if given a chance to do so, all traces of their origin; but there were also those who took pride in their noble Moorish ancestry, while they professed sincerely the Christian faith and shared the concepts and ideas prevalent among other Spaniards of their time. The frustration of the Morisco gentry at finding themselves excluded from almost every type of legitimate ambition was well understood by some political writers of the period, and in the next century the destiny of individuals cut off, because of their parentage, from a society with whose beliefs and values they identified

was given perceptive literary expression in fictional works by
Cervantes, Vicente Espinel, and Lope de Vega.[20]

Civil Wars, I is concerned with the last generation born in
independent Moorish Granada. The book was written in a
region adjacent to the former Nasrid kingdom in the years when
total expulsion of the Moriscos was being considered. This
was the time when a wave of false documentation attempted
to present the Arabs of Granada as the earliest Christians of
Spain and to narrow at the same time the gap between Christian and Moslem theology. Similarly, the interpreter Miguel
de Luna sought, with his pretended translation of an Arabic
history of the conquest of Spain, to enhance the prestige of
the Moors, giving thus greater strength to the argument that
their descendants had all the rights to be considered Spaniards.

Pérez de Hita did not intend to deceive his readers in his
playful handling of facts and fiction, but he follows a method
similar to that of Luna. Without dealing openly with the situation of the Moriscos, he implicitly exposes the incongruence of
denying the privileges of noble birth to the descendants of his
idealized characters. The built-in courtesy code of the literary
type to which he gave the finishing touches was so meaningful
from a European point of view, that the stereotype Granadine
Moor, when exported, would be seen as the most perfect example
of that refinement of sensibility and manners which linked the
brave knights of late chivalric romance to the courtier of
précieux society.

In the view he holds of the knighthood that had flourished on
both sides of the frontier of Granada, Pérez de Hita remains
within the tradition of *El Abencerraje*. In his work and in the
short novel alike, the stress is placed on the mutual respect
and goodwill arising among adversaries. Castilians appear as
more deeply concerned with the service of their king and
their faith, while the Moors fight rather with a sense of sportsmanship and are chiefly moved by the hopes, joys, or disappoint-
ments of romance. Though vehement, jealous, and impulsive,
the young Moors of both sexes in *Civil Wars, I* behave as models
of decorum, and if the knight is the epigone of medieval chivalry, the ladies, with their witticisms and coqueterie remind

one of the type that will be developed subsequently in *comedias* of urban setting.

Pérez de Hita, who knew how much resentment had been generated over the prohibition against dress in the Moorish fashion, makes a point in favor of Moorish costume, but not of the Koran-prescribed habit that women cover their faces. The *almalafa*, a loose cloak used for that purpose, is the only article of clothing well represented in the inventories of the possessions of wealthy Moriscos which is not part of the vocabulary of *Civil Wars, I*. In the book the fair ladies of Granada do not cover their faces, except in a case when Spanish customs would also condone their doing so.[21] And if all this reflects the conformity with contemporary habits or situations depicted in the new ballads, the latter do not emphasize in a comparable degree the goodwill in Moorish-Christian relations. Pérez de Hita follows his own path when he makes of the Abencerrajes models of charity and counts among their merits that they keep the Christian leaders informed of what goes on in Moorish Granada. As to the disappointment over his religion of a Moslem whose fortune has taken an adverse turn, it does appear in the romancero and may be traced to the Carolingian ballads of King Marsín, but it is rarely treated, as in *Civil Wars, I*, as a positive state of mind that leads to the acceptance of the Christian faith.

In connection with the theme of conversion, it should be emphasized that *El Abencerraje* and *Civil Wars, I* idealize in a similar way the knights of Granada. Both works highlight the loyal foe attitude, vis-à-vis the Christians, but whereas the anonymous novelette makes of the mutual respect of men professing different faiths the cornerstone of its moral message, this principle is overshadowed in the longer book by other implications. The new approach may be related to the desire that the assimilation of Moorish gentry by Christian society be effected.

In his generally attractive picture of Moorish Granada, Pérez de Hita includes from the outset signs of unbalance and corruption, while his brief allusions to the Castilian camp make it appear as a symbol of stability. Throughout the fictional plot, the Rey Chico reveals himself gradually as a weak character with a strain of sadism; the clan of the Zegrís is given an increasingly adverse characterization; stress is placed on the feuds that divide the ruling class and indeed the royal family. If the murder of the Abencerrajes is laid at the door of the last king of Granada, who was in fact their friend, it must be because the sovereign who allowed the state to collapse ought to bear the burden of guilt. After more than thirty members of the unjustly persecuted family die proclaiming that they are Christians at heart, the survivors change sides, becoming, as the author states, Christian Abencerrajes. These two words form a curious syntagm, which not only appears in the prose text, but is likewise introduced in the ballad "Mensageros le han entrado / al Rey Chico de Granada" (*Guerras civiles,* I, 277–78, chap. 17). Other clans follow suit, as the Moorish state remains torn by a self-destructive frenzy of which the episode of the accusation and imprisonment of the innocent queen is a fitting symbol.

The rulers of Granada deserve their doom, but the gentry, with the exception of the king's advisers—now the Zegrís—is free of guilt. And first individually, then by clans, they come to the realization that the moral values they hold dear are better represented by their opponents. This consideration prompts them to embrace the faith of the Christians. In consequence, they beg to join the Castilian ranks and are graciously made welcome. Since Pérez de Hita emphasized army battles much less than individual encounters or other forms of chivalric adventure, the reader gets the feeling that the conquest of Granada was not so much the outcome of a long struggle as the result of the voluntary integration of two chivalric societies under the crown of Castile.

The conversions are considered as bringing credit to both sides. It is obvious, therefore, that they make thoroughly inconsistent, by implication, the social stigma attached to the descendants of the converts. To underscore the willingness of conversions, Pérez de Hita pours out details about the specific positions granted to Granadine leaders in the court of the Catholic Sovereigns (I, 289–90, chap. 17). Queen Isabella welcomes as ladies of honor young Moorish women of noble birth; Muza and his beloved Zelima will be married by the first archbishop of Granada—a reminder of the tolerance prevailing immediately after the conquest may be read in the simple allusion to Fray Hernando de Talavera. The names of fictional Moors, like Sarracino and Abenámar, are linked to those of well-known leaders of the Castilian army, whose banners they will carry. Some of the Christian names adopted by converts are given, specifying for instance that a certain alcaide was granted, after the conquest, the right to wear arms and have access to high positions.

The terms *hidalgo* and *ahidalgado* are used time and again in combination with a Moorish name, which implies a repudiation of the principle that a lineage free from Jewish or Arabic blood is a prerequisite for being accepted as an hidalgo. Even more deliberate appears to be the expression *el nuevo cristiano don Juan* (I, 123, chap. 11)—comparable to *cristianos Abencerrajes*—which is applied to Albayaldos at the hour of his conversion and death, since the phrase combines in reverse order the name and adjective commonly designating the descendants of Moors and Jews, and carries emotional connotations that are totally antithetical to the unfavorable overtones of such a designation.[22]

Pérez de Hita used all the means at his command to make his point that the conquest of Granada was concluded in a manner which allowed hope for a harmonious future. An appeal for the social rehabilitation of the descendants of the Moors is discernible in the turn he gives to historical events, as well as in the fictional action of *Civil Wars, I*. An exhortation to accept sincerely the Christian religion is also implicitly addressed to the crypto-Moslems. In a conciliatory spirit, Pérez de Hita made a plea for the integrity of a mixed culture that was his own, and his intense concern may well have imparted to his portrayal of Moorish Granada the mythical quality that was an inspiration for many generations of writers and reading public.

CHAPTER 8

The Civil Wars of Granada, II

IT was Pérez de Hita's wish to include under a common title his fictional *Historia de los vandos de los Zegríes y Abencerrajes* and the book on the 1568 revolt of the Moriscos in the Alpujarras, based chiefly on his memories as a soldier who participated in the two-year war that finally subdued the rebels. By grouping together two works so very different in content and style, Ginés gave us an indication that in his mind they deal with the same entity: the people of Granada. Moreover, in both cases internal strife is a basic theme and defeat an inevitable outcome. This not withstanding the first book focused on a closed era through the prism of romance, whereas the history of the rebellion was written with a strong commitment to the reporter's point of view.

The author must have felt encouraged by the success in 1595, of the *Historia de los vandos—Civil Wars, I—*to write the *Segunda parte de las guerras civiles de Granada,*[1] which he concluded in November of 1597, as specified in the last chapter. An edition was planned in 1610, but it is almost certain that the book was not printed until 1619.[2]

I *Synopsis*

The work opens with a very brief account of the frustrations experienced by the descendants of the Moors of Granada from the time of the conquest until 1566, when Philip II issued a particularly severe decree intended to put an end to the secret practice of the Moslem religion and mores. It is with the angered reaction to this promulgation that the author begins his detailed narrative, relying largely in this first part on word-of-mouth reports obtained mostly among the Moriscos. Attention is given to the early organization of a conspiracy aiming at

124

the restoration in Granada of an independent Islamic state. One of the events reported is the ceremony of crowning as king a young hidalgo, who could claim to be of the lineage of the caliphs of Cordoba and who took on the royal name of Aben Humeya. The author tells about the unsuccessful attempt by the conspirators to gain control of Granada in December of 1568, and surveys the spread of the revolt. The efforts to pacify the Moriscos made by the Marqués de Mondéjar yielded some results, according to Pérez de Hita, but were finally thwarted because of the crimes committed by his troops, whom he was not able to control. A pause in the historical narrative is made to present the discouragement experienced by Aben Humeya before the arrival of a Turkish contingent, which helped him to establish a rebel state in the mountainous region of the Alpujarras.

With the first interventions of the Marqués de los Vélez, Don Luis Fajardo, whose domain was adjacent to Lorca, the narrative becomes more precise, at the same time that literary embellishments, such as long challenges and speeches, are introduced. The appearance and the psychological traits of the Marqués are impressively sketched. We hear of some Moriscos who are influential in small towns and try to keep their townspeople loyal to the king, confronting with courage the rebels, whom, however, they will eventually join. The process of military operations is followed, touching eventually on political conflict among the leaders of both sides and dwelling more extensively on episodes which interested the author, because of his direct involvement in the action, his familiarity with the area where the event took place, or simply some circumstance that appealed to his sense of drama. Showing the same preferences as the old ballads for highlighting adverse rather than successful ventures, Pérez de Hita reports in detail the death of Captain Álvaro de Flores and his men, after they had been led into an ambush in Aben Humeya's native town of Válor, as well as the defeat of the black Moorish leader Farax and the daring escape he made, through enemy fire and a forest blaze, to the rugged peaks of the sierra.

An offensive of Aben Humeya against the Marqués de los Vélez fails because of the confessions of a spy and another prisoner. In one instance the previous scene of surrender is marked by the dignity that had been awarded to similar situations in literary treatment of Moorish-Christian strife, and the story that the Morisco later tells the Marqués de los Vélez shows the suffering of lovers separated by the vicissitudes of war.

Soon thereafter the focus is again on the Morisco king, who ransacks several towns of the Marqués. Awaiting reinforcements to arrive from Africa or for the revolt to spread, he announces a series of festivities to be held at Purchena, his temporary capital. The competitions, consisting of hand-to-hand fights, races, and contests of strength, are held with as much pomp and luxury as circumstances will allow, and they highlight the rivalry and antagonism between Turks and Moriscos. The contests are followed by dances and songs, whose themes relate to the situation of the rebels. Subsequently the story of Aben Humeya will be somewhat extensively treated, though not as a separate narrative unit. Acting with increasing despotism, the king of the Alpujarras will keep by force a woman, whose lover then plots and resorts to fraud to cause his death. The Morisco king is murdered by his Turkish allies, who have been led to believe that he sought to destroy them. His rival Aben Abó is sworn in as king.

In the meantime the forces of the Marqués de los Vélez have been joined by other contingents under the command of renowned generals, including the duke of Sessa. Don Juan de Austria, the king's brother who will eventually become the victor at the battle of Lepanto, is placed at the head of the army. The struggle has now the magnitude of a civil war. Pérez de Hita reports at length on ambush, siege, looting, painful marches and fierce battles for the possession of small towns. Occasionally his enthusiasm is aroused as he records a heroic deed, but the prevalent emotion is that of horror at the atrocities he witnessed and compassion for the victims of both sides.

Ginés was not present at the long siege and seizure of Galera by Don Juan de Austria, and he announces that he will quote at length from the day-by-day chronicle written by an officer, the alférez Thomás Pérez de Evia.[3] This he does, but he also includes numerous details that were allegedly reported orally to him, mostly by Moriscos. He tells about Moorish women who fight fiercely, and men who kill their wives and children before seeking their own death in combat. The author's feelings on recounting those deeds fluctuate between amazement, admiration, and awe.

It is during the siege of Galera that Alvaro Tuzaní first appears. He is a Morisco of noble ancestry who has been brought up among Old Christians, and like so many of his kind, started by having contradictory feelings about the rebellion. But in the looting of Galera his beloved is stabbed by a greedy soldier and hence he will live only to seek revenge. Joining the king's army, he finds and kills the assassin, and in the process he spies and makes it possible for the Morisco population of the town to escape, carrying their most valued possessions. Eventually he is exposed and brought before the Spanish command, but he exonerates himself by disclosing the full truth, and is accepted in the company of Don Lope de Figueroa.

Mortal feuds among the Morisco leaders and forebodings of defeat, added to the hardships of war, create a climate of fear and uncertainty in the villages of the Alpujarras, as well as a great desire for peace. El Habaquí, a sensible and mature Morisco captain, initiates negotiations to capitulate. This leads to his assassination by one of his people, but the rebels must finally surrender. The Moorish population of the former kingdom of Granada will be deported to other parts of Spain. With the vivid memory of their grief and a comment on the loss resulting from their departure the book is closed.

II *Historical Value*

The war to subdue the rebel Moriscos was the object of three contemporary works of history: the relatively brief *Guerra de Granada* by Diego Hurtado de Mendoza,[4] a masterpiece of Spanish historiography; the detailed and comprehensive *Historia del rebelión y castigo de los moriscos de Granada* (1600) by Luis del Mármol Carvajal, and Pérez de Hita's book. All three authors either experienced the conflict or had access to direct documentation pertaining to it, Mármol being the least critical of the manner in which the Moriscos were dealt with.[5] Don Diego's book, which circulated widely in manuscript form, was

known to Mármol, and probably also to Pérez de Hita, since
a copy of the *Guerra de Granada* includes certain interpolations,
coinciding with anecdotal material found only in Pérez de Hita,
in which the nutshell version of the story of El Tuzaní appears.
Manuel Gómez Moreno considered that the author of *Segunda
parte de las guerras civiles de Granada* is a likely author of the
additions to Hurtado de Mendoza's text and that they represent an early stage in the fictional treatment of certain episodes
that characterizes his account of the war.[6] Pérez de Hita was
also familiar with the historical poem *La Austriada*, by Juan
Rufo, who dealt with the life of Don Juan de Austria and treated
extensively the Alpujarras revolt, following mainly Don Diego.
The author had served in that war, like Ginés, with whom he
shared a tendency to treat facts as literary material; occasionally
the latter either used data from the poem, mentioning his source,
or contradicted specifically Rufo's views.[7]

With respect to accuracy Pérez de Hita is the least reliable
of the three chroniclers of the Moriscos' rebellion. He seldom
recorded dates and frequently gave disproportionate space to
minor incidents, blurring the line between factual reporting and
fictional embellishment. However, his book is a valuable source
for the historian, inasmuch as certain details are known only
through him.[8] But the greatest value of his testimony lies in the
fact that he expressed, as Caro Baroja has pointed out, the
views of the common man.[9] His talent for external characterization was put to good use in his elaborate portrait of the stately
Marqués de los Vélez (*Guerras civiles*, II, 42–45, chap. 4), and
in the swift sketches of several Morisco leaders. In most cases,
the author gives us, with the profile of the man, the feelings
that the people had for him. An attitude shared by many is also
represented in Pérez de Hita's condemnation of crimes committed by both sides during the Alpujarras revolt and of retalia-
tory measures. Like Hurtado de Mendoza, he views the conflict as a civil war, but unlike him, Ginés underplays differences
arising among the Spanish leadership, although he stresses the
divisiveness of the Moriscos.[10] And if Don Diego was incom-
parably better equipped to analyze the causes of the upheaval
and to pass judgment on leaders and policies, Ginés comple-
ments significantly his testimony, thanks to his interest in people

and in what people think. The psychological climate of the war may be, to a large extent, inferred from his book, and it is not surprising that this should be a frequently quoted source in Caro Baroja's sociological analysis of Morisco society in the former kingdom of Granada.

Among Pérez de Hita's Moriscos it is the common people who act with unwavering solidarity, and some of their women carry their loyalty to extremes that make them either sublime or inhumanly cruel. In contrast, the reader becomes aware of the social dichotomy of well-to-do Moriscos, who were not very different from Spanish hidalgos elsewhere, and yet felt compelled, either by choice or the force of circumstances, to stand at the head of a revolt that many of them had not willed. The small gallery of characters appearing in the *Segunda parte de las guerras civiles* gives testimony about the existence of an almost forgotten segment of the population of Spain in the sixteenth century.

Since personal memories were the main source of his book, Pérez de Hita concentrated on developments in which he had participated, and he paid more attention to the Marqués de los Vélez than to any other general. When he dealt with events in which the people of Murcia, Lorca, and the neighboring towns took part Ginés drew largely from his own poem on the local history of Lorca.[11]

The relación by Pérez de Evia on the siege of Galera is used as a long interpolation, rather than simply as a source. Pérez de Hita's admiration for the thorough, objective, concise, and casually elegant manner in which the alférez reported events (*Guerras civiles*, II, 244, chap. 20) did not prevent him from introducing into the latter's narrative several digressions dealing with some striking incidents that had reached him by word of mouth.

It is difficult to know how much of the anecdotal material appearing only in *Segunda parte de las guerras civiles* was of a fictional nature and how much reflected stories reported to the author by the people from whom he sought information. In any case, those swift sketches reveal the guerrilla aspect of the struggle and shed light on the manner in which war was experienced by the population of the Alpujarras, providing with

respect to narrative mode an intermediate stage between the
chronicler's approach and the fictionalized portrayal of characters and situations.

III *Literary Elements*

Pérez de Hita did not forget that his main concern was to
write the history of the Alpujarras war, and he refrained in his
Segunda parte de las guerras civiles from long literary digressions, with the exception of the elaborate scene presenting the
festivals at Purchena. Nevertheless, his imagination and his gift
for capturing those essential traits that make a situation come
alive from the printed page are manifest throughout the book.
One can consider in this respect his already mentioned sketches
of historical figures, his use of a recurrent motif to bring out
a point he is trying to make, and above all his treatment of
three fictional plots, which do not develop independently but
rather are interlaced with the reporter's narrative, serving thus
to enhance the value of the book as a testimony.

Aben Humeya is not portrayed by Pérez de Hita with coherent psychological traits. However, the kaleidoscopic image
obtained by the reader from the various lights under which he
is presented conveys the complexities of his destiny. Bringing
to mind the peaceful days preceding the rebellion, the author
recalls that the stately young councilman of royal blood was
once pointed out to him during a ceremony in Granada (*Guerras
civiles*, II, 8, chap. I), and with the impression of his physical
appearance, the popularity that followed the first steps of this
youthful leader comes through. Soon thereafter, we see the
young hidalgo reacting with exaggerated sensitivity to a point
of honor and alienating himself completely from Spanish society
to join the rebels, who will crown him in a secret ceremony,
reviving Islamic protocol. The dual aspect of his personality
is expressed in the soliloquy scene,[12] staged in a landscape of
mountains overlooking the sea, which is perfectly suited to the
mood of foreboding and loneliness marking this moment of
despondency, soon to be reversed by another turn of the wheel
of fortune, as he enters his ephemeral period of power. Subsequently the name, but not the personality, of Don Fernando de

Válor will vanish. On the eve of combat the Morisco king will address his subjects as "lions of Spain," and in the last minutes of his life the memory of the affront that decided his fate creeps into his consciousness. He dies cursing the incident and proclaiming himself Christian (II, 219, chap. 17).

Presiding over the festivals at Purchena, Aben Humeya will be seen almost as the reflection of the Rey Chico, and, as was the case with the latter, his public image will subsequently suffer a deterioration not unwarranted in this instance by the facts. Following Juan Rufo's fictionalized account of events leading to the murder of the rebel leader,[13] Pérez de Hita emphasized his cruelty and self-indulgence, which justifiably provoke the hatred of one of his partisans. The jealous and wronged man is then transformed into the perfect villain of romance. The documents he forges will inevitably make the Turks seek Aben Humeya's death, an episode in which poetic justice is served, not only by the motivation leading to the well-known fact of the latter's assassination, but also by an aftermath which is not present in *La Austriada*. Pérez de Hita sees Aben Humeya's mistress in the character of the fatally attractive woman who leads men to their destruction; accordingly he introduces a minor character—the Turkish captain Hazén—who in order to win her, will in turn kill the murderer of the Morisco leader.

If the destiny of Aben Humeya is given a moralistic turn by Pérez de Hita, in the sense of guilt finding retribution, two other stories about individuals unnamed by history cast their Morisco protagonists as exemplary lovers, who eventually find understanding among the leadership of the Christian army. The first and most pleasant of such episodes is evidently conceived as a variation of the Abindarráez-Narváez theme. Pérez de Hita, however, does not mention *El Abencerraje*, and indeed the situation of the Morisco prisoner Albexarí, who is allowed to join his bride Almanzora, and thereafter becomes a loyal servant of the Marqués de los Vélez, arises among non-heroic characters and is told in a casual style, matching the surrounding harsh reality. In fact, the author takes the reader into his confidence, admitting that he has refrained from dwelling at length upon this attractive subject, because of the nature of the book, which is all about arms, fistfights, and battles.[14] Such a remark seems to aim also at giving the story a semblance of authenticity, and when the author tells later about the subsequent good fortune of the lovers, he places them squarely in the midst of the Morisco community resettled in La Mancha (II, 127, chap. 12). However, when Albexarí fights to resist capture and laments his bad fortune, he is reenacting in a transposed key the action and words of Abindarráez. With Mateo Alemán's Ozmín, he shares a willingness to join his beloved in enemy territory or in captivity, but any similarity with the *Guzmán* novelette must be coincidental, since this work appeared in 1599 after the completion, though not the publication, of *Segunda parte de las guerras civiles*. The unsophisticated Morisco couple of Pérez de Hita is indeed far removed from the stylized figures of the lovers in the two short Moorish novels—*El Abencerraje* and "Ozmín y Daraja"—but the similarity of their predicament lends to the downgraded descendants of the Nasrid kingdom's gentry some measure of prestige, borrowed from the idealized Moor of poetry and fiction.

In contrast to the amiable Albexarí, Alvaro Tuzaní appears as a heroic and tragic figure. A Morisco raised among Christians, he is an appealing representative of a mixed culture that was thwarted before taking root. His commitment is to no political entity, but to his own sense of right and dignity, and to the memory of his beloved. As with Ozmín but in contrast to Abindarráez and the Moorish knights of *Civil Wars, I*, Tuzaní has recourse to deceit in order to achieve his goal. Having succeeded in his revenge and in shielding the escape of the Moriscos of Galera, he is also able to assert his reputation as a man of honor against the double stigma of Morisco and of spy. This is all that can be salvaged by this forceful character, in whom a spark of the gallantry of the Moorish knight is still discernible, although he emerges from a realistic contemporary context. Likewise, the attitude taken by Don Lope de Figueroa is in line with Narváez's generous gesture in *El Abencerraje*, but such similarity only tends to heighten the tragic overtones of the new type of hero, whose burden of adverse circumstances may well symbolize the hopelessness of his people.

The plot of Alvaro's story originates in a scene of horror which is a leitmotiv of the book: the abandoned home or village where lies the body of a young woman, Christian or Moorish, of unblemished beauty. Ginés must have experienced the shock of finding similar sights in devastated villages and his memory still hurts when he writes, but the recurrence of the motif (*Guerras civiles* II, 19, 80, 215, 293, chaps. 2, 8, 17, 22) indicates its symbolic value in relation to the self-destructive nature of the conflict. The pathos of the scene permits one to link such passages to the aesthetics of mannerism, but in contrast with his treatment of the Rey Chico's fury, Pérez de Hita handles the motif with restraint, creating a tense poetic climate and using effectively the contrast between the surrounding horror and the delicate beauty of objects framing the face of the dead girl.[15]

The feasts held in Purchena are presented as an attempt to revive the chivalric festivals of Vivarrambla, which proves the conscious efforts on the part of Morisco leaders to identify their rebel state with the Nasrid nation. The author uses here again his characteristic technique of offering a colorful description of dress and ornaments, combined with simple, realistic reporting of the actual game or fight, and with comments bringing forth the emotion and suspense of spectators. Psychologically, the court of Aben Humeya has inherited the spirit of gallant Moorish Granada: the noble Moriscos use mottoes and devices, they are brilliantly attired, and wear the symbolic colors of love and courtship, exchanging occasionally pointed remarks or polite phrases, as they follow the ritual of parading and saluting. The same is true of the fair beauties, who are clad with a luxury comparable to that of Nasrid Granada, though with touches of "modern Moorish usage" (II, 157). But for all this picturesque and gallant setting, the games of Purchena become a symbol of nostalgia and frustration. The impossibility of bringing back the past is epitomized in the fact that all marching and fighting has to be done on foot, and the skilled sportsmen who had practiced bullfighting and juegos de cañas as members of the Andalusian gentry now must compete in plebeian fights and tests of strength, which some consider unworthy of human beings. Such notes of disappointment do not prevent the contests to go on as a colorful display of skill and physical resistance.

If the author, as was suggested by Menéndez y Pelayo,[16] recalled the games, including races and fights, described in the

Æneid, as well as the famous *prueba del tronco* ("test of the log") in *La Araucana* by Alonso de Ercilla, he deliberately stripped such epic themes of the great dignity they have in the classic and Renaissance poems. On the other hand, Pérez de Hita delights in picturing the zest, courtesy, and good spirit of the contenders, and with his keen novelistic flair, he uses the rivalry between Moriscos and .Turks to promote suspense and to create an atmosphere similar to that of his Nasrid equestrian games, so often disturbed by the strife of the Zegrís and the Abencerrajes.

As to the dances and songs of the Moriscos which follow the games they are not only mentioned, as in *Civil Wars, I,* but are actually described to some extent. Nostalgia and the will to win back the Alhambra is again a recurrent theme in several songs in Spanish traditional style, some of which were supposedly sung in Arabic. The somber mood is reestablished with the final endechas "¡Ay de Ohánez!" sung by a girl whom the war has deprived of all her kin, and who falls lifeless, after prophesying the tragic end of Aben Humeya and the Morisco people.[17]

IV *The Implicit Plea*

Scholars have given Pérez de Hita credit for reporting without bias the events of the Alpujarras war, in which he fought against the Moriscos.[18] In fact, his position implies more than just a historian's impartiality or a soldier's fairness to his foes. The conflict cut too deeply into Ginés's world to allow for single-minded identification with any one side. If he condemns unequivocally the revolt and its leaders, he places responsibility for the exasperation of the Moriscos on the policy that unnecessarily outlawed all their cherished customs and traditions. The rebels commit horrifying crimes, but the cruelty of soldiers in the king's army is the principal reason why Mondéjar's efforts at conciliation failed. Ginés cannot ignore the fact that where Moriscos ruled the Islamic religion was proclaimed and Christians martyred, and yet he explicitly states that this was a war of Christians against Christians (II, 10, chap. 1). In fact the episodes Pérez de Hita chose to expand exemplify in the protagonists a wavering religious allegiance and a high degree of assimilation to Spanish customs. El Tuzaní proclaims that his beloved, who was killed because she was a Morisca, never ceased to be a Christian (II, 336, chap. 24), and Aben Humeya is supposed to have rejected the Islamic religion before his death. This is also reported of El Habaquí, who negotiated the capitulation and was assassinated by a fanatical faction of his own people. He was to be buried with honor in his native town (II, 352, chap. 25). One might say that almost every imaginative digression in the book is controlled by a point of view not very different from that expressed years later by Fernández de Navarrete, when he suggested that Moriscos remained hostile because they had been rejected.[19]

On the other hand it is true that Pérez de Hita refers often to the rebels as a collective entity toward which his feelings fluctuate. He speaks with indignation and hatred of their crimes but considers the self-destruction of the Moorish population of Galera an example of love and heroism worthy of the Romans (II, 286–87, chap. 21). He sympathizes deeply with the defeated Moriscos who must face deportation when they crave peace and expect to return to their homes. The picture he offers of such people in their moments of joy or of despair is a fitting epilogue of his chronicle. He does not refrain from pointing out the great loss to the land and the king's interest that resulted from the expulsion of the Morisco population from the territory of the old kingdom of Granada.

Significantly, Ginés gives us then the date of the completion of the book: November, 1597. Almost thirty years had elapsed since the diaspora of 1570. Philip II would not make the decision to expel from Spain all descendants of the Moors, but this king's health was declining, and the project had powerful supporters. Those who opposed the expulsion must have felt the urgency to strengthen whatever awareness the people had of the Moriscos' worth. Pérez de Hita had implicitly expressed an attitude of sympathy in *Civil Wars, I.* The not very well matched sequel to that book was aimed, we may assume, at discrediting the projects of total expulsion. It is in this light that the attempt and failure to publish the book in 1610 must be viewed. It was only in 1619, shortly after the fall from power

of the minister who had presided over the years of the expulsion—the duke of Lerma—that the book appeared, dedicated by
one of its sponsors to a peer who had been a lonely defender
of the Murcian Morisco communities.[20]

During the seventeenth and eighteenth centuries the history
of the rebellion shared only slightly in the popularity of *Civil
Wars, I*,[21] although it inspired Calderón de la Barca to write
Amar después de la muerte o El Tuzaní de la Alpujarra,[22] a
powerful drama which in turn would promote a renewed interest in the rebel Moriscos during the Romantic period.[23] Pérez
de Hita's last book is appreciated today for its informative
value and its direct forceful style, but the nongeneric nature
of the work has restricted its public. Perhaps it should be read
as a document of persuasion as much as of information, or more
so, since the fictional elements that impair its historical consistency strengthen the testimonial message. Individual destinies
are allowed to embody the errors of the Moriscos as well as the
zest and courage they displayed and all the hope and suffering
they experienced during the three years of the Alpujarras war.
The colorful Plaza of Purchena and the looted house in Galera
epitomize the two directions in which the author engages the
reader's empathy for those Moriscos and mudéjares with whom
he shared much of his life.

CHAPTER 9

Conclusion:
The Scope of Pérez de Hita's Influence

I *The Golden Age*

PARADOXICALLY, the format of *Civil Wars, I* was not imitated in the seventeenth century, although editions attest to the success of the book. The brief list of Golden Age Moorish novels was to be completed in 1599, with Mateo Alemán's "Historia de los dos enamorados Ozmín y Daraja," included in the first part of *Guzmán de Alfarache*.[1] The action takes place at the time of the conquest of Baza (1489), and details of historical background indicate that the author documented his work carefully, probably using Pulgar's *Crónica de los Reyes Católicos*.

In length, as well as in its single plot structure and the exemplary character of the Moorish lovers whose happiness is disturbed by war and captivity, Alemán's novelette is closer to *El Abencerraje* than to Pérez de Hita's work. The latter's influence is revealed by a greater stress on the beauty and symbolism of attire, the choice of the arena rather than the frontier or battlefield as the setting for the exploits of the protagonist, and the eventual adoption of the Christian faith by the Moorish lovers, who are assimilated into Castilian society. A difference with both preceding Moorish novels is a pattern of composition, imitated from the Byzantine novel, consisting of a chain of obstacles, such as separation and imprisonment, which must be overcome by an idealized couple. Deceit is accepted as a means of defense, the sincerity of the lovers' conversion being much less apparent than in *Civil Wars, I*. Although the enamel-like quality of the interpolated novel contrasts in themes and style with the autobiography of the pícaro, it shares to some

137

extent the disillusioned outlook which inspired *Guzmán*. The conduct of Ozmín when he must resort to training his master in order to humiliate a most feared rival, instead of confronting him openly, may be seen as a symbol for the equivocal situations of hidalgos of convert parentage—whether Jewish or Moorish—to which the author belonged.

The success of Pérez de Hita's work must have contributed, though only for a short time, to the popularity of Moorish ballads, enlarging the repertoire of themes and situations. The poets' interest in this genre soon receded, however, and it is possible that, in addition to sheer exhaustion, a certain reluctance to emphasize the Moorish heritage contributed to the decline of the vogue.[2]

In the early stages of the rise of the Spanish *comedia*, there was developed the *comedia de moros y cristianos*. This type of play derived much of its appeal from a colorful portrayal of Moorish-Christian confrontation, and it emphasized the affinities and contrasts among the knights who on both sides of the frontier were supposed to have embodied the spirit of chivalry. Lope de Vega contributed more than any other dramatist to the rise of this genre,[3] paralleling *Civil Wars, I*, not only because of its related subject matter, but also by the emotional approach to such themes and the effects it sought to enhance. The comedias do moros y cristianos offer a gallery of stylized figures, most of them idealized and some caricatured, as the comical *morillo*, a type of *gracioso*. Lope's diverse characterizations reflect the popular views of the Moors and their imprint on Spanish history. He used epic themes in such dramatic works as *El cerco de Santa Fe*,[4] and elaborated, in other cases, upon the situations depicted in his own Moorish ballads, as in certain scenes of *El sol parado*. He also dramatized the Moorish fictional theme of *El Abencerraje* in *El remedio en la desdicha*,[5] and followed Pérez de Hita when he presented in *La envidia de la nobleza* a brilliant Nasrid court, torn by the Zegrís' hatred for the Abencerrajes and shattered by the holocaust suffered by this lineage. Not infrequently a fierce Moor, seeking with hatred every opportunity to confront the Christians, appears in these plays, but next to him the author places an exemplary Moorish knight, who practices Christian virtues and who voluntarily becomes a convert. This affinity of characterization with the portrayal of Nasrid Granada in *Civil Wars, I* is matched by the same brilliance of description and the charm of lyrical motifs related to the sentimental episodes.

Although Lope lost interest in his later years in the comedias, de moros y cristianos, the genre continued to be immensely popular. And, indeed, it was through late recastings and imitations of Golden Age works that those Moorish themes and types, endowed by Pérez de Hita with particular warmth, sifted down into the stream of folk plays which even today formulate the motives of Moorish-Christian confrontation. A trend paralleling the more sophisticated Moorish ballads is represented by *La Luna africana*,[6] a play based on the accusation against the Moorish queen of *Civil Wars, I*, in which no less than nine authors collaborated. On the other hand, Moslem-Christian relations are approached from a new angle by Pedro Calderón de la Barca in *El príncipe constante*,[7] which falls outside our specific concern. As to the Morisco, the comical treatment predominated, but exceptions are not lacking, one of the most interesting being Calderón's dramatization in *Amar después de la muerte* of the tragic story of El Tuzaní, related by Pérez de Hita in *Civil Wars, Part II*.[8]

II *Neoclassics and Romantics*[9]

In the second half of the eighteenth century, when the literary elite of Spain had turned away from much of the Golden Age heritage to conform to contemporary European trends, the Moorish ballads as well as *Civil Wars, I* retained their appeal and inspired jointly, along with less significant poems, the famous "Fiesta de toros en Madrid" by Nicolás Fernández de Moratín.[10] Notwithstanding the cultural dichotomy evident in the literature of the period, this eminent neoclassicist skillfully revived traditional forms and motives and he adopted an almost folkish distortion of Spanish history to describe a picturesque and zestful bullfight in a Moorish kind of Madrid, which is modeled after Pérez de Hita's view of Nasrid Granada, giving to El Cid a role similar to that of the Maestre de Calatrava in one of the equestrian exercises of *Civil Wars, I*.

Pérez de Hita's book crossed the Pyrenees early in the seventeenth century and eventually gave rise to an almost mythical interpretation of Moorish Granada as an exquisitely refined European court where précieux sophistication had first bloomed. *Almahide ou l'Esclave reine* (1660–63), a lengthy novel by Madeleine de Scudéry (also attributed to her brother Georges under whose name it was published), initiated the trend of *romans hispano-mauresques,* which combined in their romance mildly exotic touches and which did not clash with the premises of refinement in the culture they represent. Among the themes of *Civil Wars, I,* the story of the Moorish queen comes to the foreground and forms the core of a highly elaborate sentimental plot, in which the influence of "Ozmín y Daraja" may also be discerned.

More emphasis is given to epic elements in John Dryden's heroic play in ten acts, *Almanzor and Almahide* or *The Conquest of Granada by the Spaniards* (1672). Leading the Moorish army, the hero is made aware by supernatural voices of his true identity when he confronts in battle his father, the duke of Medina Sidonia. Neither this fantastic element nor the protagonist's aggressive individualism or his love for Almahide bring him close to the Spanish origin of his immediate French source, but the English poet, who must have read the "Historia de Ozmín y Daraja" and presumably also *Civil Wars, I,* drew a picture of the Moorish court at the time of an equestrian festival which is closer to Pérez de Hita's Nasrid Granada than to Scudéry's.

Changes in sensibility and taste occurring toward the end of the eighteenth century and a renewed interest in historical studies are reflected in *Gonzalve de Cordoue ou Grenade reconquise* (1791) by Jean Pierre Claris de Florian. The legend of the Abencerrajes comes once more into focus, combined with the Scudéry theme of a Christian leader's love for a princess of Granada. The sentimental tone of this work, as well as its thematic content, influenced the treatment given to Hispano-Moorish themes, not only by French but also by Spanish pre-Romantic authors. Without mentioning the less-renowned writers of the period it should be noted that Nicasio Alvarez de Cienfuegos translated poems interpolated in *Gonzalve* and that he based his tragedy *Zoraida* (1798) on the French author's interpretation of the Sultana and the Abencerrajes' story. And still in the late 1830s Martínez de la Rosa—who had borrowed in 1818 directly from Pérez de Hita the related theme of Boabdil's fury in his neoclassic tragedy *Morayma*—felt encouraged by the success of Florian's romance to write the historical novel of the decline of Granada, *Doña Isabel de Solís*.

The great esteem for Spanish, and particularly for Moorish, ballads among scholars and poets of the Romantic period, including Lord Byron in England and Victor Hugo in France, promoted a renewed interest in the work of Pérez de Hita. *Civil Wars, I* was translated into English by Thomas Rodd in 1803, and imitations or versions of the interpolated poems proliferated as well as did erudite or pseudoerudite writings related to an idealized Moorish Granada. A knowledge and interest in this material became part of the heritage of educated men and women on both sides of the Atlantic. Two resulting literary trends were first, the quasi-allegorical plot, in which Moors or Moriscos stand, individually or collectively, for contemporary subjects, and second, the blending in a literary text of legendary and fictional motifs with personal memories of a stay in Granada. Concern for ethical and sociological problems of the author's age and society underlies the dramas about Moriscos of no less significant Romantics than Samuel Taylor Coleridge, who in 1797 wrote *Osorio* (recast in 1813 with the title of *Remorse*), and Heinrich Heine, who produced his *Almansor* in 1820–21. Closer to history is *Aben Humeya* by Martínez de la Rosa—first produced in Paris in 1830, during the author's exile[11]—but, although Pérez de Hita's book on the Alpujarras war provided the background for this and other Spanish works about the Moriscos, the characters and attitudes presented could be viewed as symbols of Romantic liberal ideology.

For the Romantic generation, a visit to Granada could become a pilgrimage to the site of childhood dreams, and the experience itself became a literary topic. The finest examples of Romantic Alhambraism are due to the Frenchman François René de Chateaubriand, the American Washington Irving, and the Spaniard José Zorrilla. The myth of the Abencerrajes, seen as a symbol of adverse fortune and exemplifying the priority of honor and the excellence of a vanishing lineage, receives in Chateaubriand's *Les Aventures du dernier Abencérage* (1826) a completely new fictional formulation, reflecting also travel impressions and circumstances of the author's life.[12]

Washington Irving offered his *Chronicle of the Conquest of Granada* (1829) as a historical report, intended to correct popular views on the subject that derived from Pérez de Hita and Florian. He used, indeed, a wealth of first-hand documentation, but his work ought to be considered a creative, rather than a scholarly, achievement. Not only is the alleged original by Fray Antonio Agapida as much a fabrication as Pérez de Hita's Arabic source, but the series of defeats suffered by the Moors, which are reported in the *Chronicle,* are seen as parables or symbols of loss, amounting to exile from a land of delight. In the words of William L. Hedges[13] the fall of Granada became an emblem of mutability. Similarly, the unifying point of view of the diverse elements amalgamated in *The Alhambra*—description, historical evocation, topics of orientalism, and sketches of picturesque types and customs—is the reminiscence of radiant days gone by, and this deeper meaning transcends the book's apparently trivial subject, consisting of travel memories and reveries recorded by an exceptional tourist. For all the good humor and mild irony of the imaginative book, a feeling of loss pervades it, which is fittingly expressed by the search for Boabdil, a figure whom Irving tries to rescue from the distortions of popularized history. Not surprisingly, the author's identification with the last Moorish king becomes more important in the 1850 revised version[14] of this Romantic classic, which played in the subsequent revival of Granada themes a role comparable to that of *Civil Wars, I* in an earlier period.

In Spain, the nineteenth-century vogue of historical and legendary poems adopting the metrical form and certain stylistic traits of the ballads culminated in the *leyendas* ("poems on legendary themes") of José Zorrilla, who belonged to the younger generation of Romantics. Influenced by Victor Hugo's orientalism and the treatment of Spanish medieval themes stressing exotic and picturesque effects, he had a talent for blending foreign and traditional motives in a manner which appealed to a wide public. Zorrilla could endow his *leyendas* with the zest and vigor of the frontier and Moorish ballads, at the same time achieving striking effects of sonority and rhythm by his use of new complex metrical patterns. The emotional nuances associated with the themes of Granada were well suited to the style he developed. Early in his career he composed spirited little *orientales*, (short poems with exotic motifs) with a stylized frontier or Nasrid setting, and *leyendas* stressing either the epic accent of episodes of conquest or the lyricism of the motif of "the Moor's sigh." Greater emphasis on description as well as formal experimentation with verse forms and styles intended to parallel visual and auditory perceptions characterize the production of his mature and declining years, particularly in relation to the themes of Granada. A major project for which the author claimed to have undertaken extensive research was the book-length poem *Granada* (1852), dealing with the years preceding the conquest, and its extensive prelude "La leyenda de Alhamar," which focuses, in an evocative mood, on the early period of Nasrid history. Zorrilla's repertoire of Granadine themes comprised the heritage of the Golden Age, the romance-oriented plots derived from nineteenth-century history books and the fantastic tales abounding in the literature of his own time.

The Romantics, rather than Pérez de Hita or other Golden Age authors, were the chief influence stimulating a few writers of the period of modernism to create a very personal imagery, integrating impressions of art and landscape with literary topics related to Moorish Granada and stressing exoticism. A characteristic example was the play *El Alcázar de las Perlas* (1912) by Francisco Villaespesa, who also wrote a drama on Aben Humeya. Moriscos interested other Spanish authors, like the dramatist Eduardo Marquina, but it was the Argentinian Enrique Larreta who produced on the subject a work of great originality and merit. His novel *La gloria de don Ramiro* (1908) portrays an idealized crypto-Moslem culture as the counterpoint of the austere Philipine society. The protagonist, a man of mixed blood, agonizes between these two different concepts of life.[15]

With the fading out of modernism, the three-century cycle

of literary "Morophilia" may be considered closed. In the twentieth century the *Civil Wars of Granada* has deservedly been edited and studied as a classic, but its public narrowed after 1900, and Pérez de Hita ceased to inspire writers to use a stylized view of a past era for their own expression of ideals and perceptions in the present.

Notes and References

Preface

1. Márquez Villanueva, "El morisco Ricote o la hispana razón de estado," in *Personajes y temas del Quijote* (Madrid: Taurus, 1975), pp. 229–335.

Chapter One

1. Various historical surveys in English on Moslem Spain are available: Edwyn Hole, *Andalus: Spain under the Moslems* (London: Hale, 1958); P. M. Holt, A. K. S. Lambton and B. Lewis, *The Cambridge History of Islam*, vol. II (Cambridge: Cambridge University Press, 1970); S. M. Imamuddin, *A Political History of Muslim Spain* (Dacca, Pakistan: Najmah, 1961); idem., *Some aspects of the Socio-Economic and Cultural History of Muslim Spain* (Leiden: Brill, 1965); W. M. Watt and P. Cachia, *A History of Islamic Spain* (Edinburgh: University Press, 1965).

2. See Castro's *The Spaniards: An Introduction to their History*, trans. W. F. King and S. Margaretten (Berkeley: Univ. of California Press, 1971), chaps. 10 and 11.

3. Useful surveys are Reynold A. Nicholson, *A Literary History of the Arabs* (Cambridge: Cambridge University Press, 1930), chap. 9 and Alois R. Nykl, *Hispano-Arabic Poetry and its relations with the Provençal Troubadours* (Baltimore: Furst, 1946), chap. 6. Philosophical and aesthetic principles, as well as the formal aspects of caliphate poetry, are studied by J. T. Monroe in G. E. von Grunebaum, ed., *Arabic Poetry* (Wiesbaden: Otto Harrassowitz, 1973), pp. 125–54.

4. For a brief and comprehensive treatment of Nasrid history with useful references see Miguel Angel Ladero Quesada, *Granada* (Madrid: Gredos, 1969). Cf. also the chapter on Granada in Henri Terrasse, *Islam d'Espagne: Une rencontre de l'Orient et de l'Occident* (Paris: Plon, 1958). Recent important additions are Cristóbal Pérez Delgado, *El antiguo reino nazarí de Granada* (Granada: Anel, 1974) and Rachel Arié, *L'Espagne musulmane au temps des Nasrides (1237–1492)* (Paris: Boccard, 1973).

5. According to a widespread legend—found, e.g., in Antonio de

Guevara *Epístolas familiares,* ed. J. M. de Cossío (Madrid: Real Academia Española, 1950–52), II, 251–54—when the Moorish king watched Granada sorrowfully for the last time his mother Aixa remarked that he was shedding tears like a woman over the city he had been unable to defend as a man. See Marcelino Menéndez y Pelayo, *Antología de poetas líricos castellanos,* ed. E. Sánchez Reyes (Santander: C.S.I.C., 1944–45), VII, 173–76.

6. See below, chapter 3, notes 21–23.

7. For research on internal matters of the Nasrid Kingdom consult the reviews *Al-Andalus,* Madrid, and *Miscelánea de Estudios Arabes y Hebráicos,* Granada (hereafter referred to as *M.E.A.H.*). Also L. Seco de Lucena, "Notas para el estudio de Granada bajo la dominación musulmana," *Boletín de la Universidad de Granada* 23 (1951), 169–91.

8. See the references in chap. 3, notes 6, 7, and 8. The chivalric character of the strife was greatly stressed by Washington Irving in *A Chronicle of the Conquest of Granada* (1829), a book combining fantasy with considerable documentation. See Ma. Soledad Carrasco-Urgoiti, *El moro de Granada en la literatura* (Madrid: Revista de Occidente, 1956), pp. 238–46, and A. Soria, in *Arbor* 44, no. 168 (Dec., 1959), 144–62.

9. See articles by J. de M. Carriazo in *Al-Andalus* 13 (1948), 35–96, and in *M.E.A.H.* 4 (1955), 81–125; by L. Seco de Lucena in *M.E.A.H.* 7, no. 1 (1958), 137–40 and 11, no 1 (1962), 107–9; and by J. Torres Fontes, in *Hispania* (Madrid) 20 (1960), 55–80, and *M.E.A.H.* 10, no. 1 (1961), 89–105.

10. Julio Caro Baroja, *Los moriscos del reino de Granada* (Madrid, 1957), pp. 36–39.

11. On the use of Moorish clothes in Christian Spain, see studies by C. Bernis in *Boletín de la Real Academia de la Historia* (Madrid) 144 (1959), 199–228, and by R. Arié in *Revista del Instituto de Estudios Islámicos en Madrid* 13 (1965–66), 113–17.

The vogue of juegos de cañas in the sixteenth century is studied by C. A. Marsden in J. Jacquot, eds., *Fêtes et cérémonies au temps de Charles Quint* (Paris: C.N.R.S., 1960), pp. 389–411. For the persistence of festivals based on such customs see Carrasco-Urgoiti in *PMLA* 78 (1963), 476–91.

12. The educational approach and theory of *adab,* which helped to shape social patterns in Al-Andalus, integrated the concept of honor, as well as physical exercise, with formal study concerning food, clothing, and etiquette. Cf. Gustav E. von Grunebaum, *Medieval Islam* (Chicago: University of Chicago Press, 1954), pp. 250–57.

13. The essential reference work is Carriazo, "Historia de la guerra

de Granada," in *La España de los Reyes Católicos. Historia de España,* ed. R. Menéndez Pidal, vol. XVII (Madrid, 1969), pp. 387–914.

14. For new insight into one aspect of the unrest in Granada see F. de la Granja, "Condena de Boabdil por los alfaquíes de Granada," *Al-Andalus* 36 (1971), 145–76. An interesting document on the awareness of imminent disaster in Granada was published by M. Gaspar Remiro in *Revista del Centro de Estudios Históricos de Granada,* vol. I (1911), pp. 149–53.

15. See note 19 to chap. 3.

16. See note 8 to chap. 3.

17. For the actual proceedings see M. C. Pescador del Hoyo, in *Al-Andalus* 20 (1955), 283–344.

Chapter Two

1. Caro Baroja, *Los moriscos del reino de Granada* (Madrid, 1957). This book has been the main source for this chapter.

2. Tangentially relevant to the background of Pérez de Hita's work are A. Domínguez Ortiz, "Notas para una sociología de los moriscos españoles," *M.E.A.H.* 11, fasc. 1 (1962), 39–54; idem., "Los moriscos granadinos antes de su definitiva expulsión," *M.E.A.H.* 12–13, fasc. 1 (1963–64), 113–28; idem., "Felipe IV y los moriscos," *M.E.A.H.* 8, fasc. 1 (1959), 55–66; K. Garrad, "La Inquisición y los moriscos granadinos, 1526–80," *Bulletin Hispanique* 67 (1965), 63–77; and B. Vincent, "L'Expulsion des morisques du royaume de Grenade et leur répartition en Castille (1570–71)," *Mélanges de la Casa de Velázquez* 6 (1970), 211–46; idem., "L'Albaicín de Grenade au XVIᵉ siècle (1527–1587)," *Mélanges de la Casa de Velázquez* 7 (1971), 187–222. The material is summarized by Ladero Quesada, *Granada,* pp. 163–80. With respect to international repercussions see A. C. Hess, "The Moriscos: An Ottoman fifth column in Sixteenth Century Spain," *American Historical Review* 74 (1968), 1–25; H. C. Lea, *The Moriscos of Spain* (1901; reprint ed., New York: Greenwood Press, 1968).

3. For information and references on this family see Erika Spivakovsky, *Son of the Alhambra: Don Diego Hurtado de Mendoza 1504–1575* (Austin & London: Univ. of Texas Press, 1970), pp. 23–24. See also L. P. Harvey, "Yūse Banegas: Un moro noble en Granada bajo los Reyes Católicos," *Al-Andalus* 21 (1956), 297–302.

4. A curious letter that gives some insight into the daily life of the gentry of Granada after the conquest was published by I. de las Cagigas in *Arabica* (Paris) 1 (1954), 272–75.

5. Lope de Vega gave the protagonist of his short novel "La desdicha por la honra"—see note 20 to chap. 7—a relatively dark skin

that did not reveal him, however, as the high-class Morisco that he was. Domínguez Ortiz, in "Notas para una sociología de los moriscos," concludes that physical differentiation was nonexistent or very slight.

6. Caro Baroja, *Los moriscos*, p. 5.

7. On Talavera see the edition of his *Católica impugnación* by F. Márquez and Fr. Martín Hernández. Universidad de Salamanca, Espirituales Españoles, Series A, 6 (Barcelona: Flors, 1961). In consonance with the teachings of the first archbishop, when plans to establish the University of Granada were made in 1526, it was decided to establish a school for the sons of converts. See E. Orozco Díaz and J. Bermúdez Pareja, "La universidad de Granada desde su fundación hasta la rebelión de los moriscos (1532–1568)," in *Carlos V. Homenaje de la Universidad de Granada* (Granada: Universidad, 1958), pp. 563–93.

8. For the state of Arabic scholarship in Spain at the time of the Renaissance see the study by M. Bataillon, *Hespéris* 21 (1935), 1–17, and the introduction to James T. Monroe's *Islam and the Arabs in Spanish Scholarship* (Leyden: Brill, 1970). The history of early Arabism in Spain is also summarized in Manuela Manzanares de Cirre, *Arabistas españoles del siglo XIX* (Madrid: Instituto Hispano Arabe de Cultura, 1971), pp. 21–36.

9. See in particular Garrad, "La Inquisición."

10. For the sociological history of the Valencian Moriscos, see studies of Tulio Halperín Donghi in *Cuadernos de Historia de España* (Buenos Aires) 23–24 (1955), 5–115 and 25–26 (1957), 83–250, and *A.E.S.C.* (Paris) 11 (1956), 154–82. For Aragon see below, p. 51.

11. The article on *Aljamia* in the *Encyclopedia of Islam*, vol. I (London, 1960), has been written by Leonard P. Harvey, who is the author of an unpublished dissertation on the subject. A. Galmés has published as the first work in a series of *aljamiado* texts a version of *Historia de los amores de París y Viana* (Madrid: Gredos, 1970). For references to other recent studies see R. Kontzi in *Thesaurus* 25 (1970), 196–213.

12. Caro Baroja, *Los moriscos*, p. 129. On the general situation see Pedro Longás, *Vida religiosa de los moriscos* (Madrid: Centro de Estudios Históricos, 1915). Recent research includes that of Denise Cardaillac, "La Polémique anti-chrètienne du manuscrit aljamiado N° 4944 de la Bibliothèque Nationale de Madrid" (Thèse, Université Paul Valéry de Montpellier, 1972), and that of M. Manzanares de Cirre, "El otro mundo en la literatura aljamiado-morisca," *Hispanic Review* 41 (1973), 599–608.

13. The habit of addressing the new Christians in derogatory terms

was criticized by Antonio de Guevara, *Epístolas familiares*, ed. Cossío, II, 375–82.

14. Important documentation on this matter is in A. Gallego Burín and A. Gámir Sandoval, *Los moriscos del reino de Granada según el Sínodo de Guadix de 1554* (Granada: Universidad, 1968).

15. The essential reference book on the subject is Albert Sicroff, *Les controverses des Statuts de pureté de sang en Espagne* (Paris: Didier, 1960). Américo Castro's views on the causes and effects of the pure lineage obsesion are summarized in his book *The Spaniards*. See especially pp. 48–94.

16. Playwrights who created the comical type of the morillo and other authors have given us the caricature of this jargon. Cf. A. E. Sloman, in *Modern Language Review* 44 (1949), 207–17; Gisela Labib, "Der Maure in dem dramatischen Werk Lope de Vega's," (Ph.D. dissertation, Univ. of Hamburg, 1961), pp. 175–83; and Domínguez Ortiz, "Notas para una sociología de los moriscos."

17. The three main contemporary sources of the war are *De la guerra de Granada* by Diego Hurtado de Mendoza, *Historia del rebelión y castigo de los moriscos del reino de Granada* by Luis del Mármol Carvajal, and *Segunda parte de las guerras civiles de Granada* by Ginés Pérez de Hita, discussed below, chap. 8.

18. The complete text has been published by Garrad in *Atlante* 2 (1954), 198–226.

19. Garrad in *M.E.A.H.* 5 (1956), 73–104.

20. *Guerras civiles*, ed. P. Blanchard-Demouge, vol. II (Madrid, 1915), p. 4.

21. On this incident, reported by the historian Hurtado de Mendoza, who was related to Don Alonso, see Spivakovsky, in *Archivum* (Oviedo) 14 (1964), 212–32.

22. Such as Alonso del Castillo and Miguel de Luna. See note 25.

23. Pérez de Hita and Mármol report that he was forced to surrender a dagger which he carried against regulations at a meeting he attended as councilman. Details and chronology are not clear. Cf. notes of B. Blanco-González to his edition of Hurtado de Mendoza, *Guerra de Granada*. Clásicos Castalia, 22 (Madrid, 1970), pp. 115 and 137.

24. On the proceedings of deportation and resettlement see Vincent, "L'expulsion des morisques du royaume de Grenade," and his article in *Mélanges de la Casa Velázquez* 7 (1971), 397–98.

25. A recent study that throws light on this segment of Granadine Society is by Darío Cabanelas, *El morisco granadino Alonso del Castillo* (Granada, 1965). The essential material on the subject is summarized by the author in *M.E.A.H.* 5 (1956), 19–42. Monroe, *Islam*

and the Arabs, pp. 7–16, Caro Baroja, *Los moriscos*, chaps. 7 and 8, and Domínguez Ortiz, "Felipe IV y los moriscos," deal with this period and with remnants of the Morisco population after the expulsion. For insight into the culture of highly Hispanized Moriscos in Africa cf. J. Oliver Asín, "Un morisco de Túnez admirador de Lope," *Al-Andalus* 1 (1933), 409–50.

26. See Monroe, *Islam and the Arabs*, pp. 7–16, and T. D. Kendrick, "An example of the Theodicy Motive in Antiquarian Thought," in *Fritz Saxl. Memorial*, ed. D. J. Gordon (Edinburgh: Nelson, 1957), pp. 309–25.

27. Monroe, *Islam and the Arabs*, p. 11.

28. Domínguez Ortiz, "Felipe IV y los moriscos," believes that the expulsion had little popular support. Opinions pro and con were collected by Miguel Herrero, *Ideas de los españoles en el siglo XVII* (Madrid: Gredos, 1966), pp. 564–75. For a more analytical assessment cf. the article by C. Colonge in *Boletín de la R. Academia de Buenas Letras de Barcelona* 33 (1969–70), 137–243. References concerning Cervantes' ambiguous treatment of the subject may be read in note 20 to chap. 7. On the proceedings of the expulsion, see, in addition to works cited, Henri Lapeyre, *Géographie de l'Espagne Morisque* (Paris: SEVPEN, 1959), and Juan Reglá, *Estudios sobre los moriscos*, Anales de la Universidad de Valencia, vol. 37, cuaderno 2 (Valencia, 1964). For interesting documentation on petitions for exceptions from residents of Granada and Murcia cf. Ignacio Bauer Landauer, *Papeles de mi archivo* (Madrid: Biblioteca Hispano-Marroquí, 1923).

Chapter Three

1. A survey of this subject in William W. Comfort, *The Moors in Spanish Popular Poetry Before 1600*, Haverford Essays . . . [in honor of] F. B. Gummere, reprint ed. (Freeport: N.Y. Books for Library Press, 1967), pp. 271–303. Relevant interpretative trends on medieval literature are assessed by Francisco López Estrada, *Introducción a la literatura medieval española*, 3rd ed. (Madrid: Gredos, 1966).

2. Menéndez Pidal, *Reliquias de la poesía épica española* (Madrid: Espasa Calpe, 1951), p. xliv. Cf. also the study of the *Crónica general* in his *Estudios literarios*, Colección Austral, 28 (Buenos Aires, 1943), pp. 159–66.

3. Lida de Malkiel, "El moro en las letras castellanas" (a review of Carrasco Urgoiti, *El moro de Granada en la literatura*), *Hispanic Review* 28 (1960), 350–58.

4. Lida de Malkiel, *ibid.*

5. Catalán, "Ideales moriscos en una Crónica de 1344," *Nueva Revista de Filología Hispánica* 7 (1953), 570–82. See also his article in *Boletín de la Real Academia Española* 48 (1968), 189–236.

6. The subject and its historical background were treated by Harry A. Deferrari, *The Sentimental Moor in Spanish Literature before 1600*, University of Pennsylvania Publications ... in Romanic Languages and Literatures, 17 (Philadelphia, 1927); pp. 7–32. Cf. also López Estrada, *El Abencerraje y la hermosa Jarifa* (Madrid, 1957), chapter 2.

7. There were instances of a Christian knight challenging another to a duel under the auspices of the king of Granada. See Martín de Riquer, *Caballeros andantes españoles*, Coleccion Austral, 1397 (Madrid, 1967), pp. 158–67.

8. Memories persisted after thirty years when the Venetian Ambassador Andrea Navagiero visited Granada and wrote a frequently quoted letter on the subject, which may be read in Pérez de Hita, *Guerras civiles*, I, 332–36.

9. Preserved to this day have been Hernando del Pulgar, *Compendio de la historia de Granada*, published by A. Valladares, *Semanario Erudito* 12 (1788), 57–144; and Hernando de Baeza, *Relaciones de algunos sucesos de los últimos tiempos del reino de Granada*, Sociedad de Bibliófilos Españoles, 3 (Madrid: Rivadeneyra, 1868), as also a sequence published by Carriazo, *Al-Andalus* 13 (1948), 431–42. Carriazo also edited the sixteenth-century MS "Historia de la Casa Real de Granada," (similar to the corresponding chapters of Esteban de Garibay's *Compendio historial*), *M.E.A.H.* 6 (1957), 7–56.

10. Carrasco-Urgoiti, *Moro de Granada*, pp. 42–46.

11. The genealogist Gonzalo Argote de Molina transcribed and translated the poem "Alhambra amorosa, lloran tus castillos" in his "Discurso sobre la poesía castellana," included by Marcelino Menéndez y Pelayo in *Antología de poetas líricos castellanos* VII, 100. See also a linguistic study by J. Vázquez Ruiz, "La elegía de Boabdil," *Bol. de la Univ. de Granada* 22 (1950), 277–91.

12. For a general study of the genre see David W. Foster, *The Early Spanish Ballad* (New York: Twayne Publishers, 1971). For a selection and brief discussion see W. S. Merwin, *Some Spanish Ballads* (London: Abelard-Schuman, 1961), and C. Colin Smith, *Spanish Ballads* (Oxford: Pergamon, 1964). English translations have been studied by G. W. Umphrey in *Modern Language Quarterly* 6 (1945), 479–94, and 7 (1946), 21–43; and also by Shasta M. Bryant, *The Spanish Ballad in English* (Lexington: Univ. Press of Kentucky, 1973). See also below, n. 15.

13. Manuel Alvar has insisted on the essential affinity between the

old Castilian epic and the romances of the frontier in "Pervivencia de las gestas en el romancero fronterizo," included in his book *El romancero: tradicionalidad y pervivencia* (Barcelona: Planeta, 1970). This comprehensive survey is also useful as a reference guide. The fundamental work on the subject is Ramón Menéndez Pidal, *Romancero hispánico* (Madrid: Espasa-Calpe, 1953). For a formal analysis of the two ballad genres originated in connection with the themes of Granada see Ulrich Knoke, "Die spanische 'Maurenromanze,' " (Ph.D. dissertation, Göttingen, 1966).

14. For an interpretation of the "romancero" as the expression of an age of crisis in which the individual suffered from a sense of alienation and perplexity, see the article by J. Rodríguez Puértolas in *Philological Quarterly* 51 (1972), 85–104.

15. Translations and adaptations of this poem (including Lord Byron's "Woe is me, Alhama!") and of "Abenámar" are studied by Daniel Bodmer, *Die granadinischen Romanzen in der europäischen Literatur* (Zürich, 1955). See also Menéndez Pidal, *Romancero hispánico* II, 239–42 and Carrasco-Urgoiti, *Moro de Granada,* pp. 225–30.

16. See note 11 to chapter 1.

17. *Romancero hispánico,* II, 9–12.

18. Among the most important studies of "Abenámar" are those of Leo Spitzer in *Sobre antigua poesía española* (Buenos Aires: Universidad, 1962), and Paul Bénichou, in *Creación poética en el romancero tradicional* (Madrid: Gredos, 1968), pp. 61–92. For an Arabist's argument in favor of the theory that the ballad was composed by a bilingual Moor see Luis Seco de Lucena, *Discurso de Apertura. Investigaciones sobre el romancero* (Granada: Universidad, 1958), pp. 17–29. The point is contested by Alvar, p. 61.

19. Seco de Lucena, *Los Abencerrajes: leyenda e historia* (Granada: F. Román, 1960), pp. 29–31. The actual role of the Abencerraje clan in the politics of Granada, is in contradiction, as the author proves, to the image shaped in Spanish poetry and fiction of the sixteenth century. The background of the most important frontier ballads has been studied in Arabic sources by Seco de Lucena, who summarizes his views in *Orígenes del orientalismo literario* (Santander: Publicaciones de la Universidad Menéndez Pelayo, 1963).

20. Cf. the article by G. Cirot in *Bulletin Hispanique* 31 (1929), 268–70.

21. As in "La mañana de San Juan / al tiempo que alboreaba," published in "Pliegos sueltos" and included in the *Segunda parte de la Silva de varios romances* (Zaragoza, 1550); there are also subsequent editions. Cf. A. Rodríguez Moñino, ed., *La silva de romances (Bar-*

celona, 1561) (Salamanca: Universidad, 1969), p. 137. See also note 34 to chap. 6.

22. See the article by Cirot, *Bulletin Hispanique*, 34 (1932), 5–26. The subject is surveyed in Carrasco-Urgoiti, *Moro de Granada*, pp. 36–40, and Alvar, *El romancero*, pp. 145–51.

23. For an exhaustive study on the Santa Fe ballads see Catalán, *Siete siglos de romancero* (Madrid: Gredos, 1969), pp. 100–132.

24. Such is the case in Lorenzo de Sepúlveda's *Romances* (c. 1549) and Alonso de Fuentes, *Los cuarenta cantos* (Sevilla, 1550). Cf. Rodríguez Moñino's edition of Sepúlveda's *Cancionero de romances* (*Sevilla, 1584*) (Madrid: Castalia, 1967).

25. Timoneda, *Rosas de romances*, facsimile edition, ed. Rodríguez Moñino and D. Devoto in Floresta. Joyas Poéticas Españolas, 8 (Valencia: Castalia, 1963). Among other romances on the war of Granada, the collection *Rosa española* includes "Junto al vado del Genil / por un camino seguido" on the theme of public demonstrations of grief, motivated here by Boabdil's defeat and capture.

26. This is correctly stressed by López Estrada, *El Abencerraje y la hermosa Jarifa*, p. 116.

27. Introduction to *Los temas ariostescos en el romancero y la poesía española del Siglo de Oro* (Madrid: Castalia, 1968), pp. 19–20. See also the same author's *L'Arioste en Espagne* (Bordeaux, 1966), pp. 245–52.

28. Chevalier, *Temas*, pp. 326–28.

29. For the significance of this collection from which Moncayo borrowed several ballads on the themes of Granada, see Menéndez Pidal, *Romancero*, II, 115–16, and the introduction by Rodríguez Moñino to his edition of Rodríguez, *Romancero historiado* (*Alcalá, 1582*) (Madrid: Castalia, 1967).

30. *Tesoro de varias poesías* (Madrid, 1580), and *Romancero* (1583). A modern edition of the latter work was published by Sociedad de Bibliófilos Españoles, 19 (Madrid, 1880).

31. *Primera parte del romancero y Tragedias* (Alcalá, 1587).

32. See introduction to *Romancero del Abencerraje*, ed. López Estrada, Biblioteca Anaya, 68 (Madrid, 1965).

33. For a characterization of his style in a similar type of ballad see Chevalier, *Temas*, pp. 21–26.

34. Research on the new ballads has flourished since 1950. Most significant have been the studies by J. F. Montesinos, cited in note 39 to chap. 6, Menéndez Pidal, *Romancero Hispánico*, and the editions and bibliographical studies by Antonio Rodríguez Moñino. Among these *La Silva de romances* and the edition of Sepúlveda, *Cancionero de romances* quoted above are concerned with the transitional period.

D. Saunal studied the question of assonance in *Mélanges à la mémoire de Jean Sarrailh* (Paris: Institut d' Études Hispaniques, 1966), II, 355–75. Knoke, op. cit. analyzes the evolving styles of the Moorish ballads; Alvar assesses the history and problems of the genre. A survey by J. Fradejas Lebrero, "El romancero morisco," *Cuadernos de la Biblioteca Española de Tetuán*, no. 2 (1964), 39–74.

35. In subsequent collections Moncayo included fewer narrative ballads of the type he had borrowed from Lucas Rodríguez and stressed the more lyrical kind of romance intended for singing. This type usually appeared anonymously, although the authors were established writers. The *Flores* that followed the 1589 collection included poems in the genre, but their number decreased gradually. See for such matters Menéndez Pidal, *Romancero*, II, 125–26 and 160, as well as the articles by Montesinos cited in note 39 to chap. 6.

36. On the relationship between such spectacular festivals and the Moorish ballad, see R. Benítez Claros, "Antecedentes moriscos del género aúlico," *Cuadernos de Literatura* 1 (1947), 247–54.

37. "Algunos problemas del romancero nuevo," reprinted in *Ensayos y estudios de literatura española* (México: Andrea, 1959). See pp. 87–91.

38. Along with the cult of beauty and the analysis of sentiment, Dámaso Alonso stressed in the late Petrarchan poets whose mannerism he analyzed, "una masa de metáforas y metonimias siempre reiteradas, una tendencia a la imagen suntuaria y colorista, un gusto por ciertos esquemas distributivos de la materia en el verso y en la estrofa, en especial por la regular distribución de materia en el verso en plurimembraciones y pluralidades, etc., y, sobre todo, por la bimembración, ya simple, ya por contrarios." In *Poesía española*, 5th ed. (Madrid: Gredos, 1966), p. 386. A penetrating analysis of Lope de Vega's Moorish ballads in *La Dorotea* (which was not yet available at the time this chapter was written) may be read in Alan S. Trueblood, *Experience and Artistic Expression in Lope de Vega: The Making of La Dorotea* (Cambridge: Harvard University Press, 1974), pp. 52–72.

39. Knoke, "Maurenromanze" pp. 243–49. This critic discusses the manneristic traits of the Moorish ballad, as does E. Moreno Báez, article cited in note 31 to chap. 5.

40. As in "Con los francos Vencerrajes / el Rey Chico de Granada," in Lucas Rodríguez, *Romancero historiado*. See on the topic Knoke, "Maurenromanze," pp. 282–83.

41. Góngora excelled in this approach. Cf. Robert Jammes, *Études sur l'Oeuvre poétique de don Luis de Góngora y Argote* (Bordeaux: Université, 1967), pp. 387–88.

42. See Alvar, pp. 98–122, on the Zaide ballads, some of which have survived in oral tradition. Cf. also Bénichou, *Romancero judeo-español de Marruecos* (Madrid: Castalia, 1968), pp. 260–62 and 319–24. Lope de Vega's Gazul ballads and their autobiographical content have been studied by M. Goyri, in *Nueva Revista de Filología Hispánica* 7 (1953), 403–16, and by Menéndez Pidal, *Romancero hispánico*, II, 126–30. On attributions to Lope of poems inserted by Pérez de Hita, see notes 35, 37, 39 and 41 to chap. 6.

43. See Jammes, pp. 376–98. On the theme of captivity in the new romancero cf. Albert Mas, *Les Turcs dans la littérature espagnole du Siècle d'Or* (Paris: Centre de Recherches Hispaniques, 1967), II, 247–65, and Bénichou, *Creación poética*, pp. 160–84.

44. Such poems are "¡Ah! mis señores poetas, / descúbranse ya esas caras" and Góngora's "Ensíllenme el asno rucio / del alcalde Juan Llorente." Included in *Romancero general*, ed. A. Durán, vol. I, Biblioteca de Autores Españoles, 10 (Madrid, 1849), numbers 245 and 251.

45. *Op. cit.* p. 129.

46. Fradejas, "Romancero morisco." The ballad referred to is "¿Por qué, señores poetas·/ no volvéis por vuestra fama?" (Durán, number 246).

47. See the study by Martínez Ruiz cited in note 16 to chap. 7.

Chapter Four

1. "'L'Abencérage'. Un texte retrouvé," *Bulletin Hispanique*, 59 (1957), 369–95. The volume was in the library of the Academia de la Historia in Madrid.

2. "El 'Abencerraje' de Toledo, 1561," *Anales de la Universidad Hispalense*, 19 (1959), 1–60.

3. Published in facsimile by G. Cirot in *Bulletin Hispanique* 25 (1923), 172–73 and plates. The text was then edited and studied by H. Mérimée, "*El Abencerrage* d'après diverses versions publiées au XVIᵐᵉ siècle," *Bulletin Hispanique* 30 (1928), 147–81.

4. This was first established by Mérimée, *loc. cit.*

5. The colophon is dated January 7, 1562. See López Estrada, *El Abencerraje y la hermosa Jarifa: Cuatro textos y su estudio* (Madrid: Rev. de Archivos, 1957), p. 375. Study and text of this version of *El Abencerraje* are on pp. 46–64 and 376–413. Most editions of *La Diana* subsequent to that of Cuenca, 1561, include the Moorish novel.

6. For references on Villegas see below, note 24. The *Inventario* version of *El Abencerraje* has been published many times. For research purposes López Estrada's edition cited in note 5 is recommended. The same editor prepared *El Abencerraje y la hermosa Jarifa*, Biblioteca

Anaya, 64 (Madrid, 1971), and previously in collaboration with John
E. Keller, who translated the text, *Antonio de Villegas' "El Abencerraje,"* University of North Carolina Studies in Comparative Literature, 33 (Chapel Hill, 1964). Another reliable edition, with introduction and notes in English by Claudio Guillén, is *"Lazarillo de
Tormes" and "El Abencerraje"* (New York: The Laurel Language
Library, 1966).

7. "De Granada partió el moro / que se llama Ben Zulema."
It was studied by Menéndez Pidal in "Un nuevo romance fronterizo,"
Homenaje a Almeida Garret (Genoa, 1900), pp. 4–15 (reprinted in
Los romances de América. Colección Austral 55) and by López
Estrada, *Bol. de la R. Academia Española* 38 (1958), 421–28.

8. Cf. López Estrada, *El Abencerraje,* pp. 79–83. See also above
p. 28 and note 19 to chap. 3.

9. The text of the song is as follows:

Nascido en Granada,   Nascido en Granada
criado en Cártama,   de una linda mora,
enamorado en Coín,   criado en Cártama,
frontero de Álora.   enamorado en Coín
(*Inventario*)   frontero de Álora.
                                       (*Corónica*)

En Cártama me he criado,
nascí en Granada primero,
mas fuy de Álora frontero,
y en Coín enamorado.

. . . .

(*Diana*)

I quote from López Estrada, *El Abencerraje: cuatro textos,* pp. 315,
355, 380.

10. Published by G. I. Dale in *Modern Language Notes* 39 (1924),
31–33, and by López Estrada, *El Abencerraje,* pp. 415–21.

11. See comments on the "tradicionalidad" of short stories in Maxime Chevalier, *Cuentecillos tradicionales en la España del Siglo de
Oro* (Bordeaux: Institut d'Études Ibériques et Ibéro-Américaines de
l'Université, 1971), pp. 3 and 15–17.

12. On the possible priority of this text see Carrasco-Urgoiti in
Revista Hispánica Moderna 34 (1968), 242–55.

13. Whinnom, "The Relationship of the Three Texts of 'El Abencerraje' ", *The Modern Language Review* 54 (1959), 507–17.

14. For editions of the text *Parte de la corónica* see notes 1 to 3 of
this chapter.

15. "El Abencerraje de Toledo," pp. 51–52.

16. "Individuo y ejemplaridad en *El Abencerraje," Collected Studies in honor of Américo Castro's Eightieth Year* (Oxford: The Lincombe Lodge Research Library, 1965), pp. 2–23.

17. This crisis is examined in Carrasco-Urgoiti, *El problema morisco en Aragón al comienzo del reinado de Felipe II,* Estudios de Hispanófila, 11 (Valencia, 1969).

18. A book by Piérre Geneste on Urrea will be forthcoming. Cf. the summary of research on this author in Chevalier, *L' Arioste en Espagne* (Bordeaux: Université, 1966), pp. 71–84.

19. See on this matter Carrasco-Urgoiti, "Las cortes señoriales del Aragón mudéjar y *El Abencerraje,"* in *Homenaje a Casalduero* (Madrid: Gredos, 1972), pp. 115–28.

20. See Guillén, p. 18, n. 40.

21. A second tender scene is introduced and serves as frame for an Italianate poem that Abindarráez is said to have sung in Arabic for Jarifa. This and other variants are surveyed by López Estrada, *El Abencerraje: cuatro textos,* pp. 46–65.

22. Article cited in note 13.

23. Irving, "Recollections of the Alhambra," *The Knickerbocker* 13 (1839), 485–94. Reprinted in *Wolfert's Roost and Other Papers* (New York: Putnam, 1855). See below, note 44.

24. Bataillon, "¿Melancolía renacentista o melancolía judía?" *Estudios hispánicos: Homenaje a Archer M. Huntington* (Wellesley, Mass.: Wellesley College, 1952), pp. 39–50. Reprinted in *Varia lección de clásicos españoles* (Madrid: Gredos, 1964). See also López Estrada's studies on Villegas in *Bol. de la R. Academia Española* 29 (1949), 99–133, and the introduction to his edition of *Inventario,* Joyas Bibliográficas, 13 (Madrid, 1955–56).

25. "Salmacis et Trocho dans L' Abencérage," in *Hommage à Ernest Martinenche* (Paris: d'Artrey, 1939), pp. 355–63. Reprinted in his *Varia lección.*

26. See Crawford's article in the *Revista de Filología Española* 10 (1923), 281–87.

27. *El Abencerraje: cuatro textos,* pp. 71–78, and "Sobre el cuento de la honra del marido, defendida por el amante, atribuido a Rodrigo de Narváez," *Revista de Filología Española* 47 (1964), 331–39.

28. López Estrada, loc. cit.; Guillén, p. 12, and J. Gimeno Casalduero, *"El Abencerraje y la hermosa Jarifa:* composición y significado," *Nueva Revista de Filología Hispánica* 21 (1972), 1–22. Cf. pp. 16–17.

29. See comments concerning Mateo Alemán's use of the topos in Edmond Cros, *Protée et le Gueux* (Paris: Didier, 1967), pp. 281–84.

30. Article cited in note 13, pp. 512–13.

31. López Estrada, "Tres notas al *Abencerraje*," *Revista Hispánica Moderna* 31 (1965), 265–73.

32. See references in note 36. Whinnom, loc. cit., remarked that, while the suppression of "Senecan" passages in a later version would have been difficult to understand, it is comprehensible that the author of *Inventario* should have chosen to accent this aspect of the tale.

33. See the introduction of Ma. Rosa Lida de Malkiel, *La originalidad artística de La Celestina* (Buenos Aires: Eudeba, 1962). The likelihood that *La Celestina* was intended to be read aloud to an interested group and the importance at the time of oral exposition, even among circles with a highly developed culture, has been recently stressed by Stephen Gilman, *The Spain of Fernando de Rojas* (Princeton: University Press, 1972), p. 319.

34. López Estrada, *El Abencerraje: cuatro textos* is an excellent guide to the sources of the novel. Useful research on the subject was carried on by Cirot, *Bulletin Hispanique* 31 (1929), 131–38 and 40 (1938), 433–47.

35. See above, pp. 46–47 and notes 24 and 25 of chap. 3.

36. López Estrada, pp. 185–97, and Gimeno, 20–22.

37. See comments by Guillén, pp. 11–12. A study which focuses on the different terminology used in praise of each knight is R. F. Glenn, "The moral implications of *El Abencerraje*," *Modern Language Notes* 80 (1965), 202–9.

38. See above pp. 00 and note 19 to chap. 3.

39. This influence was first noted by Elena Primicerio in her edition of *El Abencerraje* (Naples, 1929). See Cirot in *Bulletin Hispanique* 40 (1938), 284. The passage in question is found in Carino's tale, Prose VIII of *Arcadia*.

40. Guillén, pp. 5–6, comments on the artistic pertinence of an allusion made by Abindarráez to the myth of Salmacis and Troco—i.e., Hermaphroditus—that had puzzled some scholars.

41. López Estrada, Guillén, and Gimeno offer interesting and somewhat divergent interpretations of this theme, as well as of the Neoplatonic foundation of *El Abencerraje*.

42. See, for example, the comments made by A. Soons on the contrast between *El Abencerraje* and Mateo Alemán's "Historia de Ozmín y Daraja" in *Romanische Forschungen* 78 (1966), 267–69. Cf. also studies by Donald McGrady cited in note 1 to chap. 9.

43. I quote from the introduction of his edition cited above *"Lazarillo de Tormes" and "El Abencerraje,"* p. 40.

44. Cited in note 28 above.

45. See below p. 140. The early diffusion of the theme of *El Aben-*

cerraje has been studied in the articles by B. Matulka in *Hispania* 16 (1933), 369–88, and by E. Moreno Báez in *Archivum* 4 (1954), 310–29. See also Carrasco-Urgoiti, *Moro de Granada*, pp. 102, 128, 136, 252 passim, and the edition and study of Francisco Balbi de Correggio's poem *Historia de los amores del valeroso moro Abinde Araez y de la hermosa Xarifa Abençerases* (Milán, 1593) in Homero Serís, *Nuevo ensayo de una biblioteca española de libros raros y curiosos* (New York: Hispanic Society of America, 1964–69), I, 148–68.

Chapter Five

1. Introduction to Pérez de Hita, *Guerras civiles de Granada* (Madrid: Centro de Estudios Históricos, 1913–15), I, ix–xvii. When using this study, Espín Rael's later findings should also be considered. I refer to Pérez de Hita's *Guerras civiles* by indicating in parentheses within the text volume and page of this edition.

2. Espín Rael, *De la vecindad de Pérez de Hita en Lorca desde 1568 a 1577 años* (Lorca, 1922). The data we summarize here come mainly from this source.

3. Nicolás Acero y Abad, *Ginés Pérez de Hita: Estudio biográfico y bibliográfico* (Madrid, 1888), pp. 7–18. As was pointed out by José P. Tejera y R. de Moncada, *Biblioteca del Murciano* (Madrid, 1924–1957), I, 597–600 and 617, and II, 19–27 and 225, Acero's work, made up of previously published articles, is far from being an entirely acceptable study.

4. Espín Rael, pp. 17 and 69.

5. Cf. Blanchard-Demouge, Introduction to Pérez de Hita, *Guerras civiles* and Espín Rael, pp. 9–13 and 65–68.

6. Espín Rael, pp. 22–24.

7. So it was reported in a seventeenth-century manuscript used by the well-informed scholar from Granada Francisco de Paula Valladar in his biography of *Hernán Pérez del Pulgar el de las hazañas* (Madrid, 1892). Mentioned, along with other sources, by Espín Rael, pp. 49–50, 57 and [71].

8. See below, p. 85, and notes 40–42 to this chapter.

9. Both volumes are reproduced by A. Pérez Gómez and M. Muñoz Cortés in *Justas y certámenes poéticos en Murcia*, 3 vols., Biblioteca de Autores Murcianos, 2–4 (Murcia, 1958–59), Pérez de Hita's sonnets are in I, 184–85. They are included in Juan Alonso de Almela, *Reales exequias a la muerte de Felipe II* (Valencia, 1600).

10. Espín Rael, "Resumen biográfico," p. 69 and following. He cites articles by Soria Gabardo in Murcia's newspaper *La Verdad* quoting the marriage license of a Ginés Pérez de Hita resident of El Palomar,

and Jerónima Botía, widow of Ginés Navarro. They were married in Molina de Segura, 1612. Pérez de Hita mentions the Botía family in *Civil Wars, II,* 147. In 1572 an Isabel Botía was a member of Pérez de Hita's household in Lorca: Espín Rael, p. 47.

11. *Guerras civiles, I,* xvi. The text of the aprobación is in II, xxxv.

12. See below, note 42.

13. Blanchard-Demouge, *Guerras civiles,* I, xv, considers it likely that this book was the poem on the history of Lorca and indicates that the death of Don Lope de Figueroa occurred in August, 1585. Only after this date could Pérez de Hita have visited El Tuzaní in his retirement.

14. See below, p. 132 and note 22 to chap. 8.

15. I have examined with more detail Pérez de Hita's position regarding the Moriscos in *Actas del Cuarto Congreso de la Asociación Internacional de Hispanistas* (forthcoming).

16. In addition to Sancho Panza, several characters in the Cervantes *entremeses* may be considered. See Américo Castro, *Cervantes y los casticismos españoles* (Madrid: Alfaguara, 1966), pp. 113–29.

17. See on this point Espín Rael, pp. 10–15.

18. Although this episode was inspired by a topic of chivalric literature (see below, p. 99), Pérez de Hita seems to have been the first author to use it in connection with the conquest of Granada. On this theme in sixteenth-century Spanish literature, cf. R. W. Tyler in *Actas del Segundo Congreso Internacional de Hispanistas* (Nijmegen, 1967), pp. 635–41.

19. In October of 1609, the city council of Murcia requests that people threatening the Moriscos of Granadine origin be punished; see Florencio Janer, *Condición social de los moriscos de España* (Madrid: Imp. de la R. Academia de la Historia, 1857), pp. 317–20. One of the councilmen who signed the petition had the family name of Almodóvar, a lineage mentioned by Pérez de Hita (II, 55, chap. 5) as having the right to be considered noble and Old Christian, even though for three generations New Christian women had married into this family.

20. On Don Diego's position see chap. 17 of the biography by Spivakovsky, quoted above, chap. 2, note 3.

21. Cf. above, chap. 3.

22. Cf. Francisco de B. San Román, *Lope de Vega, los cómicos toledanos y el poeta sastre* (Madrid, 1935).

23. This aspect is studied in Carrasco-Urgoiti, "Les Fêtes équestres dans *Les Guerres civiles de Grenade,*" *Les Fêtes de la Renaissance,* vol. III, ed. J. Jacquot and E. Konigson (Paris: C.N.R.S., 1975), pp 299–312.

24. Cf. comments by Espín Rael, pp. 49–50.

25. "Libro de la población y hazañas de la mui novilíssima y leal ciudad de Lorca," Biblioteca Nacional, MS. 19, 610. The text of the first part is included in Acero y Abad, pp. 206–394. The three last cantos of the second part, describing a contemporary celebration in Lorca, were summarized by Espín Rael, pp. 33–38. See analysis of the poem in Blanchard-Demouge, I, xvii–xxviii, and II, xxiii–xxv.

26. On Spanish versions see introduction by A. Rey to Leomarte, *Sumas de Historia Troyana*, Anejo de la Revista de Filología Española, 15 (Madrid, 1932).

27. Cf. note 9 to this chapter.

28. Espín Rael, pp. 39–44.

29. See Frank Pierce, *La poesía épica del Siglo de Oro* (Madrid: Gredos, 1961), pp. 280–89.

30. See Blanchard-Demouge, I, xxviii.

31. The point is stressed by E. Moreno Báez on p. 354 of "El manierismo de Pérez de Hita," in *Homenaje a Emilio Alarcos García* (Valladolid: Universidad, 1965–67) II, 353–67.

32. See below, pp. 105 and 122.

33. Pérez de Hita states that a friend of his was the author of the ballad "Mas tredages [sic] marineros / de Huéscar y otro lugar." The poem is about the struggle for the town of Galera (II, 298–99, chap. 22), and it builds an allegory on the basis of the double meaning of the word *Galera*, which also signifies a ship, imitating the old ballad of the "Infante Arnaldos." See Menéndez Pidal, *Romancero hispánico*, II, 62.

34. See above, pp. 46–47, and note 24 to chap. 3.

35. Cf. Menéndez Pidal, *Romancero hispánico*, pp. 64–65, and Caro Baroja, *Ensayo sobre la literatura de cordel* (Madrid: Revista de Occidente, 1969), pp. 120–21. It is known that, while residing in Murcia, Pérez de Hita published two ballads in pamphlet form; see Antonio Rodríguez Moñino, *Diccionario de pliegos sueltos poéticos* (Madrid: Castalia, 1970), #439. From the names of characters mentioned—Princess Calidonia and her father, King Agolandro—it is easy to surmise that one of the poems was connected with the ballad on Reinaldos de Montalbán, "Cuando aquel claro lucero / sus rayos quiere enviar" (Durán, *Romancero*, number 368). The locus amœnus and the tournament in which a Christian triumphs over the infidels are topoi appearing both in the ballad on Reinaldos, which had first been published in *Tercera parte de la Silva* (1551), and in Pérez de Hita's *Civil Wars of Granada*.

36. An example is the festivals held by Aben Humeya in Purchena

which are described in chap. 14 of the *Civil Wars, Part II*. See below, chap. 8.

37. For a survey of this type of folk drama in modern times and its roots in Golden Age festivities and dramatic literature see my article cited in n. 11 to chap. 1. The last part of the Lorca festivities described by Ginés toward the end of the "Libro de Lorca" is a simulated battle of Moors and Christians. See note 25 to this chapter.

38. The song in Pérez de Hita had been included by Pedro de Flores in *Sexta parte de Flor de romances* (Lisbon, 1593), folios 368–69. Reprinted by Rodríguez Moñino in *Las fuentes del Romancero general* (Madrid: Real Academia Española, 1957), vol. VII. It was included in the *Romancero general* (1600) and must have been popular, for a seventeenth-century manuscript, "Cancionero" of P. Siguerondo, in the library of the Hispanic Society of America contains a version "a lo divino" of the *Guerras civiles* serenade, which begins "Lágrimas que no pudieron / Madalena así ablandar." This is MS number CCXIII, #44, f. 16 v. See Rodríguez Moñino, *Catálogo de manuscritos poéticos en la Hispanic Society of America* (New York: Hispanic Society of America, 1965–66), II, 423.

39. Pérez de Hita's use of the stanza called *rima provenzal* by Gil Polo was noted by Menéndez Pelayo in his study of *Diana enamorada*. *Orígenes de la novela* (Madrid, 1925), p. cdlvi. Another example that may be mentioned is that of the Murcian poet Diego Beltrán Hidalgo, who adopted this metrical form in a pastoral "Lamentación" to the death of Philip II, included in the memorial volume of 1600 to which Ginés also contributed. Text of the poem and comments by Muñoz Cortés and Pérez Gómez in *Justas*, I, 118–26 and III, 203.

40. Blanchard-Demouge observed that the sum of seventy *ducados* involved in the transaction is equivalent to the 800 silver *reales* mentioned in the 1610 privilegio in favor of Dorado that was used for the publication of the *Segunda parte de las guerras civiles de Granada* (Cuenca: Domingo de la Iglesia, 1619). See *Guerras civiles*, I, lxxxix–xci.

41. All references to earlier editions are founded on conjecture prompted by the preliminary material that has been mentioned. See note 46 of this chapter.

42. This was Christiano Bernabé, who was active as printer or bookdealer from 1592 to 1603. See Fermín Caballero, *La imprenta en Cuenca* (Cuenca: El Eco, 1869), pp. 114–15.

The dedication signed by a Christiano Bernabé *archero de S.M.*, appears in a copy, at the library of the Hispanic Society of America, of the edition printed in Cuenca by Domingo de la Iglesia, 1619. The Biblioteca Nacional copy of the same edition reproduced by

Blanchard-Demouge does not include the Bernabé dedication to the duke of Infantado. Instead it contains a dedication to a canon of Cuenca, Andrés del Pozo Palomino, by a publisher called Andrés Miguel, as well as laudatory verses addressed to both. This copy however does carry a *tassa* of 1619 mentioning as solicitor the Archero Christiano Bernabé. The Barcelona, 1619, editions by Estevan Liberós and Sebastián de Cormellas include the latter's dedication to the duke of Infantado and none of the material relating to del Pozo or Miguel.

43. Cf. Henri Lapeyre, *Géographie de l'Espagne morisque* (Paris: SEVPEN, 1959), p. 195. The duke was Don Juan Hurtado de Mendoza. See Cristina Arteaga, *La casa del Infantado, cabeza de los Mendoza* (Madrid: Duque del Infantado; 1940–44), II, 17–32.

44. Carrasco-Urgoiti, *Problema morisco en Aragón*, pp. 27, 36, 61 and 73–75.

45. Text in *Guerras civiles*, I, xcviii. Data on Berrío, who was praised by Cervantes and Lope de Vega are in Francisco Rodríguez Marín, *Luis Barahona de Soto* (Madrid: Sucs. de Rivadeneyra, 1903), pp. 36 and 170, and *Nuevos datos para las biografías de cien escritores* (Madrid, 1923). The type of play known as "comedia de moros y cristianos" was reportedly started by a Berrío, according to Agustín de Rojas in his "Loa de la comedia" included in *Viaje entretenido*. See Carrasco, *Moro de Granada*, pp. 78–79.

46. Acero, p. 73, and Blanchard-Demouge, *Guerras civiles*, II, xxxiii interpret Molina's description of a printed second part as a reference to the history of the rebellion, but all data correspond to the Alcalá, 1604, edition of *Historia de los vandos*. Moreover, if the latter were the first part reviewed by Molina, why should a text that had been frequently printed be submitted in manuscript form?

Chapter Six

1. Pérez de Hita's departures from the fantasized history of his time are also inconsistent with later established facts, and Blanchard-Demouge's attempt to identify his alleged Arabic source with Aben Aljatib (*Guerras civiles*, I xxviii–li) is not well founded. See on the matter Moreno Báez, pp. 355–57. The non-Arabic immediate source of names of clans in the book is established by Seco de Lucena, *Boletín de la Universidad de Granada* 23 (1951), 169–79. The fictional nature of Pérez de Hita's work is confirmed by Carriazo's comments in "Historia de la guerra de Granada," pp. 814 and 823–24.

2. The first part was published in Granada, 1592. The praise of Granada appears in first part, book I, chap. 12 (vol. I, folio 42).

Luna, like Pérez de Hita, refers to the conquerors of Spain, Tarif and Muza, with the titles of "Capitán" or "General." See on this author the studies of Cabanelas and Monroe mentioned in notes 25 and 26 to chap. 2.

3. *Guerras civiles*, I, 2. As indicated by Pérez de Hita, Balagis or Abalagis is a character of the *Crónica sarracina* who becomes king of Sevilla. After conquering the city, he takes as his wife Queen Eliata, who had been married to the Visigothic king Rodrigo. Corral, *Crónica del rey don Rodrigo* (Sevilla? 1499), Segunda Parte, folios 71–76 (chapters 180–96).

4. His method is to quote the first and last sentence of Garibay's section on each monarch. Pérez de Hita may have followed the *Compendio* using the Antwerp, 1571, edition when he dealt with various legends on the origin of Granada, although certain details seem to indicate that he had read the *Crónica General* of Alfonso X. Blanchard-Demouge (pp. xli–xlii) includes also the conquest of Alhama and the story of the queen of Granada—historically the renegade Zoraya, or Zorayra—who became after the conquest Doña Isabel de Granada among the themes of *Civil Wars*, I originating in Garibay. Mention of this author is made by Pérez de Hita in connection with early Nasrid monarchs (*Guerras civiles*, I, 3) and the prestigious office of Alguacil Mayor held under them by the Abencerrajes (I, 37, chap. 5). He probably referred to a passage in Garibay's *Compendio*, book XL, chap. 16 on the appointment of a member of this family "que entre los moros era de muy claro linaje, porque los Abençarraxes fueron en la ciudad de Granada de grande autoridad y estima, y de antigua parentela." Esteban de Garibay, *Compendio historial* (Antwerp, 1571), p. 1124. The historian also reports on unrest in Granada and the Moors' awareness that their civil strifes would bring them disaster; he also tells of a surprise killing in the Alhambra by order of king Mohamad (Boabdil) of some of his most prominent subjects whom he suspected of conspiring against him (chap. 35, p. 1151 and chap. 39, p. 1156).

5. See above, p. 45.

6. He had, of course, gathered abundant documentation for his "Libro de Lorca." On the ballad see note 24 to this chapter.

7. Cf. above, pp. 45 and 57.

8. "Entre los moros guerreros / granadinos naturales" by Lucas Rodríguez, appeared in his *Romancero historiado* and in Pedro de Moncayo's *Flor de varios romances nuevos y canciones* (Huesca, 1589).

9. The legendary theme of the laurel in the Generalife will still inspire the French Romantic poet Théophile Gautier. Cf. Carrasco-Urgoiti, *Moro de Granada*, pp. 270–71.

10. See note 3 to chapter 2.

11. Abundant documentation on the subject in Ladero Quesada, *Castilla y la conquista del reino de Granada* (Valladolid: Universidad, 1967), and *Los mudéjares de Castilla en tiempos de Isabel I* (Valladolid: Instituto Isabel la Católica, 1969). See note 19 to chapter 3 on the historical Abencerrajes.

12. Blanchard-Demouge, in her edition of *Guerras Civiles*, I, xxxvii and xli.

13. Ibid., pp. xlix–1. Actually, the two last chapters of Pulgar's *Crónica* were added after his death (Carriazo, pp. 879 and 896). Having appeared in Latin, ascribed to Antonio de Nebrija, the *Crónica* of Pulgar was published in Spanish—with additional chapters—in Valladolid, 1565, and in Zaragoza, 1567. Cf. Blanchard-Demouge, pp. xxxvii–xxxviii and xlix–1. On the legend of "the Moor's sigh" cf. note 5 to chap. 1.

14. Alfonso de Salazar called Xarton the alleged author of an Arabic text which he claims to be the original of *Lepolemo*, published in Toledo, 1563. In connection with *Don Quijote*, the significance or lack of significance that should be attached to references to spurious sources thereof, found in the works of earlier authors, including Pérez de Hita, has been discussed by G. Stagg, "El sabio Cide Hamete Venengeli," *Bulletin of Hispanic Studies* 33 (1956), 218–25; by B. Wardropper, "Don Quixote: Story or History?" *Modern Philology* 63 (1965), 1–11; by A. Castro, "El cómo y el por qué de Cide Hamete Benengeli" in *Hacia Cervantes*, 3rd. ed (Madrid: Taurus, 1967), pp. 409–419; and recently by Márquez Villanueva, "Fray Antonio de Guevara y Cide Hamete," in *Fuentes literarias cervantinas* (Madrid: Gredos, 1973), pp. 183–257 and by Harvey, *The Moriscos and Don Quijote*. Inaugural lecture in the chair of Spanish . . . at University of London King's College, Nov. 1974 (London, 1975?).

15. Márquez Villanueva, *Fuentes cervantinas*, pp. 241–53.

16. See above, p. 39, and notes 25–27 to chapter 2.

17. See Moreno Báez, "El manierismo de Pérez de Hita," pp. 354, 364 and 365.

18. Ruta, "Ariosto y Pérez de Hita," *Archivum Romanicum* 17 (1933), 665–80.

19. G. Valli, "Ludovico Ariosto y Ginés Pérez de Hita," *Revista de Filología Española* 30 (1946), 23–53.

20. Chevalier, *Los temas ariostescos en el romancero*, pp. 326–28. "En siendo Agricán vencido / de aquel poderoso Orlando" is the most devout version. "Que en agua santa le lave / con voz débil, mal distinta," of the *Romancero general* (1600), number 1064, is a pious

account of Albayaldos' conversion, consistent with Pérez de Hita's approach to the episode.

21. See his discussion of Pérez de Hita in Chevalier, *Arioste en Espagne,* pp. 274–76.

22. Deferrari, *The Sentimental Moor,* pp. 66–68. The beginning of Gazul's encounter with the champions of the Sultana, the reference to a Narváez who is alcaide of Antequera, and the gesture of the lover crowning himself with roses in the imagined garden scene (*Guerras civiles,* I, 222–25, 255 and 171, chaps. 14, 16, and 13) are also considered as possibly influenced by *El Abencerraje.*

23. See Menéndez Pidal, *Romancero hispánico,* II, 131. Frontier ballads are discussed above, pp. 43–46, and in notes 12–14 to chap. 3.

24. The battle of Alporchones (1452), which is the subject of "Allá en Granada la rica," had been treated by Pérez de Hita in canto 14 of his poem "Libro de Lorca" (text in Acero, pp. 330–40). According to this earlier account, which remains closer to the chronicler's point of view, Alavez was captured and subsequently killed, when he refused to enter Lorca as a prisoner. Pérez de Hita included also in *Guerras civiles* (I, 8–9, chap. 1), a dialogue in *redondillas* between the Castilian captive Quiñonero and the Moorish captain Alavez, expanding the questions and answers of the ballad, which are also found in the manuscript poem. Since the author states that the anniversary of this victory was celebrated each year in Murcia and in Lorca (I, 12, chap. 2), and verbal confrontations are essential to commemorative folk plays of the Moorish and Christian type, it is quite plausible that the dialogue was part of such a piece.

On the Alporchones ballad see Menéndez Pidal, ibid, I, 307–9; Seco de Lucena, *Investigaciones sobre el romancero,* and Charles Aubrun's review of the latter study in *Bulletin Hispanique* 61 (1959), 306–7. Seco de Lucena (pp. 29–40) considers "Allá en Granada la rica" to be a sixteenth-century poem and deems it possible that it was composed by Pérez de Hita. Aubrun, who views the ballads as poetry composed by individual authors, had concluded in an earlier study that "Alporchones" was written shortly after 1543.

25. Cf. Menéndez Pidal, ibid., II, 34–35. The occasion for the ballad is not clear, but more than one historical figure of Moslem Granada bore the name of Reduán. Cf. Seco de Lucena in *Al-Andalus* 21 (1956), 285–96.

26. A crucifix is used as an emblem in this and in other ballads. Cf. Bénichou, *Creación poética,* p. 33.

27. See note 23 to chap. 3 and below, p. 138.

28. Variants with the refrain appear in musical collections as well as in the late version in *Guerras civiles.* Cf. Montesinos, "Algunos

problemas del romancero nuevo," note 15. Ballads on the theme of the loss of Alhama had an extraordinary persistence in oral tradition, their imprint being still recognizable in a traditional song of American Sephardic Jews who migrated from the Balkan countries. See S. G. Armistead and J. H. Silverman in *Nueva Revista de Filología Hispánica* 13 (1959), 88–98.

29. On "Abenámar" see note 18 to chap. 3. A longer version of "Estando el rey Don Fernando" had appeared in an undated sixteenth-century *pliego suelto*. See Menéndez Pidal, ed., *Pliegos poéticos españoles de la Universidad de Praga* (Madrid: Joyas Bibliográficas, 1960), vol. II, no. 54. The main historical motif behind "Río Verde" dates back to 1448, but it appears to have been written in the sixteenth century, using historical references and integrating with the old theme the death of Don Alonso at the hand of insurgent Moriscos, which occurred in 1601. Cf. Seco de Lucena, *Investigaciones*.

30. See above p. 99. More standard long versions of "Ay Dios, qué buen caballero"—opening with ·lines close to the fragment in *Civil Wars* and ending with the death of the unconverted Moor— were published in the Zaragoza, 1550 and 1552, editions of *Segunda parte de la Silva de romances* (Rodríguez Moñiño, *La Silva*, p. 137) and in pliegos sueltos now easily available: *Pliegos . . . Praga*, no. 68, and J. A. García Noblejas, ed., *Pliegos poéticos góticos de la Biblioteca Nacional* (Madrid: Joyas Bibliográficas, 1957–61), no. 87. For an assessment of this type of pamphlet see Rodríguez Moñino's introductory study to his *Diccionario de pliegos sueltos*.

31. This poem, also on the Maestre, appeared in the same editions of *La Silva* mentioned in note 30 and in pliegos. Pérez de Hita changed the assonance, and his version has survived until this century in oral tradition: Menéndez Pidal, *Romancero Hispánico*, I, 316. On the slim historical basis of these poems and the Santa Fe ballads, with which they share the theme of challenge and duel and a characterization of the Moor stressing arrogance and hatred, see references 22 and 23 to chap. 3. The same might be said of the ballads on Don Manuel Ponce de León which Pérez de Hita does not include, although he makes of the protagonist an important character of his book.

32. Knoke, pp. 154–55.

33. Deferrari, pp. 47–48. "En la ciudad de Granada / grandes alaridos dan"—included in the Antwerp, n.d. and 1566, editions of Sepúlveda's *Cancionero*—uses the topos to describe the distress of the Moors on the day of Ferdinand's and Isabella's entrance into Granada.

34. Cf. Menéndez Pidal, *Romancero hispánico*, II, 36. For a comparison of the variants of "La mañana de San Juan," as well as of

fictionalized versions, including those found in the *Romancero his-toriado* of Lucas Rodríguez and *Civil Wars*, see López Estrada, "La conquista de Antequera en el romancero y en la épica de los Siglos de Oro," *Anales de la Universidad Hispalense* 16 (1955), 135–92.

35. Rodríguez, *Romancero historiado*, ed. Rodríguez, Moñino, pp. 153–54. The ballad was included by Pedro de Moncayo in his first *Flor de varios romances nuevos y canciones* (Huesca, 1589), as were other Lucas Rodríguez poems which have thematic elements in common with Pérez de Hita. Among them is the glosa "Entre los moros guerreros," mentioned above (note 8), the ballad "Con los francos Vencerrajes," and a small cycle on the adventures of Albenzaide and Tarifa, which is similar to Pérez de Hita's love stories and also includes a duel of three Christian champions fighting in favor of a Moorish woman. Such similarities indicate a trend in the fictionalized revival of Moorish subjects, but they do not prove that Pérez de Hita knew all those narrative poems, which included some inspired by *El Abencerraje*. The ballad "En el Alhambra en Granada / donde el Rey Chico vivía," which deals with the same trivia involving Muça, Daraxa, and Abenhamete reported in chap. 5 of *Civil Wars, I*, appeared in the first *Flor* but was omitted in Moncayo's subsequent collections and the *Romancero general*. The poem was reprinted in the *Jardín de amadores*. Cf. Montesinos in *Bulletin Hispanique* 54 (1952), 402.

As Montesinos observed, the 1589 collection represented a transition from the period characterized by an abundant production of narrative poems on Moorish subjects, written by mediocre poets, to the new vogue of lyrical Moorish ballads intended to be sung. The success of this trend, started by young poets of Lope's generation, made Rodríguez's poems obsolete, and they were not included in Moncayo's subsequent collections. See Montesinos "Algunos problemas del romancero nuevo," *Romance Philology* 6 (1953), 231–47. Reprinted in his *Estudios y ensayos de literatura española* (México: Andrea, 1959), pp. 75–98. See also Rodríguez Moñino's introduction to his edition of Lucas Rodríguez.

The main collections of traditional ballads continued to be printed, in spite of the proliferation of pamphlets and of anthologies of ballads and songs in the new style that followed Moncayo's first *Flor* of 1589. Rodríguez Moñino, *Las series valencianas del romancero nuevo y cancionerillos de Munich* (Valencia: Instituto Alfonso el Magnánimo, 1963), pp. 9–11.

36. The Padilla ballads appeared in his *Tesoro de varias poesías* (1580). They are included in Durán, nos. 82 and 83.

37. These are "Afuera, afuera, afuera" and "Ocho a ocho, diez a

diez," which were also printed in an undated pliego of six ballads. See Rodríguez Moñino, *Pliegos*, p. 437.

Both Moncayo collections include "Ensíllenme el potro rucio" and "Por arrimo su albornoz," of which Pérez de Hita quotes only initial fragments—in the second case after the different opening lines of "En las huertas de Almería / estava el moro Abenámar." The same is true of "Por la plaza de Sanlúcar," appearing in *Civil Wars* with the name of the lady changed from Celinda to Lindaraja, and of "Sale la estrella de Venus," which is substantially unaltered. The two first Moncayo collections have been edited by Rodríguez Moñino in *Las fuentes del Romancero General*, vols. I and II.

"Afuera, afuera, afuera," "Ensíllenme el potro rucio," "Por la calle de su dama," and "Sale la estrella de Venus" have been attributed to Lope de Vega (see below, note 39). So have two poems in the *Flor* of 1591—"Estando toda la corte / de Almanzor, rey de Granada" (see note 40) and "De los tropheos de amor / ya coronadas sus sienes"—which are respectively related in theme to Pérez de Hita's "Estando toda la corte / de Abdilí rey de Granada" and "Adornado de preseas / de la bella Lindaraja," found in *Guerras civiles*. A topos of another poem in Pérez de Hita—"De honra y trofeos lleno / más que el gran Marte lo ha sido"—may have been suggested by the ballad attributed to Lope, "En el tiempo que Celinda / cerró airada la ventana," which appeared in the Moncayo collections of 1589 and 1591. For a study of such relationship, see M. Goyri de Menéndez Pidal, "Los romances de Gazul," *Nueva Revista de Filología Hispánica* 7 (1953), 403–16.

The four ballads in Pérez de Hita on the Zaide-Zaida cycle are copies or adaptations of widely popularized poems by Lope (see above, p. 50) and are not found, however, in the two first Moncayo collections. "Mira, Zaide, que te aviso" and "Di, Zaida, ¿de qué me avisas?" were published in two *quadernos* printed in Valencia in 1593 (Rodríguez Moñino, *Pliegos*, pp. 606–7), as well as in Moncayo's *Tercera parte de la Flor* (Valencia, 1593). Within the latter volume, "Mira, Zaide, que te digo" appears in the section added by Felipe Mey to Moncayo's collection. A facsimile edition is in Rodríguez Moñino, *Fuentes del Romancero general*, vol. III. See also Montesinos' notes to Lope de Vega, *Poesías líricas* (Clásicos Castellanos, 68 and 75), I, 194, and Rodríguez Moñino, *Series valencianas*. (We indicate in the text of chapter 6 the pages of *Guerras civiles* where ballads here mentioned appear.)

38. This poem is only related in its first six lines to "Galiana está en Toledo / labrando una rica manga," which appears in the collections by Moncayo of 1589 and 1591.

39. On attributions to Lope de Vega of Moorish ballads, see, in

addition to studies mentioned in note 37, J. Millé, "Apuntes para una bibliografía de las obras no dramáticas atribuidas a Lope de Vega," *Revue Hispanique* 74 (1928), 345–572 (specifically pp. 353, 356, 402, and 460), and Montesinos' review of this study in *Revista de Filología Española* 19 (1932), 73–82. Coming back to the subject many years later, the latter critic advised caution: See Montesinos, *Estudios sobre Lope* (México: El Colegio de México, 1951), p. 325. See also his studies "Algunas notas sobre el romancero *Ramillete de Flores*," *Nueva Revista de Filología Hispánica* 6 (1952), 352–78; "Notas a la Primera Parte de *Flor de romances*," *Bulletin Hispanique* 54 (1952), 386–404; and "Algunos problemas del romancero nuevo," cited in note 35. Such reservations do not apply to "Sale la estrella de Venus," "Mira, Zaide, que te aviso," and "Di, Zaida, de que me avisas." Critics agree that these poems were composed by Lope.

40. Doña María Goyri, "Los romances de Gazul," indicated that "Estando toda la corte / de Almanzor, rey de Granada," published by Moncayo in the *Flor* of 1591, refers under the name of Gazul to a young nobleman, son of the marqués de la Algaba. The text in Pérez de Hita may be an imitation of this poem or perhaps an independent composition written on the same occasion.

41. Goyri, "Los romances de Gazul," pp. 403–16; and Alvar, *El romancero*, pp. 98–103.

42. "Petrarchan" applied here as it has been used and defined by Dámaso Alonso in his stylistic analysis of sixteenth-century manneristic poetry. See note 38 to chap. 3.

43. *muera* is the correct reading. Lope, *Poesías líricas*, ed. Montesinos, I, 47.

44. Paul Bénichou, *Romancero judeo-español de Marruecos* (Madrid: Castalia, 1968), pp. 260–62 and 319–24.

45. Montesinos assessed the literary circles and the attitudes underlying the poetry of the period in "Lope de Vega, poeta de circunstancias" and "Lope y su tiempo," *Estudios sobre Lope*, pp. 292–312.

46. Cf. below, pp. 140–43.

Chapter Seven

1. Robert Scholes and Robert Kellogg. *The Nature of Narrative* (New York: Oxford, 1966), p. 228.

2. Madeleine de Scudéry (1607?–1701). Her works were published under the name of her brother Georges, who may actually have written *Almahide*. In any case, this long novel is a characteristic product of précieux style. Cf. Carrasco-Urgoiti, *Moro de Granada*, pp. 105–11.

3. When writing the history of the rebellion, Perez de Hita explained that he inserted romances "por no quebrar el estilo de la primera parte" (*Guerras civiles*, II, 10, chap. 1).

4. These terms are used as defined by Northrop Frye, *Anatomy of Criticism* (Princeton University Press, 1957), pp. 303–7.

5. A comprehensive survey of views held in Pérez de Hita's time by the Spanish reading public, as well as by individual scholars, on the subject of truth and verisimilitude in literary works may be read in Alban K. Forcione, *Cervantes, Aristotle and the Persiles* (Princeton: Princeton University Press, 1970), pp. 11–87.

6. "The chief difference between narrative and scene is accordingly of the general-particular type: summary narrative is a generalized account or report of a series of events covering some extended period and a variety of locales, and seems to be the normal untutored mode of story-telling; immediate scene emerges as soon as the specific, continuous, and succesive details of time, place, action, character, and dialogue begin to appear. Not dialogue alone, but concrete detail within a specific time-place frame is the *sine qua non* of scene." Thus Norman Friedman, "Point of View in Fiction," in Robert M. Davis, ed., *The Novel: Modern Essays in Criticism* (Englewood Cliffs, N. J.: Prentice Hall, 1969), pp. 142–71. p. 153.

7. In 1570 the count of Bailén had requested, like other noblemen, that his Morisco vassals be allowed to remain in the land he possessed in the former kingdom of Granada; when the authorization was denied, he obtained permission to resettle these families in his Castilian states. See B. Vincent in *Mélanges de la Casa de Velázquez* (Madrid) 7 (1971), 397–98.

8. The genealogy of the fourth count of Bailén, who fought as a captain in Orán, is given in Alonso López de Haro, *Segunda parte del nobiliario genealógico* (Madrid, 1622), pp. 118–19.

Next to illustrious patrons, such as Ponce de León or Fajardo, mention is made in *Civil Wars* of hidalgo families known personally to the author, like Almodóvar, Pérez de Hita, or Botía (*Guerras civiles*, I, 274 and II, 55 and 146–47.)

9. Cf. above, p. 105.

10. See, for instance, comments by Alvar, p. 159.

11. "Cuál será aquel caballero, / de los míos más preciado." Published in 'a pliego suelto ascribing the glosa to Padilla (possibly Pedro de Padilla. Cf. Rodríguez Moñino, *Pliegos*, p. 38).

12. The publication of *Civil Wars, I* in 1595 and the advent to the throne three years later of the young king Felipé III were factors encouraging the subsequent proliferation of *relaciones de fiestas*. (Cf. Benítez Claros, article cited in note 36 to chap. 3).

However, some of the manuscript and printed texts reviewed by Jenaro Alenda, *Relaciones de solemnidades y fiestas públicas de España* (Madrid: Sucs. de Rivadeneyra, 1903), indicate that the genre, with its emphasis on descriptive detail, was already flourishing in the sixteenth century. See nos. 84, 251, 266, 280, 281, 322, 310, and 331.

13. See note 11 to chap. 1.

14. The point is considered in my article cited in note 23 to chap. 5.

15. Cf. R. Ricard, in *Bulletin Hispanique* 53 (1951), 131–56.

16. J. Martínez Ruiz, "La indumentaria de los moriscos según Pérez de Hita y los documentos de la Alhambra" *Cuadernos de la Alhambra* 3 (1967), 55–124. As a result of conscientious tabulating, Martínez Ruiz notices the absence of *libreas* (of which forty-four are mentioned in *Civil Wars, I* against forty *marlotas*) in the inventories of Morisco-owned clothing and jewelry, and he observes also the omission of *almalafas* in Pérez de Hita's generally accurate description of the appearance of Moorish characters (pp. 62-66 and 89–90).

17. Cf. the article cited in note 31 to chap. 5 For a lucid discussion of mannerism, see Wylie Sypher, *Four Stages in Renaissance Style* (New York: Doubleday, 1955), pp. 100–170. With reference to Spanish Golden Age literature, critical approaches and terminology are examined by O. Macrí in *Thesaurus* 15 (1960), 1–70.

18. This genre has been surveyed by Alfredo Hermenegildo, *Los trágicos españoles del siglo XVI* (Madrid: Fundación Universitaria, 1961).

19. See above, pp. 74–79, and note 15 to chap. 5.

20. For an assessment of the Morisco episodes in *Don Quijote,* "El coloquio de los perros," and *Los trabajos de Persiles y Sigismunda* see Américo Castro, *El pensamiento de Cervantes,* ed. J. Rodríguez Puértolas (Barcelona: Noguer, 1972), pp. 280–89 and 320–24; A. Oliver, "El morisco Ricote," *Anales Cervantinos* 5 (1955–1956), 249–55; and V. Llorens, "Historia y ficción en el *Quijote,*" *Papeles de Son Armadans,* no. 84 (March, 1963), pp. 235–58. Another view is in Gustaf Freden, *Tres ensayos cervantinos* (Madrid: Insula, 1964), pp. 7–31. Additions: Harvey, study cited in note 14 to chapter 6, and Márquez Villanueva, *Personajes y temas del Quijote* (Madrid: Taurus, 1975), pp. 229–335.

On Lope de Vega's "La desdicha por la honra," which appeared in the same volume as *La Circe* in 1624 and is included in his *Novelas a Marcia Leonarda,* see study by Marcel Bataillon in *Nueva Revista de Filología Hispánica* 1 (1947), 13–42 (Reprinted in *Varia lección*). Lope's short novel as well as Espinel's Valencian Morisco who turns into a Turkish pirate (*Marcos de Obregón*, Relación Segunda, Descansos 8–13) are discussed by Albert Mas, *Les Turcs dans la littérature espagnole du Siècle d'Or* (Paris: Centre de Recherches Hispaniques, 1967), I, 487–97 and 542–49.

21. Haxa, appearing in mourning at the court of the Rey Chico (*Guerras civiles*, I, 157, chap. 12), wears the end of her *almayzar* in front of her face, in the same manner as Spanish ladies often used their *manto*. This custom, though possibly of Moorish origin, was quite common.

On the omission of the garment called *almalafa* see note 16 to this chapter.

22. The Sevilla, 1613, edition, which departs frequently from the text of the princeps, refers also to the dying Albayaldos as "nuevo convertido," the usual expression designating a Morisco. The princeps in this passage reads "valeroso caballero," Blanchard-Demouge lists variants in *Guerras civiles*, I, 317–20.

Chapter Eight

1. The full title reads: *Segunda parte de las guerras civiles de Granada, y de los crueles vandos, entre los conuertidos moros y vezinos ch[r]istianos: con el leuantamiento de todo el Reyno y ultima reuelion, sucedida en el año de 1568, L assi mismo se pone su total ruyna, y destierro de los moros por toda Castilla. Con el fin de las granadinas guerras por el rey nuestro señor, don Felipe Segundo deste nombre.* See note 42 to chap. 5 concerning variations in preliminary material of the Cuenca and Barcelona editions of 1619.

2. See above, and notes 40–41 to chapter 5.

3. Like Pérez de Hita, the alférez Thomás Pérez de Evia contributed two sonnets to the *Reales exequias* (1600), ed. J. A. de Almela, on the occasion of the death of Philip II.

4. Hurtado de Mendoza, *De la guerra de Granada*. Critical edition by M. Gómez Moreno. Memorial Histórico Español, 49 (Madrid: Real Academia de la Historia, 1948). Another edition, with notes comparing data given by the three historians of the rebellion, is that of B. Blanco-González. Clásicos Castalia, 22 (Madrid, 1970).

5. Cf. Caro, *Los moriscos del reino de Granada*, p. 146. The possibility that Mármol may have written to counteract the effect of Don Diego's book has been considered. Cf. B. Sánchez Alonso, "La literatura histórica en el siglo XVI," in *Historia general de las literaturas hispánicas*, ed. G. Díaz Plaja, III (Barcelona: Barna,

1953), pp. 310–11. Both works—Mendoza's and Mármol's—are included in *Historiadores de sucesos particulares*. Biblioteca de Autores Españoles, 21.

6. Gómez Moreno, introduction to Hurtado de Mendoza, *Guerra de Granada*, pp. xxvii–xxxii. He publishes excerpts of the Antonio Porcel MS., containing the material added to Hurtado de Mendoza, which is related to Pérez de Hita's text, pp. 24–55.

7. Blanchard-Demouge in her introduction to *Guerras civiles*, II, xv–xxiii, studies the influence of *La Austriada* on several episodes told by Pérez de Hita.

8. Pérez de Hita indicates, e.g., that the first Turks arrived in February of 1569. Cf. Blanco González in his edition of Hurtado de Mendoza, *Guerra de Granada*, p. 124, n. 71. Cf. also p. 210, n. 259.

9. *Los moriscos*, p. 169.

10. Caro Baroja, ibid., pp. 50–51, shows the existence of such divisions, related in part to old feuds between traditionally opposed families.

11. Blanchard-Demouge, pp. xxiii–xxv.

12. The poem has been discussed above, p. 84, and in note 39 to chap. 5.

13. See a comparative study of the treatment of this episode by Hurtado de Mendoza, Rufo and Pérez de Hita in Mas, I, 269–77.

14. "y si no fuera porque esta historia es toda coscorrones y armas y batallas, tratáramos las ternezas destos dos amantes y sus estremados amores" (*Guerras civiles*, II, 153, chap. 14).

15. The Marqués de los Vélez wrote that he had reports of murders of women committed by his own soldiers, as well as by the Moriscos during the struggle for Oháñez. See Gregorio Marañón, *Los tres Vélez* (Madrid: Espasa Calpe, 1960), p. 75.

16. *Orígenes de la novela*, chap. 7, p. ccclxv. The passages referred to appear in the fifth canto of the *Æneid*, which had been translated by Gregorio Hernández de Velasco, and in the canto 2 of the first part of *La Araucana* published in 1569.

17. Less interesting are the ballads, for the most part original, inserted at the end of each chapter. See above, p. 82.

18. See, e.g., Moreno Báez, "El manierismo de Pérez de Hita," p. 354.

19. ". . . con todo eso me persuado a que, si antes que estos hubieran llegado a la desesperación que les puso en tan malos pensamientos, se hubiera buscado forma de admitirlos a alguna parte de honores . . . fuera posible que por la puerta del honor hubieran entrado al templo de la virtud y al gremio y obediencia de la Iglesia católica." Discurso VII, *Conservación de monarquías y*

Discursos políticos (1625). Biblioteca de Autores Españoles, 25 (Madrid: 1866), p. 466.

20. See above, p. 85 and notes 42–43 to chap. 5.

21. See bibliography in the edition of Blanchard-Demouge.

22. See A. Valbuena-Briones, "La guerra civil de Granada a través del arte de Calderón," *Homenaje a William L. Fichter* (Madrid: Castalia, 1971), pp. 735–44.

23. Romantic interpretations of the plight of the Moriscos appear in works by Coleridge, Trueba y Cossío, Martínez de la Rosa, and Estébanez Calderón, among others. Cf. Carrasco-Urgoiti, *El moro de Granada en la literatura*, pp. 284–89, 296–300, 307–8 and 319–37. See also below, pp. 141–42.

Chapter Nine

1. See annotated edition by Francisco Rico, in *La novela picaresca española* (Barcelona: Planeta, 1967), I, 194–244. Cf. also Moreno Báez, *Lección y sentido del Guzmán de Alfarache. Revista de Filología Española*, Anejo 40 (Madrid, 1948), pp. 183–85; see also Donald McGrady, *Mateo Alemán* (New York: Twayne Publishers, 1968), pp. 147–57; Angel San Miguel, *Sentido y estructura del "Guzmán de Alfarache" de Mateo Alemán* (Madrid: Gredos, 1971), pp. 245–52; articles by McGrady in *Revista de Filología Española* 48 (1965), 283–92; A. Soons in *Romanische Forschungen* 78 (1966), 567–69; and G. Mancini in *Prohemio* 2, no. 3 (Dec., 1971), 417–37.

2. See above, p. 51 and note 35 to chap. 3.

3. The diverse interpretations of the Moor given in his theater have been well studied by Gisela Labib in the doctoral dissertation cited in note 16 to chap. 2. On images of Granada in Lope's plays see Emilio Orozco Díaz, *Granada en la poesía barroca* (Granada: Universidad, 1963), pp. 55–67.

4. Cf. the article by Carrasco-Urgoiti in *Homenaje a Fichter*, pp. 115–25.

5. The theme of *El Abencerraje* in Spanish Golden Age literature has been studied by Moreno Báez in *Archivum* 4 (1954), 310–29. See other references in note 45 to chap. 4.

6. Cf. Carrasco-Urgoiti in *Papeles de Son Armadans*, no. 96 (March, 1964), pp. 255–98.

7. Cf. Wardropper in *Modern Language Review* 53 (1958), 512–20.

8. See note 22 to chap. 8.

9. Unless otherwise indicated, what follows is based on my previous study *El moro de Granada en la literatura*. A recent book on the

subject is Neal A. Wiegman, *Ginés Pérez de Hita y la novela romántica* (Madrid: Plaza Mayor, 1971).

10. See the study on the taurine works of Moratín, by J. C. Dowling in *The South Central Bulletin* (Tulsa, Okl.) 22, no. 4 (1962), 31–34.

11. On the premiere, cf. Dowling in *Homenaje a Rodríguez Moñino* (Madrid: Castalia, 1966), I, 147–54.

12. Controversy on this subject is summarized by F. Letessier in his edition of Chateaubriand, *Atala, René, Les Aventures du dernier Abencérage* (Paris: Garnier, 1962), appendix 3. The novel was written long before its publication.

13. Hedges, *Washington Irving: An American Study, 1802–1832* (Baltimore: Johns Hopkins Press, 1965), p. 254.

14. Ibid., p. 256. See also Stanley T. Williams, *The Spanish Background of American Literature* (New York: Dryden, 1955), II, 6–45; and A. Soria in *Arbor* 44 (1959), 144–62. On Spanish translations of *The Alhambra* see A. Gallego Morell in *Revista Hispánica Moderna* 26, No. 3–4 (Jul.–Oct. 1960), 136–42. Irving's version of *El Abencerraje* is discussed above, p. 64.

15. Cf. Lida de Malkiel, "El moro en las letras castellanas" (cited in note 3 to chap. 3).

Selected Bibliography

PRIMARY SOURCES

1.   Editions of *Civil Wars of Granada, Part One*

Historia de los vandos de los Zegries y Abencerrajes Caualleros Moros de Granada, de las Ciuiles guerras que huuo en ella, y batallas particulares que huuo en la Vega entre Moros y Christianos, hasta que el Rey Don Fernando Quinto la ganó. Agora nuevamente sacado de un libro Arauigo, cuyo autor de vista fue vn Moro llamado Aben Hamin, natural de Granada. Tratando desde su fundacion. Tradvcido en castellano por Gines Perez de Hita, vezino de la ciudad de Murcia. [Coat of arms]. Con Licencia y Priuilegio. En Çaragoça. Impresso en casa de Miguel Ximeno Sanchez. M. D. LXXXXV. A costa de Angelo Tabano.

Historia de los vandos de los Cegries y Abencerrages.... Traduzido en castellano por Gines Perez. Corregida y emendada en esta segunda impression. Con licencia y priuilegio. Impresso en Valencia en casa de Pedro Patricio, año 1597. Another edition was published by the same printer in 1604.

Hystoria de los vandos de los Cegries y Abencerrajes... Dirigido a Don Fernando de Castro. En Lisboa Impresso por Pedro Crasbeck 1598. A costa de Dominguos Martines mercader de libros. Reprinted in 1603 by Antonio Alvarez.

Historia de los vandos de los Zegries y Abencerrages.... Con licencia en Alcalá de Henares en casa de Juan Gracian, ... 1601. This is the earliest extant Castilian edition. It is based on Zaragoza, 1595 and carries an aprobación by El licenciado Berrio dated in Madrid, June 17, 1598. The same publisher reissued the book, at least in 1604, 1610, and 1619. Other editions have been mentioned.

Historia de los vandos de los Zegries y Abencerrages.... En Barcelona, 1604. Con licencia. A costa de Raphael Nogues Librero.... Joan Amello Impressor. Other Barcelona editions were published in 1610 and 1647 (the latter in H. S. A. Hispanic Society of America).

Historia de las Guerras civiles de Granada.... Paris, 1606. The author's name does not appear. The editor, a "sieur Fortan," gave

French equivalents of certain words as marginal notes. Permission to print was obtained in Rouen, 1603. The edition is dedicated in Paris, 1606, to the "Marquesa de Vernoeil." It served as basis for the editions of Paris, 1660, and Anvers, 1714.

Historia de los vandos de los Zegris y Abencerrages.... En Sevilla por Matias Clauijo, 1613. This edition offers a text considerably altered by stylistic corrections and brief occasional interpolations. It is the basis for subsequent editions, including Málaga, 1613; Sevilla, 1625 (H. S. A.), 1633, 1638; Madrid 1645, 1655, 1662, 1680, and 1690, as well as all eighteenth- and nineteenth-century editions. See introductory study and appendix by Blanchard-Demouge for the main variants and further bibliographical details.

Not counting mention of unconfirmed printings, Blanchard-Demouge lists nine eighteenth-century editions, to which may be added Sevilla, 1762, and Córdoba, n. d. (by the late eighteenth-century publisher Juan Rodríguez de la Torre), both in the Biblioteca Nacional. *Guerras civiles de Granada* was included in series inspired by the Romantic· revival. Listed by José Simón Díaz in *Bibliografía de la literatura hispánica,* vol. I, are Bibliotheca Española, ed. C. Maucke Chémnitz (Gotha: Steudel & Keil, 1805–12), vols. 1–2; Colección de los Mejores Autores Españoles, vol. 45 (Paris: Baudry, 1847), and Biblioteca Granadina, vols. 1–3 (Granada: M. Sanz, 1848). The three series include the second part. Similarly, an edition with learned introduction (Madrid: León Amarita, 1833) which was attributed, according to Palau, to Serafín Estébanez Calderón, and *Novelistas anteriores a Cervantes,* ed. B. C. Aribau, Biblioteca de Autores Españoles, 3 (Madrid, 1849). All of these are modernized editions based on Sevilla, 1613. For other modern printings see José M. Tejera y R. de Moncada, *Biblioteca del murciano.*

Ginés Pérez de Hita. *Guerras civiles de Granada.* Edited, with introduction and notes, by P. Blanchard-Demouge, vol. I (Madrid: Centro de Estudios Históricos, 1913). This edition reproduces, with the old spelling, the text of the princeps. Main variants of Sevilla, 1613, are listed in appendix. The volume includes a detailed bibliographical, as well as historical and critical, study. Unless otherwise indicated, we follow this source with reference to bibliography.

2. Translations of *Civil Wars of Granada, Part One*

Civil Wars, I was first translated anonymously into French (Paris, 1608). The abridged version of the novelist Mlle de la Roche Guilhén, appeared in Paris, 1683. A third French translation was produced by A. M. Sané (Paris, 1809). A. Palau, *Manual del librero hispano-americano*, lists the Portuguese translation of Hyeronimo Moreira de Carvalho (Lisboa: Occidental, 1735). Thomas Rodd published his English text of *The Civil Wars of Granada* in London, 1803. A German version, based on the French by Sané, appeared in Bremen, 1810 (Palau). Direct translations from the Spanish into German were produced by Karl August Wilhelm Spalding (Berlin, 1821), and by Paul Weiland (Munich, 1913). As indicated above, pp. 00–00, Rodd and more eminent authors of the Romantic period published separately a considerable number of translations or adaptations of the ballads in Pérez de Hita's book.

3. *The Second Part of the Civil Wars of Granada*

Segunda parte de las Guerras Cíviles de Granada, y de los crueles vandos, entre los conuertidos Moros y vezinos Ch[r]istianos: con el leuantamiento de todo el Reyno y ultima reuelion, sucedida en el año de 1568 . . . por Gines Perez vécino de Murcia. . . . En Cuenca, por Domingo de la Iglesia año de 1619.

The edition is dedicated to a different patron in each of the two extant copies of Cuenca: Domingo de la Iglesia, 1619. Preliminaries vary accordingly. The variant represented by a copy in the Hispanic Society of America is addressed to the duke of Infantado, Mayordomo del Rey, and the dedicatory epistle is signed by Christiano Bernabé, who describes himself in the text as "Archero de Corps de su Magestad." The copy in the Biblioteca Nacional, which was repro-duced by P. Blanchard-Demouge, carries a dedication to the canon of Cuenca, Alonso del Pozo Palomino by Andrés Miguel, as well as three laudatory sonnets indentifying the latter as a publisher. The name of Christiano Bernabe [Bernabé?] appears, however, in the Tassa, which was granted at his request on April 17, 1619. The same year the book appeared in Barcelona, issued separately by Estavan Liberós "a costa de Miguel Manescal," and by Sebastián de Cormellas. Both variants of the Barcelona edition include the inscription to the duke of Infantado and none of the material related to Pozo Palomino and Miguel.

The next edition was apparently that of Madrid: Juan García In-fanzón, 1696. The book was printed in Madrid in 1724 and 1731. It reappeared jointly with *Civil Wars, Part One* in the nineteenth-century editions already mentioned, including *Novelistas anteriores a Cer-vantes*, B.A.E., 3.

Ginés Pérez de Hita, *Guerras civiles de Granada*. Edited, with introduction and notes, by P. Blanchard-Demouge, vol. 2 (Madrid: Centro de Estudios Históricos, 1915).

4. Manuscript Poems

"Libro de la Poblazion y Hazañas de la mui novilissima y leal ciudad de Lorca. Compuesto por Gines Perez de Hita Vezino de esta dicha ziu [dad] año de 1572." 216 ff. Biblioteca Nacional, MS. 19,610. The first part was published by Acero y Abad (see Bibliography, Secondary Sources).

"Los diez y siete libros de Daris del Belo troyano agora nuebamente sacado delas antiguas y verdaderas ystorias en verso por Guines [sic] Perez de Hita, V[ecino] dela çiudad de Murçia; año de 1596." 505 ff. Biblioteca Nacional, Madrid, MS. 9,847.

SECONDARY SOURCES

1. Studies on *El Abencerraje*

BATAILLON, MARCEL. "Salmacis y Trocho en *El Abencerraje*." In *Hommage à Ernest Martinenche*, pp. 355–63. Paris: d'Artrey, 1939. Clarifies an allusion to the fable of Hermaphroditus in a passage which was considered to be incorrectly rendered in the *Inventario* version. The originality and priority of this version is advanced mainly on the basis of its excellence. For additions in support of López Estrada's views on the plausibility of Villegas' authorship of *El Abencerraje* see *Bulletin Hispanique* 62 (1960), 198–206.

CARRASCO-URGOITI, MARÍA SOLEDAD. "El relato corto 'Historia del moro y Narváez' y *El Abencerraje*." *Revista Hispánica Moderna* 34 (1968), 242–55. Submits that the *relato* represents an early stage in the literary treatment of the frontier incident reported.

—————. "Las cortes señoriales del Aragón mudéjar y *El Abencerraje*." In *Homenaje a Casalduero*, pp. 115–28. Madrid: Gredos, 1972. Discusses literary currents and political tensions in the circle to which the unknown writer of *Parte de la Corónica* belonged, assessing the possible relevance of these currents and tensions to the genesis of the novel.

CIROT, GEORGE. "A propos de la nouvelle de l'Abencerrage." *Bulletin Hispanique* 31 (1929), 131–38. Historical accuracy and error in the setting of the novel are discussed, and the main inconsistency is tentatively explained.

CRAWFORD, J. P. WICKERSHAM. "Un episodio de *El Abencerraje* y una 'Novella' de Ser Giovanni." *Revista de Filología Española* 10 (1923), 281–87. Finds in a novel of Ser Giovanni Fiorentini's *Il Pecorone*, published in 1558, the source of a story about Narváez appearing only in the *Inventario* version.

DALE, GEORGE IRVING. "An unpublished version of the *Historia de Abindarráez y Jarifa*." *Modern Language Notes* 39 (1924), 31–33. First scholarly edition of the manuscript text "Historia del moro y Narváez."

GIMENO CASALDUERO, JOAQUÍN. "*El Abencerraje y la hermosa Jarifa*: composición y significado." *Nueva Revista de Filología Hispánica* 21 (1972), 1–22. An expert analysis of artistic forms and concepts: five nuclei articulate structurally the themes of love and heroism. These converge in the exaltation of a neo-Senecan virtue exemplified by the main characters and set forth as a goal for every person.

GLENN, RICHARD F. "The moral implications of *El Abencerraje*." *MLN* 80 (1965), 202–209. A discussion of the novel's ethical content, based chiefly on the semantic comparison of words used in the text to signify the characteristics of the Christian and the Moorish knight.

GUILLÉN, CLAUDIO. "Individuo. y ejemplaridad en *El Abencerraje*." In *Collected Studies in honor of Américo Castro's Eightieth Year*, pp. 2–23. Oxford: The Lincombe Lodge Research Library, 1965. An enlightening interpretation of the art of composition and the style of *El Abencerraje*, the components of which, according to the author, consistently create an image of cleavage counterbalanced by a symbol of union. This artistic form embodies an exemplary meaning which it is possible to relate to the experience of the converso class. Facts concerning the background of *Inventario* and *Parte de la Corónica* are examined in support of this view.

————. "*Lazarillo de Tormes*" *and* "*El Abencerraje*." Introduction and notes by C. Guillén. New York: The Laurel Language Library, 1966. Summarizes conclusions of the preceding study and asesses the influence of the novel in shaping the literary type of the noble Moor.

KELLER, JOHN E. and LÓPEZ ESTRADA, FRANCISCO. *Antonio de Villegas' "El Abencerraje."* University of North Carolina Studies in Comparative Literature, 33. Chapel Hill: University of North Carolina Press, 1964. Texts in Spanish and English of the *Inventario* version and a reliable summary of research on the novel and its influence.

LÓPEZ ESTRADA, FRANCISCO. "Estudio y texto de la narración pastoril

'Ausencia y soledad de amor' del *Inventario* de Villegas." *Boletín de la Real Academia Española* 29 (1949), 101–133. Opposes Menéndez Pelayo's contention that Villegas' pastoral tale and *El Abencerraje* could not have been written by the same person.

————. *El Abencerraje y la hermosa Jarifa: Cuatro textos y su estudio.* Madrid: Publicaciones de Revista de Archivos, Bibliotecas y Museos, 1957. A fundamental work covering the following topics: (a) study of literary and historical factors leading to the stylized image of the Moor of Granada and of Christian-Moorish confrontation; (b) analysis of ideological and formal elements of *El Abencerraje*, seen in the context of contemporary trends; (c) comparative study of the versions of the novel, and discussion of the background, the linguistic traits, and the style of each text; (d) an edition of the three versions of the novel (*Parte de la Corónica* in the fragmentary form available at the time) and of the short story.

————. "El 'Abencerraje' de Toledo, 1561. Edición crítica y comentarios." *Anales de la Universidad Hispalense* 19 (1959), 1–60. A critical edition of the *Parte de la Corónica* text and a study supplementing with respect to this version the preceding book. Establishes the New Christian connections of the Maecenas of the edition. The question of text priority is left open, though favoring *Inventario* as the most likely primary version.

————. "Sobre el cuento de la honra del marido, defendida por el amante, atribuido a Rodrigo de Narváez." *Revista de Filología Española* 47 (1964), 331–39. Discusses a version in a seventeenth-century manuscript of the story told in praise of Narváez's virtue, which appears only in the *Inventario*. The traditional character of the tale is stressed and the influence of *Il Pecorone* noted by Crawford is considered doubtful.

————. "Tres notas al *Abencerraje*." *Revista Hispánica Moderna* 31 (1965), 265–73. Notes a coincidence with Brunetto Latini's *Tesoro* and another with *La cárcel de amor* by Diego de San Pedro. Discusses the semantics of *contemplación* as used in the *Inventario* and *Diana* texts.

MATULKA, BARBARA. "On the European Diffusion of the 'Last of the Abencerrajes' Story in the Sixteenth Century." *Hispania* 16 (1933), 369–88. Deals with the Spanish poem by Balbi de Correggio and considers Italian and French versions of the novel.

MÉRIMÉE, HENRI. "*El Abencerraje* d'après diverses versions publiées au XVIᵐᵉ siècle." *Bulletin Hispanique* 30 (1928), 147–81. Concludes that the relationship between the three texts can only be explained by their dependence on a now lost prototype.

MORENO BÁEZ, ENRIQUE. "El tema del Abencerraje en la literatura española." *Archivum* (Oviedo) 4 (1954), 310–29. In addition to the novel, several romances and Lope de Vega's play *El remedio en la desdicha* are discussed.

RUMEAU, ARISTIDE. " 'L'Abencérage,' un texte retrouvé." *Bulletin Hispanique* 59 (1957), 369–95. Reports the discovery in the Real Academia de la Historia of a long lost copy of the edition printed in Toledo, 1561, of the *Parte de la Corónica* version. The text is reproduced.

SERÍS, HOMERO. "Balbi de Correggio, Francisco." In *Nuevo ensayo de una biblioteca española de libros raros y curiosos*, I, 148–69. New York: Hispanic Society of America, 1964. Study and excerpts of the poem by Balbi on the subject of *El Abencerraje*, plus a critical survey of research on the Moorish novel and its influence.

SOONS, ALAN. "Deux moments de la nouvelle mauresque: *El Abencerraje* (avant 1565) et *Ozmín y Daraja* (1599)." *Romanische Forschungen* 78 (1966), 567–69. Underscores contrasts between the Christian-Stoïc inspiration of *El Abencerraje* and the pessimistic and allegedly conformist outlook of Mateo Alemán's novelette.

WHINNOM, KEITH. "The relationship of the three texts of 'El Abencerraje.' " *The Modern Language Review* 54 (1959), 507–17. Extensive tabulating and study of variants lead to the conclusion that *Parte de la Corónica* was the earlier text, that it was followed by the version in *La Diana*, and that both these texts were known to the writer of the *Inventario* version.

2. Studies on Pérez de Hita

ACERO Y ABAD, NICOLÁS. *Ginés Pérez de Hita. Estudio biográfico y bibliográfico*. Madrid: Hernández, 1888. A miscellany of not always reliable data. Contains some material worthy of consideration, mainly the first part of Pérez de Hita's "Libro de Lorca."

ALVAR, MANUEL. *El Romancero: Tradicionalidad y pervivencia*. Barcelona: Planeta, 1970. Includes valuable studies on the ballads · in *Civil Wars, I*. Their role in shaping the themes and style of the work is considered.

BLANCHARD-DEMOUGE, PAULA. Introductory studies on the two volumes of Pérez de Hita, *Guerras civiles de Granada* (Madrid: Centro de Estudios Históricos, 1913–15). A worthy scholarly contribution, although arguments in favor of the authenticity of Pérez de Hita's Granada, as well as the attempts to identify the Arabic author of the alleged original, are doubtfully valid. The

study of Spanish historical sources is adequate, and the collections
from which most ballads of part one were borrowed have been
specified. The connection between the relaciones de fiestas and
Pérez de Hita's art is established. For biographical purposes
these studies should be used in conjunction with the later findings
by Espín Rael. Volumes I and II of Blanchard-Demouge's edition offer a detailed bibliography and a critical consideration of
the most important editions.

BODMER, DANIEL. *Die granadinischen Romanzen in der europäischen
Literatur.* Zürcher Beiträge zur vergleichende Literaturgeschichte,
5. Zürich: Juris-Verlag, 1955. A monograph on translations and
adaptations, chiefly of the Romantic period, of the most important
ballads inserted in *Civil Wars, I.*

CARO BAROJA, JULIO. *Los moriscos del reino de Granada. Ensayo de
Historia social.* Madrid: Instituto de Estudios Politicos, 1957. A
fundamental study of conflicts reported in *Second part of the
Civil Wars of Granada.* The testimonial value of this book is
stressed.

CARRASCO-URGOITI, MARÍA SOLEDAD. *El moro de Granada en la lite-
tura. Del siglo XV al XX.* Madrid: Revista de Occidente, 1956.
A comparative survey of the treatment and interpretations given
in various literatures to themes formulated in the work of Pérez
de Hita and other Golden Age authors.

————. "Ginés Pérez de Hita frente al problema morisco." *Actas del
IV Congreso de la. Asociación Internacional de Hispanistas,* in
press. Submits that the defense of the status quo and the attempt to restore the prestige of the descendants of the Nasrid
elite is discernible in the two books of *Civil Wars of Granada.*

————. "Les Fêtes équestres dans *Les Guerres civiles de Grenade.*"
In *La Fêtes de la Renaissance,* III, ed. J. Jacquot and E. Konigson, pp. 299–312. Paris: C.N.R.S., 1975. Comments on literary
motifs and elements of the Spanish contemporary scene incorporated by Pérez de Hita into his portrayal of the Nasrid court.
The persuasive value of this composite image is considered.

CHEVALIER, MAXIME. *L' Arioste en Espagne (1530–1650): Recherches
sur l'influence du "Roland furieux."* Bordeaux: Inst. d'Études
Ibériques et Ibéro-Américaines, 1966. Reexamines with modern
criteria Ariosto's influence on Pérez de Hita.

CIROT, GEORGE. "La maurophilie littéraire en Espagne au XVIme
siècle." Articles in *Bulletin Hispanique,* from vol. 40 (1938) to
vol. 46 (1944). A reliable study encompassing various genres
and taking into consideration historical sources and background.
Pérez de Hita is duly considered.

DEFERRARI, HARRY AUSTIN. *The Sentimental Moor in Spanish Literature before 1600.* Univ. of Pennsylvania Publications ... in Romanic Languages and Literatures, 17. Philadelphia, 1927. Surveys extensive material and may still be used with profit, but the author's views on the authenticity of the literary type studied should be considered with caution.

ESPÍN RAEL, JOAQUÍN. *De la vecindad de Pérez de Hita en Lorca desde 1568 a 1577 años.* Lorca: Imp. de Luis Montiel, 1922. Publishes and discusses significant documents proving that the writer was established as an artisan during the years preceding and following the Alpujarras war.

FESTUGIÈRE, PAUL. "Ginés Pérez de Hita: Sa personne, son oeuvre," *Bulletin Hispanique* 46 (1944), 145–83. A general presentation.

GÓMEZ MORENO, MANUEL. Introduction to Diego Hurtado de Mendoza, *Guerra de Granada.* Memorial Histórico Español, 49. Madrid: Real Academia de la Historia, 1928. Includes authoritative discussion of *Segunda parte de las Guerras civiles de Granada.* Additions to Mendoza's work in the Porcel MS are transcribed. It is suggested that this text may have been a source of Pérez de Hita or possibly his own fragmentary draft.

KNOKE, ULRICH. *Die spanische 'Maurenromanze.'* Ph.D. dissertation, University of Göttingen, 1966. An expert analysis of frontier and Moorish ballads giving special consideration to the group inserted in *Civil Wars, I.*

LIDA DE MALKIEL, MARÍA ROSA. "El moro en las letras castellanas." *Hispanic Review* 28 (1960), 350–58. A review article assessing the field covered in Carrasco, *Moro de Granada*, and contributing significant views and additions.

MARTÍNEZ RUIZ, JUAN. "La indumentaria de los moriscos según Pérez de Hita y los documentos de la Alhambra." *Cuadernos de la Alhambra* 3 (1967), 55–124. Analyzes abundant documentation proving that Pérez de Hita's portrayal of Nasrid Granada relies heavily on description of the type of clothing which had been owned by wealthy Moriscos in his time. Also a worthy contribution to lexicography.

MAS, ALBERT. *Les Turcs dans la littérature espagnole du Siècle d'Or.* 2 vols. Paris: Centre de Recherches Hispaniques, 1967. An erudite study in which the literary treatment of certain episodes—including the story of Aben Humeya—in *Second Part of the Civil Wars of Granada* is analyzed.

MENÉNDEZ PELAYO, MARCELINO. *Orígenes de la novela.* Nueva Biblioteca de Autores Españoles, I. Madrid: Bailly-Bailliere, 1925. The survey of sixteenth-century historical novels includes enlightening remarks on *Civil Wars of Granada*. Information available at the time on the shaping of the Granada legends and their subsequent diffusion is summarized.

MENÉNDEZ PIDAL, RAMÓN. *Romancero hispánico*. Madrid: Espasa Calpe, 1953. Includes scattered but important remarks on Pérez de Hita's role as collector and adapter of ballads. The revival of interest in his work in the late 1700s and the Romantic period is also considered.

MORALES OLIVER, LUIS. *La novela morisca de tema granadino*. Madrid: Fundación Valdecilla, 1972. Categorizes and comments in detail on the themes, motifs, and stylistic patterns of *Civil Wars I* and *II*. Also a general survey of background and sources, covering *El Abencerraje* and Mateo Alemán's "Historia de Ozmín y Daraja."

MORENO BÁEZ, ENRIQUE. "El manierismo de Pérez de Hita." In *Homenaje a Emilio Alarcos*. II, 353–67. Valladolid: Universidad, 1965–67. In light of recent interpretations of epochal trends, the structure and style of *Civil Wars, I* is convincingly characterized as manneristic.

RUTA, EMMELINA. "L'Ariosto e Pèrez de Hita." *Archivum Romanicum* 17 (1933), 665–80. A survey of themes found in both writers. This is largely superseded by Valli and Chevalier.

SECO DE LUCENA, LUIS. *Los Abencerrajes: Leyenda e historia*. Granada: Impr. F. Román, 1960. Summary of research conducted by the author in Arabic sources on facts and distortions behind the legendary theme.

————. "Notas para el estudio de Granada bajo la dominación musulmana." *Boletín de la Universidad de Granada* 23 (1951), 169–91. Discusses the historical element or the lack of it in the names of the powerful families of Granada mentioned by Pérez de Hita.

————. *Discurso de Apertura*. Universidad de Granada: curso 1958–59. *Investigaciones sobre el romancero: Estudio de tres romances fronterizos* ["Río Verde," "Abenámar," and "Alporchones"]. Granada: Universidad, 1958. Proposes later dating than Menéndez Pidal's. Pérez de Hita's authorship of the Alporchones ballad is deemed possible.

TEJERA Y R. DE MONCADA, JOSÉ PÍO. *Biblioteca del murciano*. 3 vols. Madrid: Revista de Archivos, Bibliotecas y Museos, 1924–57. Includes exhaustive bibliography of Pérez de Hita's works, which supplements Blanchard-Demouge's.

VALLI, GIORGIO. "Ludovico Ariosto y Ginés Pérez de Hita." *Revista de Filología Española* 30 (1946), 23–53. A competent study of *Orlando Furioso*'s influence on Pérez de Hita.

WIEGMAN, NEAL A. *Ginés Pérez de Hita y la novela romántica.* Madrid: Plaza Mayor, 1971. A dissertation considering Pérez de Hita and the themes derived from *Civil Wars of Granada* in works by five authors of the late eighteenth and nineteenth centuries.

Index[*]

Abderrahman I, 17, 18
Abderrahman III, 19
Aben-Abó, 38, 126
Aben-Humeya, 37, 38, 74, 84, 125,
130, 131, 133-35, 141. *See also*
Pérez de Hita, Ginés, *Civil Wars
of Granada, II,* Martínez de la
Rosa, Francisco
Abencerraje, El, 46, 53-72, 113, 115,
120-21: "Historia del moro y Narváez," 58-60, 62; historical elements, 57-58; literary topics, 63,
65-66, 69-70; Moriscos (possible
plea in their favor), 62; Neo-
Senecan ethics, 66, 67, 71; New
Christians (as possible author and
patrons), 60-62, 64-65; song of
Abindarráez, 58; traces in later
works (imitations, translations and
adaptations), 47, 64, 95, 105, 107,
120, 132, 166n22, 168n35

VERSIONS:

Corónica, 53, 54, *60-63,* 64-66,
71, 85
Diana, La (posthumous ed. of
Montemayor's novel), 53, *63-
64,* 65-66, 101, 155n5, 157n21
Inventario (Antonio de Villegas),
54, 63, *64-67,* 157n24-27
See also Abencerrajes, legend of;
Irving, Washington; Narváez,
Rodrigo de; Padilla, Pedro de;
Pérez de Hita, Ginés; Rodrí-
guez, Lucas; Vega, Lope de, *El
remedio en la desdicha*

Abencerrajes, legend of the, 27-29,
45, 55, 57, 59, 66, 68, 69, 88-91,
95-96, 102, 105, 106, 113, 115,
116, 121-23, 138, 140-42, 152n19,
164n4. *See also Abencerraje, El*
Abindarráez. *See Abencerraje, El;*
Padilla, Pedro de; Pérez de Hita,
Civil Wars I, Moorish fictional
characters
Acero y Abad, Nicolás, 159n3, 161-
n25
Acosta, José de, 78
Aguilar, Alonso de, 32, 91, 93, 97,
104. *See also* ballads; Pérez de
Hita, *Civil Wars of Granada I,*
INSERTED BALLADS: "Río Verde,
Río Verde"
Aixa (Queen of Granada), 27, 146-
n5
Albaicín (section of Granada), 22
Alemán, Mateo, "Historia de Ozmín
y Daraja," 71, 132, 137, 140,
158n42
Alfonso VI of Castile, 41
Alfonso X of Castile, 41, 164n4
Alfonso XI of Castile, 42
Alhakem II, 19
Alhamar I of Granada, 21-24, 87,
143
Alhambra (Castle in Granada), 22,
24, 26, 28, 91, 95, 103, 115, 134,
142, 151n11, 164n4
Almanzor, 17, 20
Almotamid (King of Seville), 20
Alonso, Dámaso, 154n38
Alvar, Manuel, 51, 151n13

---

[*] The Index has been compiled with the cooperation of Gloria Vaquero
de Magalhães.

189

190